DIS  RD'

BIG WALLS, SWIFT WATERS

BIG WALLS, SWIFT WATERS

EPIC STORIES FROM YOSEMITE SEARCH AND RESCUE

BY CHARLES R. "BUTCH" FARABEE

YOSEMITE CONSERVANCY
Yosemite National Park

◄ At 12:13 p.m. on October 4, 1977, park rangers first learned a French climber on the Salathé Wall of El Capitan had fallen 10 feet, possibly breaking his ankle. By 3:00 p.m., the first of several loads of rescuers were airlifted to the top. At 4:15 p.m., Mike Graham, a renowned climber of the 1970s and '80s, began to be lowered the 800 feet to the victim. Within 80 minutes, Mike and the victim were both back on top, soon to be flown to the Valley. Note that in the photo, Mike does not have a helmet on. Today such vital protection would be mandatory. NPS photo by Tim Setnicka.

Photos on preceding pages:

page 1 (top)
YOSAR rescue trucks line El Capitan Meadow and the Helicopter Rescue Team debriefs after their technical short-haul training day, as the downdrafts and clouds descend the face of the monolith in May 2014. The park helicopter, H-551, sits in the foreground. NPS photo by David Pope.

page 1 (bottom)
Rescue Technician Jon Gleason punches through rapids below Happy Isles Bridge in June 2007. NPS photo by David Pope.

page 2 (top)
Rescuer Skye Detray prepares to release a kayak caught in a fallen tree in the Merced River in June 2010. NPS photo by David Pope.

page 2 (bottom)
Ranger Leslie Reynolds (left) gathers gear and gets ready to be short-hauled to Union Point in 2004. NPS photo by Keith Lober.

page 3
Park helicopter H-551 short-hauls (see Glossary on pages 206–09) a would-be rescuer as YOSAR prepares for Big Wall missions in this training exercise in May 2013. NPS photo by Barry Smith.

YOSEMITE NATIONAL PARK

Twin Lakes

Lundy Lake

Benson Lake

Cherry Lake

Mt. Conness

White Mtn.

Saddlebag Lake

120

Tueeulala & Wapama Falls

Hetch Hetchy

Reservoir

GRAND CANYON of the TUOLUMNE RIVER

Mt. Dana

Tioga Pass Entrance

Tuolumne River

Hetch Hetchy Entrance

Mather

Harden Lake

White Wolf

Mt. Hoffmann

Marmot Dome

Cathedral Peak

Tuolumne Meadows

Lyell Fork

MATHER DISTRICT

Yosemite Creek

May Lake

Tenaya Lake

CATHEDRAL RANGE

120

Big Oak Flat Entrance

Tuolumne Grove

Merced Grove

Crane Flat

El Capitan

Yosemite Falls

Yosemite Village

Half Dome

Merced

Merced Lake

Mt. Lyell

YOSEMITE VALLEY

Glacier Point

Vernal & Nevada Falls

River

VALLEY DISTRICT detail below

Foresta

Bridalveil Fall

CLARK RANGE

Merced

River

El Portal

140

Arch Rock Entrance

Badger Pass

Chinquapin

WAWONA DISTRICT

Lower Merced Pass Lake

Chilnualna Falls

Wawona

South Fork

Mariposa Grove

South Entrance

41

N

0   5 Miles

VALLEY DISTRICT

The Cascades

El Capitan

Yosemite Falls

Lost Arrow Spire
Yosemite Point Buttress

Clouds Rest

CANYON

Quarter Domes

Half Dome

TENAYA

Yosemite Village

Washington Column
Royal Arches

Foresta

Ribbon Fall

The Rostrum

Merced River

Leaning Tower

Bridalveil Fall

Sentinel Dome

Taft Point

Glacier Point

Clark Point

Vernal Fall

Illilouette Fall

Emerald Pool

Nevada Fall

LITTLE YOSEMITE VALLEY

El Portal

Arch Rock Entrance

0   1 Mile

CONTENTS

Ranger Dov Bock signals to H-551, hovering above, that she is ready to be lifted into a gorge above Lower Yosemite Fall for a victim of a 20-foot fall in 2010. NPS photo by David Pope.

It is 3,000 feet to the Bottom
And no undertaker to meet you
TAKE NO CHANCES.
There is a difference
Between bravery and just plain
ORDINARY FOOLISHNESS.

▶ For some 50 years, approximately 1920 to 1970, Red Cross Advanced First Aid was the level of training for medical emergencies for park rangers. In this c. 1940s photo, a ranger is applying his 24 hours of training to someone with a head injury at least. It is unknown what happened, but note that the ranger still has his Stetson "Flat Hat" on.

FOREWORD

BY JACK MOREHEAD

I witnessed Search and Rescue (SAR) in Yosemite from four different perspectives—from seasonal ranger to ranger to chief ranger to superintendent.

My first introduction to SAR occurred in 1954 when, fresh out of college, I started working at Yosemite as a seasonal. I interviewed with Chief Ranger Oscar Sedegren. Skiing, hiking, and camping came up, and he asked if I was a climber. I had some experience, but was no expert. "Do you know what a rope and carabiners are? You know how to rappel?" When I said yes, he said, "Good, you are now on the Yosemite Mountain Rescue Team." A rather amazing start.

What a summer! There were stranded climbers, as well as one major search for Orvar von Laass. Park staff would always do the initial SAR, but when help was needed we called the Sierra Club, particularly with climbing. We searched every reasonable spot for von Laass, multiple times. I even recall climbing and searching with David Brower, soon to be a prominent environmentalist. But we never did locate Orvar. I spent that winter working as a ski instructor at Badger Pass, and the next summer as a seasonal ranger in Yosemite Valley.

In the fall of 1955, I was drafted and sent to Fort Carson, Colorado, for basic training. At that time the Mountain and Cold Weather Training Command (remnants of the 10th Mountain Division) was there in the summer and at Camp Hale in the winter. Fortunately, I transferred into it where I served for two years as an instructor in climbing, mountain warfare, and skiing. While I absolutely hated being in the army, I was fortunate to be in an outstanding part of the military, especially since the skills I was learning were transferable to my hoped-for National Park Service (NPS) career.

I returned to Yosemite, better equipped for rescues. I was alone in a patrol car one day when the call went out that someone was yelling for help above Mirror Lake; being the closest, I responded. We only had a few portable radios, all surplus from World War II, and they were heavy, bulky, and mostly unreliable. A far cry from today's radios and extensive relays. When I left my car, I had radioed I was off to rescue the stranded visitor. I had no means of communication other than shouting. I took a rope, a few pitons, and carabiners.

▲ Jack Morehead, chief ranger, 1971–74. NPS photo.

◄◄ (opposite) Yosemite has always aggressively tried to prevent accidents. This c. 1930 sign at Glacier Point paints a direct and graphic warning, common in that era, which predates railings in the area. Notice the three people out beyond the sign on that overhanging rock. Surprisingly, few people have actually fallen from the lethal cliffs here, contrary to what the sign might imply.

I reached the young man several hundred feet up the Half Dome apron, roped him up, and safely descended. As I was hiking back, an apparition appeared on the trail. It was Tommy Tucker, the assistant district ranger, totally engulfed in ropes, helmets, slings, pitons, and carabiners. Even though he really hated climbing, he had gathered all the equipment he could carry and was coming to help me out.

▲ The U.S. Forest Service began experimenting with two-way radios for use with fires in 1919. In 1933, Yosemite obtained its first radio, demonstrated here in 1934 by Chief Ranger Forest Townsley. Weighing 15 pounds, it was portable, with a range of up to 20 miles. Initially there was not much faith in its applicability, since telephones seemed to work better. On May 20 to 21, 1934, this system was first used on a search and rescue.

We didn't have the use of helicopters then, either. I vividly remember one rescue we made of a visitor who had somehow made his way about halfway up Michael's Ledge (Lower Brother), then couldn't get back down. Three of us reached him from the top, all of us totally out of water. We made our way back up to the top of Yosemite Falls. By that time it was totally dark, but Ranger Dick McLaren had brought a string of horses up to meet us. That ride down the trail's switchbacks in darkness was one of the most frightening things I have ever experienced.

We used search dogs on occasion, but our experience was limited. I was involved in one SAR in which a young boy was separated from his family descending the Yosemite Falls Trail. All the adults reached the bottom, then discovered the boy was missing. It was now dark. We located two bloodhounds, and at first light we returned. Just above the Lower Yosemite Fall, one hound hesitated, sniffing off the trail. The trainer wasn't at all sure, but just to be thorough, I rappelled down. I heard the boy's voice coming from a near-vertical crack where he had spent the night. We never would have located him without the dogs.

It was also during this period (1957 to '58) when we first discussed improving our water rescue. On one occasion a visitor fell into the river below Vernal Fall. Several of us spent at least a week wading in the freezing river with wooden poles with metal hooks on the end, poking into cracks, crevasses, and caves trying to hook her body. Scuba had not yet arrived.

My wife and I married in the Yosemite Chapel in April of 1958. Wayne Merry and Warren Harding, occasional climbing partners of mine, were among the invited guests. After the ceremony they and Royal Robbins did a first ascent which they named "Pat and Jack Pinnacle." It is now a popular area for climbers, with numerous routes.

My next experience with Yosemite SAR came during 1971 to '74, when I served as chief ranger. Wow, had things changed for the better! Equipment was much advanced, radios vastly improved, and rescue techniques had evolved. We began working closely with Naval Air Station Lemoore developing advanced rescue techniques. The NPS was also using some of the best of the Camp 4 climbers to assist us. They were talented, experienced, in fantastic physical condition, both male and female, an invaluable aid to the park's SAR program. Ranger Pete Thompson was heading the program. In 1971 he told me that he was confident the park now had the ability and experience to rescue someone from literally any cliff in Yosemite—and I believed him.

This was quickly proved when a climber midway up El Capitan was severely injured. Pete somehow had two 4,000-foot ropes shipped to the park. Bev Johnson, an incredible climber, made the initial roped descent to the injured party. Pete even had spotters count her spins as she descended the sometimes overhanging cliff, so that the ropes could later be unwound before the injured climber was secured and Jim Bridwell brought him to the ground below.

Finally, I returned yet again to Yosemite in 1986 as superintendent. By then the SAR scene was vastly changed from my first experiences in 1954. Helicopter use was now almost routine. Communications were, for the most part, excellent. Climbing and rescue techniques had advanced tremendously. Semipermanent quarters were now provided in Camp 4 to house the local climbers selected and trained for SAR missions. Organization of SAR followed the Incident Command System adopted by the NPS for emergencies. Yosemite's SAR team was now a well-organized, well-trained, highly specialized part of the Ranger Division. They were now functioning at a level we could not have believed possible back in the early days.

It has been a great privilege to have experienced this phenomenal development of the SAR program. I'm doubly pleased to now learn that it is being recorded for you in this book.

▼ While on the South Face of Washington Column on October 3, 1975, a 28-year-old climber fell, fracturing his right ankle. He was lowered 700 feet using a Tragsitz, a European-designed rescue harness, not often used at that time in this country. In this photo, the victim piggybacks the rescuer, John Long, a super climber of the 1970s and '80s. The lowering rope was 1,200 feet in length and was pulled up from the bottom. NPS photo by Tim Setnicka.

INTRODUCTION

From the little two-way radio strapped snugly to my chest came this: "Butch, do you know there's a fire near your rappel ropes?" Now *there's* a question you don't hear every day! Tied off gingerly to our lines maybe 800 feet up a cliff face and about to jab a syringe's worth of pain-killing Demerol into a dirty, badly scraped human thigh with one hand, while gripping for dear life onto a rock with the other, you do not want to hear the words "fire," "near," and "rope" all in the same sentence.

Of the many daily challenges I faced as a National Park ranger in Yosemite, I probably enjoyed search and rescue the most—well, except for maybe during the times when I was scared, tired, cold, hot, wet, hurting, hungry, overwhelmed, thirsty, grossed out, missing my family, was needed elsewhere, and/or . . . all of the above. Which was often. In June of 1971 when my wife, Anne, and I first arrived at our home in "downtown" Yosemite Valley, I was the new Valley District night shift supervisor, GS-9. I had just been transferred in from an isolated little ranger station in Death Valley National Monument, due mostly to my rather recent three years in the Tucson Police Department and the professional training I'd received there in law enforcement. The Yosemite Valley night shift was arguably the busiest field ranger operation in all of the National Park System. It was a zoo, and I would love it!

Tim Setnicka, the park's multitalented search and rescue officer, calmly went on, "The tree you're tied to is burning. Can't tell. We'll check!" Actually, I'm not sure he was calm or even what he really said, as I was mostly still stuck on "fire near your rappel ropes."

In the nearly 10 years I was in Yosemite (from 1971 to 1981) I made a great many misdemeanor and felony arrests, settled campground disputes and family fights, fought forest and building fires, drove fire trucks and ambulances, drugged problem bears, started IVs, stabilized broken spines, jumped from helicopters onto cliffs, used scuba under waterfalls, swam through rapids, rode patrol horses, was a dog catcher and traffic cop, climbed cliffs, and pronounced people dead while serving as a coroner. And on a good day, Friday night to be exact, and much to my delight, I quite often gave scheduled interpretive talks about search and rescue in the park's main auditorium. Down through the years, this is what rangers have been largely doing, from at least 1898, when the United States

> **"The saving of human life will take precedence over all other management actions as the Park Service strives to protect human life and provide for injury-free visits."**
>
> **—The National Park Service *Management Policies 2006*, Section 8.2.5.1, "Visitor Safety and Emergency Response"**

◀◀ Rangers brace for holiday weekends. On Friday, May 26, 2006, a 20-year-old from Capitola, California, dropped his camera over the railing at Glacier Point. It landed just below. He climbed over to retrieve it and fell 1,600 feet. Rangers George Paiva (left) and Eric Gabriel were short-hauled onto the ledge to recover the young man's body. NPS photo by David Pope.

Cavalry left Yosemite National Park for the Spanish-American War. (That is a whole different and very interesting story.)

> Just 30 minutes before Tim radioed this little piece of bad news, Ron and I had been lowered 75 feet by cable out of a Vietnam-era navy chopper onto a bus-sized brushy ledge at the top of the Glacier Point Apron. This part of The Apron, as it is generally called, is a mixture of both smooth face and broken-terraced granite rising maybe 900 feet directly above Yosemite's Curry Village. The cliff face is a favorite challenge of intermediate climbers, as many of its routes are only moderately difficult and doable in a day. My partner was Ron Kauk. Broad shouldered and impeccably chiseled, with long hair and zero fat, he was already a superstar among the Yosemite "Rock Jocks." But at just 19, this was a first for him.

Why was I brought into Yosemite? On the Fourth of July, less than a year before I arrived, Yosemite suffered one of the watershed events in the history of the National Park Service. It is known both affectionately and derisively as the "Yosemite Riot" and "Stoneman Meadow Massacre." In the background were Vietnam, Kent State, Watergate, Woodstock, the draft, political radicals, race riots, a sexual revolution, and more. An antiestablishment, counterculture hippie era fueled by LSD, marijuana, wine, cynicism, rage, and rebellion was in full bloom and very much alive and doing well in the park, as it had been for a year or three. On that one fateful day in 1970, any semblance of order swiftly dissolved and a confrontation between rangers and the antiestablishment crowd turned into a free-for-all and then before long, a humiliating full rout. That night: Hippies—1, Rangers—0.

The incident was an ugly, lose-lose scar on the hearts of those rangers who endured it—and a highly embarrassing wake-up call for the agency. The National Park Service was now forced into the twentieth century. And in due course, this was the principal reason I, with my law enforcement background, was there.

> Flying in, we spotted our two climbers, tightly huddled on what appeared to be, well, pretty much nothing—a coffin-sized ledge, sloping perilously down at a 30-degree angle, seemingly a million feet above the Valley floor. Ron and I watched as our ship—with only yards to spare for its main rotor blades—slowly backed away from the rock wall, still towering 1,000 feet overhead. Damn, that Lemoore rescue crew was good! The two of us then hustled to tie our ropes to one of the few real trees available. We expected to be joined quickly by Setnicka and Werner Braun, another young, wiry Yosemite climbing prodigy. Critical to this rescue, those two would add essential gear and needed support. But we had to go now;

YOSEMITE BY THE NUMBERS

With an operating budget of $30 million in 2016, Yosemite National Park had 5,028,868 visitors within its almost 1,200 square miles, 95% of which is designated as wilderness. The National Park Service and concessions combined have some 2,900 summer employees. There are 214 miles of paved roads, 800 miles of trails, over 1,100 buildings, 1,500 campsites, and 1,400 lodging units. On an average August day in 2016, the busiest month, more than 23,000 people visited the park. They camped, slept, ate, hiked, biked, climbed, swam, drove, and played tourist, all while marveling at just how lucky they were to be in one of the most awe-inspiring spots on the planet.

starting down, I was banking on Ron, my superclimber partner, knowing what was below—our rappel ropes were only 165 feet long, and this was a 900-foot-high cliff!

Most visitors spend some time in the half-mile-wide by seven-mile-long Yosemite Valley and the Village within. This is a small city with all of the attendant bells and whistles. There are water, sewer, electrical, and bus systems, a 24-bed jail, an urgent care center that once was a 20-bed hospital, two fire stations, restaurants and cafés, a high-end hotel and low-cost tent cabins and a swimming pool, to mention but a few of the Valley's many fixtures and amenities.

And it might go without saying, if it were not for the park's nearly 1,200 square miles of wilderness, full of rivers, cliffs, domes, valleys, waterfalls, meadows, trees, trails, roads, and bears and snakes, there would not be nearly the need for SAR that there is.

Rapelling down the 150 feet to the trapped pair, we still had absolutely no idea why they'd been screaming so loudly for help that July morning in 1976. We found a man and woman in their early twenties, both safely tied off. She was fine; he had a broken shoulder and was hurting a whole lot. Ron tied off above her, and I settled in, my rear end half over and off the little, sloping ledge. It was shaky at best, at least for me. While I was saying hello to my newfound friend Mike and his partner, the navy whumped, whumped, whumped in overhead; Tim and Werner would soon join us, but it was time to get busy.

The first real record I could find even hinting at a search and rescue incident for Yosemite was for May 28, 1871, when San Francisco restaurateur Giacomo Campi died "while climbing a rickety ladder beside Vernal Fall. . . . [He] stopped to offer assistance to a lady. She declined his hand. He stepped back to bow graciously but stepped into empty air and fell 35 feet to fracture his skull. That summer the rickety ladders were replaced by wooden stairs and a railing." There were surely other accidents before and during this era, given that everyone rode horses, carried guns, and camped out; women wore skirts while hiking; and super lightweight, rain- and windproof protection would not be invented for almost another century.

I radioed Lewis Memorial Hospital, literally within eyesight across the Valley. Dr. Jim Wurgler, a great friend of the park, quickly answered—no surprise since he worked with us on a more-than-daily basis. Moments later he authorized use of a painkiller and said he'd stand by. Ron and I both listened for our backup team while waiting for the painkiller to kick in. It was then that my park radio came to life and Tim put "fire" and "rope" in the same sentence! So let me now cut to the chase and tell you what happened.

PRIMARY SOURCES

Circumstances of a death, serious fire, or an unusual event in the park often ended up in the local newspaper. The author utilized logbooks the rangers maintained from the 1930s and into the 1950s, which include notable events such as deaths, births, fires, vehicle wrecks, serious injuries, and so forth. But these are merely log entries, not separate, detailed reports. A few such reports on serious events have been found from the mid-1950s, but it was not until the late 1960s that SAR reports became standardized.

▲ SAR Officer Pete Thompson unloads a Stokes litter with equipment for rescuing Blair Glenn, a climber seriously hurt on El Capitan. Taken on May 29, 1972, this photo may show the first time the Naval Air Station Lemoore Helicopter SAR Unit was in Yosemite. Over the next 30 years they came to the park at least 200 times (see page 110). NPS photo.

My new buddy Mike and his partner had camped on the brushy ledge that Ron and I had just been lowered onto and had built a small fire to pass the cool night before. By the time the navy tried to lower the next two rescuers, the winds had become squirrelly and the helo was forced to retreat, unable to deliver the second team. Unseen by anyone, air stirred by that helo had reignited the embers from their campfire of the night before. Now, from below, they could see the fire near our ropes. Once more the Lemoore crew tried; though they were still not successful, luckily they could see the fire was actually no danger to us. Within another two hours, the winds calmed down and Setnicka and Braun joined us.

There were now six of us near the little ledge. I put Mike's bad arm in a sling and strapped it to his chest—he was actually one very tough dude, which is good because he'd have to be for the next step. Fortunately, he did not feel as much pain as when we first arrived; we spent the next couple of hours making our way back up the two ropes we had come down hours before. Ron and Werner served as the victim's broken arm. As we finally reached the large ledge we had originally been lowered to, the sun was setting and the winds had fully died down. All six of us were winched safely back aboard the navy helicopter.

So what is a search and rescue (a "SAR")? Well, there is probably a textbook answer, but I will not drag you through it; instead I'll provide some real-life examples to illustrate. The need for a SAR is generally obvious; however, there are often fine lines to be drawn and complicated, knotty variables to be considered. And even if an incident does not start out as a search and rescue, once further details are learned, it could turn into one. But regardless of how it is defined, the park will provide the best, most efficient answer to the crisis at hand. On the opposite page are some real-life scenarios to help you better understand what might or might not be a SAR.

For every one of these real-life scenarios, I could identify many more. The decision to declare a SAR and initiate a response is definitely not taken lightly, although, when in doubt, the ranger(s) will generally favor going, rather than not. Many factors will come into play when sounding the alarm, and the speed and the degree with which responders deploy also vary. Variables considered might include the present and/or forecasted weather; age and known health of the victim, including prescription medicines they might be taking; how reliable the reporting party seems; number and characteristics of people in the group; time of day; severity of injury or illness suffered; victim's experience and training; specific equipment the involved party may have; location of the incident; experience level of the ranger making the first decisions; and availability of SAR staff

▲ Organizing and rigging anchor systems to raise or lower a litter or a person is often complicated and requires an understanding of the uses and merits of equipment. The system shown here is still being put together and the anchors are not visible. It will be built for maximum safety through redundancy of the various pieces. Each piece is capable of holding several thousand pounds and of withstanding a great deal of stress from different angles. See this equipment in use on page 193. For an example of anchor points, see the photo on page 41. NPS photo by Keith Lober.

IS IT A SAR?

A climber is hurt halfway up El Capitan and needs help.	YES
A man breaks an ankle a mile up the trail and cannot get back.	YES
Lightning strikes a hiker on Half Dome and CPR is now being performed.	YES
A swimmer is stuck on a rock in the middle of dangerous rapids.	YES
A wilderness camper is very badly burned when her gas stove explodes.	YES
A small child has not been seen around her remote campground for 30 minutes.	YES
A runner cuts a switchback and becomes stuck, uninjured, above a cliff.	YES
A horse falls in the backcountry and the rider breaks her back when thrown off.	YES
While playing by the railing above Vernal Fall, a teenager slips over and disappears into the mist and boulders below.	YES Sadly, this will be a recovery, not a rescue.
A driver is badly hurt when his car goes off the Tioga Road and ends up 200 feet down a steep embankment.	YES
An Alzheimer's patient has not been seen after visiting the bathroom in the Lodge cafeteria.	PROBABLY Emergency personnel will respond immediately and assess.
A 69-year-old man has chest pains in the Bridalveil Fall parking lot.	PROBABLY NOT But emergency personnel will respond immediately.
A woman in Fresno calls saying her husband is two hours overdue from a two-day road trip to the park.	PROBABLY NOT But the park will alert rangers on patrol.
The regional aviation officials call and say a small plane is missing somewhere in the Sierra but they are not sure where.	NO But the park will alert relevant stations and assign an investigator.

▼ Before the daily quota system was instituted on Half Dome, this was a busy day. The shadows of people make it look even busier than it was. NPS photo by Keith Lober.

▲ Valley rangers carry out a patient from near Lower Yosemite Fall in the early 1970s. The responding rangers are not wearing identifying SAR clothing, as it didn't exist then. NPS photo by Butch Farabee.

and equipment (see "A Yosemite SAR from Start to Finish" on pages 80–81). It may not be an easy evaluation.

Even when the ranger making the initial decision rounds off in favor of calling out the troops, intent on being prompt and efficient, there is always the fear of overkill. When talking to a SAR manager, you'll hear that actually overkill is not often a problem, but there are genuine concerns about a helicopter crashing or a ranger who is going "lights and sirens" hitting a tree. These things have happened.

There is also a dark side to search and rescue that needs to be mentioned, one that may take a profound toll on the people in this field. Without a doubt, there is a genuine sense of reward and satisfaction one feels for having done a notable service. But it is not all heroics, with everyone walking away pounding their chests. You may actually walk away telling yourself you should have done more. There is way too much ugliness, death, gore, sorrow, fear, hardship, guilt, and stress, all of which may build up over time. There is a real possibility of losing your life or limbs. There is torment and grief for you when telling a family that a loved one is dead or cannot be found. Lives will change forever. No one who has ever taken a drowned child from beneath the water or carried a young mother with irreparable brain damage from a cliff will ever totally get over it. Knowing that the lives of victims, your coworkers, and yourself may depend on you is a true burden. First responders are infamous for high divorce rates, family breakups, alcoholism, and long-term

▼ Here, searchers, mostly volunteers, are gathering to look for a Honduran man last seen not far from Glacier Point. From June 8 to 11, 2008, the 22-year-old was lost in the Yosemite wilderness. Ultimately, nearly 200 members of 14 different county and mountain rescue teams, including aerial spotters and dog teams, looked for him. He was found safe and in good shape. NPS photo by David Pope.

emotional scarring. After 40 years, I still tear up thinking about futilely performing CPR for more than 60 minutes on a six-year-old who was accidentally gored by a startled deer. His father looked on with fingers crossed.

Appearing throughout this book is the acronym YOSAR, which stands for Yosemite Search and Rescue. Some will say that since YOSAR does not appear on any park organizational chart, it does not really exist. That's a far too narrow perspective. I believe YOSAR is alive and well, in both the abstract—as a conceptual "machine"—and in the concrete—when yellow-shirted rescuers with YOSAR on their backs race up a cliff. Regardless, both interpretations signify dedication, professionalism, effort, heart, attitude, and training. Search and rescue is a team sport and the park's team is YOSAR.

Once begun, the search for a missing child or the rescue of an injured hiker quickly ramps up, and a lot of people see it through to the end, including rangers, climbers, dispatchers, administrators, maintenance workers, volunteers, outside agencies, and other contributors and disciplines. Some functions are obvious: the ranger on horseback riding out or the chopper flying up canyon. These you note; others you probably will not, such as the dispatcher calling for more aid and tracking volunteers as they go out. Crews readying the helicopter or refueling it upon return. Dog teams finding a quiet spot to organize. A semitrailer arriving with showers and a mobile kitchen set up to feed a hundred searchers. All of these, along with dozens of other duties and functions, need to be competently performed, coordinated, and documented. At the end of each and every SAR in Yosemite National Park, the hoped-for outcome by all in YOSAR is one of safe and efficient success.

To quote one of the near-legendary thoughts that Horace M. Albright, second director of the National Park Service, proffers in his 1922 book, *Oh, Ranger!*:

> They are a fine, earnest, intelligent, and public-spirited body of men [and women], the rangers. Though small in number, their influence is large. Many and long are the duties heaped upon their shoulders. If a trail is to be blazed, it is "send a ranger." If an animal is floundering in the snow, a ranger is sent to pull him out; if a bear is in the hotel, if a fire threatens a forest, if someone is to be saved, it is "send a ranger."

SAR VOLUNTEERS

There are many volunteer as well as professional SAR groups without which land-management agencies such as the National Park Service would be crippled. They range from search dogs to ham-radio operators to mounted horse units to cave-rescue specialists to scuba divers to sheriff's posses to those who focus on mountain and wilderness search and rescue. Each team is advanced in its organization and proficient in the skills and roles its members gladly contribute. In California, these varied groups are coordinated by the state's Office of Emergency Services, although there are exceptions such as the Civil Air Patrol (see the box on page 91) and various military units. These groups are dispatched after they have met a specific level of competence and training. Yosemite uses these teams when requiring lots of personnel or special expertise, such as for searches and winter rescues.

2010: A TYPICAL YEAR

Is there really a typical year in Yosemite SAR? The short answer is both yes and no! There are many similarities among the years, as has been the case for the past half century. Each year has probably seen major rescues off El Cap, and one or two climbers, often more, will fall to their deaths from park cliffs. People will accidentally stray too far into the rivers and need to be pulled out, and several may drown or even go over a waterfall. Others will take an easy day hike and twist an ankle or have a heart attack. Cross-country skiers and those just playing in the snow will do much the same thing. A kid with autism or a senior citizen with dementia will wander away and spend the night out, alone and confused. Each SAR is different in its own way, but a great many will be almost identical to one that happened the year before or even 40 years before. In 2010, there were 245 SAR missions—lots were mundane, some tragic, and many incredibly epic. Here are thumbnail sketches of a variety of them.

SAR #001   JANUARY 10
KNEE INJURY

A 28-year-old woman sustained a knee injury approximately 2 miles from the isolated Ostrander Ski Hut, southeast of Badger Pass. The veteran ranger there skied out to begin fashioning a temporary sled to transport her. Several rangers also went in by snowmobile, and the victim safely arrived at Badger Pass at about 3:00 p.m.

SAR #003   JANUARY 17–23
MASSIVE WINTER STORM

A series of winter storms with significant tropical moisture and strong dynamics caused major impacts and damage throughout the park. The wilderness received upwards of 8 feet of new snow, with the Valley receiving 18 inches of very heavy, wet snow. Trees and large limbs fell all over the Valley and along every road into the park. Ambulance response was curtailed, buildings and campgrounds were evacuated, and convoys of visitors were escorted from the park as trees and deep snows were chainsawed or plowed off the roads. Due to the nature of this event, all emergencies during this time were put under SAR #3. The emergency lasted for five days.

SAR #016   MARCH 28
STUCK BETWEEN ROCKS

A 61-year-old man became stuck in a tight spot on Reed's Pinnacle, and as reported by his 20-year-old climbing partner, had asked for help. Two rangers responded only to find the man had been assisted by a second climbing party and had become unstuck. The rangers saw them both down.

Rescuers carry equipment for a rescue hike through patches of snow down to the rim of El Capitan in 2010. NPS photo by David Pope.

A rescuer on snowshoes pulls a rescue toboggan with gear for a SAR in February 2005. NPS photo.

SAR #024 APRIL 17
BROKEN PELVIS

A 39-year-old man fell approximately 15 feet at about the midway point of the Royal Arches Route. A blitz team of two rangers climbed to the victim in just over 30 minutes. Rescuers feared a broken femur and asked for a CHP helicopter for a hoist. The rescue was complicated by a protected nesting peregrine falcon nearby as well as a dead but hazardous tree at the scene. In less than four hours the victim was down and being transported to a hospital in Modesto.

SAR #027 MAY 1
STUCK ON ROCK

A 42-year-old man ventured onto a large rock in the water just below the Vernal Fall's footbridge and had become stuck. He was unable to climb safely off due to the surrounding steep and loose terrain, and the river was high with snowmelt. He was secured and a technical raising ultimately lifted him off.

SAR #032 MAY 7
CLIMBER FELL 300 FEET

A 31-year-old man fell over 300 feet to the ground while rappelling. Approximately a dozen rescuers responded; when they arrived they initiated CPR and advanced life-support measures. A medical helicopter was requested due to the mechanism of injury. Within 45 minutes of the original call, the man was pronounced dead by a local doctor. This was the second death of the year, the first being a 59-year-old female hiker who suffered a fatal heart attack on the Yosemite Falls Trail on March 13.

In June 2010, an injured hiker (seated) is made ready to be flown from a remote part of the park. NPS photo by David Pope.

SAR #057 JUNE 6
REPORT OF POSSIBLE DEAD BODY

A visitor to the park on May 31 took some personal video from the Illilouette Fall area. Getting home and viewing the footage, he believed he observed a dead body on a ledge. Video was emailed to rangers that day and it looked credible. A powerful telescope was used, vehicle licenses were checked, footprints in the area were looked for, and finally SAR personnel rappelled into a dangerous area to look at the ledge. No smells and no further clues were found.

SAR #067 JUNE 18
TWISTED KNEE

A 53-year-old woman twisted her knee, which was incapable of bearing weight. She was 6 miles from and 3,000 feet above Yosemite Valley. A wilderness ranger was first on scene. The victim thought she could walk with crutches, which were provided, but she wore out after 2 miles. Two rangers on horseback ultimately packed her out. She refused to go to the hospital.

A Good Samaritan aids a woman trapped in the river below Mirror Lake, April 6, 2007. NPS photo.

SAR #073 JUNE 21
RATTLESNAKE BITE

A 61-year-old man was struck in the small toe by a rattlesnake. There was no warning by the snake; the fangs pierced the victim's sneakers. Within five minutes, eight SAR team members and a paramedic were en route, and within 30 minutes of the strike the victim was hallucinating. The victim was carried to the road, transferred to a local hospital and provided with antivenom, and then flown by air ambulance from the Valley to Modesto for more advanced care.

SAR #092 JULY 5
SWIFT WATER RESCUE

A 911 call came in reporting a possible drowning with people still in the water. Within five minutes rangers were on scene and observed nine individuals on an island in the Merced River. All were accounted for, with no drownings. The group was rafting in three rafts, and hit a log jam in the river. There was only one life jacket for the entire group, and three rafters were younger than 13. A swift-water rescue was initiated, and all were safely taken off the island within 30 minutes of rangers arriving on scene. There were only minor injuries and no one needed further medical attention.

SAR #120 JULY 16
STRANDED HIKER / BODY RECOVERY

A stranded hiker was reported above Columbia Point. The 61-year-old man was located and was told by loudspeaker to remain in place and wait for the rescuers. Once rescuers arrived on scene, the victim could not be located. The search for the man was suspended for the night, thinking that he had made it out successfully. The next morning a report was received of an overdue hiker in the same area. The park helicopter launched, and the stranded/missing hiker was soon located deceased at the base of a nearby cliff.

Ranger Dov Bock (left) and the victim of SAR #128 are lifted by helicopter short-haul from the snowfield on Mount Ritter. NPS photo by Keith Lober.

SAR #124 JULY 18
SLIPPED OVER WATERFALL

While exploring the cascades in the Inner Gorge between Upper and Lower Yosemite Falls, two 26-year-old hiking friends slipped on wet, mossy rock and both fell over the same 20-foot waterfall. One injured his knee, but both ended up in a safe spot. Rangers responded at dark and provided equipment to spend the night. The next morning, the man with the injury was short-hauled out while the second victim was hiked out.

SAR #128 JULY 21
MUTUAL AID SHORT-HAUL

A 62-year-old hiker crossing the glacier below Mount Ritter on the east side of Yosemite, just outside of the park, injured his knee and was having difficulty walking. There was no spot to land the park helicopter, and snow depth and conditions precluded carrying him to one. A short-haul was deemed necessary, and rangers lifted him out and to the Mammoth Airport.

On November 18, 1975, rangers aid a climber being hoisted into a Naval Air Station Lemoore helicopter. NPS photo by Tim Setnicka.

A TYPICAL YEAR

SAR #134   JULY 25
PARTY OF FOUR LOST

A 49-year-old and his three younger companions accidentally walked off the Half Dome Trail after descending from the summit. Upon their first 911 call, they were told to walk east back to the trail from Lost Lake. The party did not follow instructions given to them by the park dispatcher and had walked farther west, eventually traveling down a steep embankment and again calling 911 for assistance. Rescue personnel were dispatched, eventually finding the party down the steep ravine. They were escorted to safety.

SAR #149   JULY 31
BREATHING TROUBLES

A 31-year-old man was having trouble breathing, coupled with dizziness and the inability to stand up, and thus could not get off the top of Half Dome. An off-duty Sacramento Fire Department paramedic happened to be on top and relayed vital information to rangers. The patient was later determined to have sustained a spontaneous pneumothorax. Several rangers hiked to the top of Half Dome and prepared the victim to be flown off the next morning.

SAR #154   AUGUST 2
SOS SIGNAL

In the evening park dispatch received a report of a potential SOS signal in the area of North Dome. Rangers established contact with the party via loudspeaker and flashing lights. Rangers determined that one member of the party was injured and unable to walk. SAR personnel climbed up to the area via the Royal Arches climbing route and located a party of five backpackers who had become lost. All spent the night on top and then a short-haul helicopter evacuation was performed the next morning.

SAR #174   AUGUST 15
REPORTED KIDNAPPING

A ranger responded to a possible "5150," referring to a psychiatric patient, on the Panorama Trail. A 43-year-old woman reported her husband "had been kidnapped and beaten up by some unknown assailants. . . . She had been chased by these assailants but had gotten away from there." A search was initiated for her husband, but rangers suspected the woman was on drugs. Some 21 law enforcement and SAR personnel as well as the park helicopter spent considerable time looking for both the husband and potential assailants. Ultimately the man was found. Both admitted to having taken methamphetamine and were subsequently arrested on various charges.

In June 2010, an injured and trapped man (see circle) is short-hauled to safety. NPS photo.

SAR #189 AUGUST 24
HIGHLY TECHNICAL SHORT-HAUL FROM EL CAPITAN

While climbing The Nose route on El Capitan, a 47-year-old Korean climber pulled a rock onto himself, fracturing his right femur. He was part of a four-man team, and there was a language barrier between climbers and rangers. It was also the hottest day of the year, over 100 degrees. In the two-day mission, some 15 rescuers were involved. Two rescuers were lowered by ropes from the summit. A throw bag (see page 107) was thrown from the park helo to a rescuer on scene, and the victim was short-hauled from the cliff to the meadow below. The remaining three climbers also needed to be evacuated, which required several lowerings from the scene to the ground.

SAR #198 SEPTEMBER 3
POSSIBLE HUMAN REMAINS

A ranger received a thirdhand report of a backpack being found in a remote part of the park. This ranger, along with a few SAR-Siters (see page 56), hiked in that night and located the pack and the seven-year-old remains of Fred Claassen lying nearby. It appeared that he had fallen down a cliff. The 46-year-old man had disappeared during a solo four-day backpacking trip in July 2003. A massive search at that time had failed to find him.

SAR #209 SEPTEMBER 13
VEHICLE COLLISION

Two vehicles collided head-on, injuring several people and trapping one, a 66-year-old man. Mono County Fire and Paramedics were asked to assist as were both the park helicopter and an air ambulance from Modesto. The gentleman had to be extricated from his vehicle and then flown to Modesto using the two helicopters. The others were taken to Mammoth Hospital.

SAR #219 SEPTEMBER 22
A FALL ON THE MIST TRAIL

A ranger hiking down from Vernal Fall on the Mist Trail came across a 62-year-old man who had fallen, striking his head. The man was now hyperventilating after losing consciousness at least twice. A team of rescuers reached him, and a short-haul was deemed critical. With a park medic as an attendant, the park helicopter performed the tricky maneuver. The victim was ultimately flown to Modesto by an air ambulance.

SAR #225 SEPTEMBER 25
FELL OFF A LOG

An 83-year-old woman walking along the South Fork Merced River in Wawona became fatigued and sat down on a log. She slipped off and was unable to get up. Once she was lifted to her feet, she was still unable to walk, again due to fatigue. A litter team was organized and carried her out on a wheeled litter.

Litter attendants prepare to descend to an 18-year-old injured climber off the 8th pitch of The Prow on Washington Column on June 14, 2010. NPS photo by David Pope.

A TYPICAL YEAR

SAR #251 DECEMBER 13
CLIMBER DISLODGES ROCK

While climbing the 11th pitch of El Capitan's Tangerine Trip, a 24-year-old woman dislodged a refrigerator-sized rock, pulling it down onto herself. It struck her head, shoulder, and back, although she did not lose consciousness. In fact, she tried to self-rescue, although it was later determined she had fractured a vertebra and sustained serious muscle injuries. She was in a party of three. A SAR team was flown to the summit by a National Guard Chinook helicopter the next morning. Two rangers were lowered to the victim. All three climbers and the two rescuers were then lowered all the way to the bottom of the cliff. The patient was then hoisted by a California Highway Patrol helicopter from the base of El Capitan to the Valley floor.

All four photos are from the rescue of an injured woman off El Capitan on December 13, 2010. NPS photo by David Pope (top). NPS photos by Keith Lober (left, below). NPS photo (bottom).

A safety sign from 1947.

The YOSAR Helicopter Rescue Team, including the helicopter crew that supports it, practiced heli-rappel and short-haul techniques on May 20 and 21, 2014. Here, two of the team prepare to be lifted from El Capitan Meadow. Notice the rope hanging below H-551. NPS photo by David Pope.

PART 1
THE ADVENTURE BEGINS

THE UNITED STATES ARMY

Between 1891 and 1914, the United States Army, under the direction of the Department of the Interior, managed much of Yosemite National Park. During this time, the army was involved in a number of significant search and rescue operations.

SAVING PUBLIC LANDS

In late 1890, President Benjamin Harrison signed into law the creation of three national parks: Sequoia on September 25, and both General Grant and Yosemite on October 1. A few weeks later Secretary of the Interior John W. Noble wrote to Secretary of War Redfield Proctor asking for military troops to be sent to these new parks. Military troops were already being used in Yellowstone, America's first national park, and it seemed to be working well. Noble wanted troops stationed in these areas all year round, and to that end he had formulated and established rules and regulations for how this would work. Secretary Proctor was agreeable, but the whole plan became much more official when President Harrison made a formal request for Proctor to assist Secretary Noble.

▲ John Muir is synonymous with preservation and love of this country's natural heritage. He was the first president of the Sierra Club. President Theodore Roosevelt was also a champion of wild places and important cultural sites. He established the U.S. Forest Service, signed the Antiquities Act, and set aside some 20 national park areas, preserving them for the future. This photo shows Muir (right) and Roosevelt on Yosemite's Glacier Point in 1903.

THE ARMY HEADS TO YOSEMITE Feeling they were unnecessary that first winter, the army did not send men to the California parks. But the following spring, Troops I and K left the Presidio in San Francisco and, mostly by train, headed toward Yosemite. Under command of Captain Abram Epperson "Jug" Wood, 63 soldiers arrived in Yosemite on May 19, 1891. A permanent camp (which has been called Camp A. E. Wood since Wood's death in 1894) was formed on the western edge of Wawona, where the Wawona Campground is currently located.

There was angst and great suspicion of the federal government and of the army, and ultimately a realized fear among the residents of nearby San Joaquin Valley that mining, timber harvesting, hunting, and grazing would be halted. Locals had little or no understanding of the role and character of a national park. Captain Wood, an 1872 graduate of West Point, didn't really know that much more, but seemed eager to enforce the laws and rules and regulations, as ordered.

DEALING WITH TRESPASSERS

Timber and wildlife poaching did exist at the time, but were sporadic and incrementally being shut down. Hard rock and placer miners had already picked through the crags and streams of the Sierra, finding little of real value. But trespass of sheep and cattle was particularly rampant, and so mounted patrols were soon detailed to all sections of the park.

AN INAUSPICIOUS BEGINNING Four sheepherders were arrested that June for grazing on park land and brought to Wawona. They were confined while Captain Wood contacted the nearest United States attorney, Charles Garter in Visalia, west of Sequoia. Garter received Wood's request for prosecution under criminal laws for trespass on U.S. government land. Faced with these new circumstances, Attorney Garter forwarded the request on to the attorney general in Washington, DC for a higher decision. He was informed, and so told Captain Wood, that the Act of October 1, 1890, creating the park, only warranted removal of trespassers, not their criminal prosecution. Frustrated, Captain Wood released the sheepherders.

DEVELOPING A PLAN This incident highlights that, from the very beginning, protection of these three parks was hindered by the lack of a substantial penalty that could be assessed to a violator of the rules and regulations. The first encounters with these grazing trespassers resulted merely in their expulsion with warnings, which was not much of a deterrent. It was all too easy for the sheep and cattlemen to return again when the troops were gone. Soon, the soldiers developed a plan that quickly discouraged this trespass and in short order led to the elimination of grazing while troops were there. When a patrol captured a herd in the heart of the park (sometimes there were 3,000 to 4,000 animals), the animals were driven out the northern boundary, while the herders were brought several days' journey in the other direction. Warned by Wood, the men were ejected out the southern boundary.

While both sheep and cattle herders grazed their animals in the park, sheep were much more damaging. Indeed, John Muir called them "hoofed locusts."

▼ Between 1890, when Yosemite was established, and 1916, when the National Park Service was created, the park's officials answered directly to the secretary of the interior. In 1916, the secretary oversaw more than 30 separate park areas, including Yosemite. Congress promulgated rules and regulations for residents and visitors. Notices like this were tacked to sign boards and gathering spots.

RULES AND REGULATIONS

OF THE

Yosemite National Park.

DEPARTMENT OF THE INTERIOR,
Washington, D. C., June 1, 1896.

1. By act of Congress approved October 1, 1890, the tract of land in the State of California described as townships one (1) and two (2) north, and townships one (1), two (2), three (3), and four (4) south, all of ranges nineteen (19), twenty (20), twenty-one (21), twenty-two (22), twenty-three (23), and twenty-four (24) east, also townships one (1), two (2), three (3), and (4) south of range twenty-five (25) east, and also townships three (3) and four (4) south of range twenty-six (26) east, excepting therefrom that tract of land known as Yosemite Valley granted to the State of California for a public park by act of Congress approved June 30, 1864, as the same has been surveyed out and accepted by said State, have been set apart for a public park, and the same shall be known as the "YOSEMITE NATIONAL PARK."

2. The Park by said act is placed under the exclusive control of the Secretary of the Interior, and these rules and regulations are made and published in pursuance of the duty imposed on him in regard thereto.

3. No person other than transient visitors will be permitted to be within the Park without written authority from the Secretary of the Interior.

4. No person shall cut, break, remove, impair, or interfere with any trees, shrubs, plants, timber, minerals, mineral deposits, curiosities, wonders, or other objects of interest in the Park; and all of the same shall be retained in their natural condition.

5. The wanton destruction of the fish and game found within the Park and their capture or destruction for the purposes of merchandise or profit are forbidden by said act; and no one shall carry into or have in the Park any fire-arms, traps, nets, tackle, or appliances, or fish or hunt therein without a license in writing signed by the Secretary or Superintendent of the Park.

6. No one shall start or kindle, or allow to be started or kindled,

ESTABLISHING A PRESENCE

The summer of 1891 was spent patrolling and establishing a presence. The camp in Wawona was a semipermanent installation consisting of some 60 or so tent floors and canvas tents with wooden bunks and tables. There was a blacksmith shop, a storehouse, a quartermaster sergeant's house, and two saddle shops.

THE CAMP IN WAWONA Because of snow in the high country, Captain Wood left the park on November 1 and returned his command to San Francisco. The next six years, from 1892 to 1897, troops were dispatched in either April or May, and left in late fall. The troops at that time had little to do with Yosemite Valley, as it would not be annexed into Yosemite National Park until June 11, 1906.

In fact, "state officials had made it abundantly clear they did not want Army troops permanently encamped in the valley . . . according to Gabriel Sovulewski, the Yosemite commissioners forbade army patrols entering the valley from Wawona from camping farther up the valley than Bridalveil Meadow and strictly limited their movements in the valley, off or on duty." Sovulewski had a long, distinguished career in Yosemite, first coming with the U.S. Army in 1895 and retiring in 1936 as a lead supervisor. He and his wife are buried in Yosemite Cemetery in the Valley.

▲ Between June of 1891, when the army first arrived in the park, and May of 1906, when the Valley was annexed into Yosemite National Park, soldiers only patrolled the Sierra outside the Valley, such as here in the Mariposa Grove of Giant Sequoias. Above, about 40 soldiers from the 6th Cavalry, Troop F, pose with their patrol horses on the Fallen Monarch in 1899.

U.S. ARMY'S CAMP YOSEMITE On June 22 of 1906, 11 days after the Valley was annexed, Major Harry C. Benson moved the army headquarters from Wawona to Yosemite Valley. The HQ occupied more than four acres immediately west of Yosemite Creek (largely where the Yosemite Valley Lodge, opened in June of 1956, now stands). Over the next seven or eight years, the U.S. Army's Camp Yosemite emerged. Ultimately, it consisted of two long, narrow barracks, bath and lavatory houses, accessory structures, a small wooden hospital, 156 tent frames, and a parade ground to accommodate the cavalry. Separate officers' quarters were built in a rough circle between the camp and the nearby cliff face to the north known as Swan Slab. Upwards of 10 of these houses remained in that spot into the mid-1960s. Park visitation for 1906 was 5,414, most ending up in Yosemite Valley.

NEW AND EXPANDED DUTIES In addition to their patrols, the removal of sheep and cattle, and creating a federal presence in the new park, the troops did a great many other things. They fought fires, blazed and built trails, established remote patrol cabins, implemented temperature and water measurements, and undertook some of the first fish plantings in the Sierra. They were also involved in several significant search and rescue missions.

BUFFALO SOLDIERS

In 1866, Congress created six African American regiments in the U.S. Army, soon consolidated down to four: the 9th and 10th Cavalry and the 24th and 25th Infantry. Most were posted in the west and southwest and were almost always commanded by white officers, although some noncommissioned officers came from the ranks. It is claimed that the Plains Indians who first saw these men—often in battle—nicknamed them "buffalo soldiers" because their dark, curly hair reminded them of buffalo fur. The black soldiers, knowing the buffalo was robust and revered by the Indians, took this as a title of respect.

HONORABLE, VALIANT, AND TOUGH In 1899, 1903, and 1904, Buffalo Soldiers from the 24th Infantry and 9th Cavalry patrolled the parks. They stopped poaching and timber theft, confiscated firearms, fought fires, and curbed illegal grazing of cattle and sheep. They oversaw construction of roads, trails, and other infrastructure, including the first nature trail and arboretum. Most fought in the 1898 Spanish-American War and the Philippine-American War from 1899 to 1903. From the very beginning, the Buffalo Soldiers brought great credit to the army, quickly proving to be honorable, valiant, tough, and highly skilled.

▲ Buffalo soldiers from the 24th Mounted Infantry pause while on patrol.

THE ARMY LEAVES

Between Captain Wood and Major Benson, there were 15 other acting superintendents for Yosemite National Park from the War Department between 1891 and 1906. In the *Acting Superintendent of the Yosemite National Park—1906* report to the secretary of the interior by Major Harry C. Benson, he declares: "Due to the fact that last year trespassing was made an unprofitable business no trespassing has been attempted upon the park's lands this year." Encroachment by sheep, horses, and cattle seemed to have been stopped. The army, with the assistance of Rangers Archie Leidig and Charles Leonard (these two are a whole separate, interesting story), was able to solve the only serious protection problem that faced Yosemite. Eight years after the invasion of John Muir's "locusts" had been halted, the secretary of the interior in his 1914 annual report wrote that army troops were no longer needed in the California parks. On July 9, 1914, the United States Army relinquished control of Yosemite. (However, they remained in Yellowstone until 1918.)

HIS FATE UNKNOWN

Who: Mr. F. P. Shepherd • When: 1909

The Story: One of the park's first of many notable searches sadly did not end in a rescue, but in a tragic mystery.

On Thursday, June 17, 1909, a 37-year-old jeweler from San Francisco left the comfort of McCauley's Glacier Point Mountain House and headed for nearby Sentinel Dome—generally a moderate and straightforward hike.

F. P. Shepherd was among the 13,812 visitors to the park that year. When a heavy curtain of water-filled fog rolled in through the tall pines of Glacier Point, his two female companions quickly abandoned their adventure; the recent immigrant from England went on alone.

A THOROUGH SEARCH Every day for almost a week that June, readers of the *San Francisco* *Chronicle* eagerly followed the dogged labors of the United States Army in their attempts to locate Shepherd. Although the search took place more than a century ago, the intensity and methods are still admirable. Within an easy walk of the Mountain House lie some of the most perilous drop-offs in all of Yosemite. The danger of what these searchers were doing was surely not lost on them. More interesting for you today, however, may be the colorful, flamboyant prose and literary license characteristic of newspapers of that era. The following excerpts will reflect how the search for Shepherd progressed, at least as seen in the *Chronicle*.

• • •

Nothing seemed to daunt these brave soldiers. They scaled the faces of dizzy precipices, they were lowered with windlasses over the rocky walls where not even a goat could get a foothold, and dangled between earth and heaven without fear or complaint. They shrank from no risk, no matter how perilous, their hearts seemed to be in the search.

It is a task attended with the utmost danger, as one slip on the part of the soldiers would send them to a terrible death thousands of feet to the rocks below. It is feared now that he may have been attacked by wild beasts or that in trying to find his way in the thick fog at night he may have fallen over some cliff and been dashed to death. If he is still alive he will be in a deplorable condition, as he is without food and blankets . . . the chilling rain which has fallen in and around the valley will leave him in a badly weakened physical state.

◀ These soldiers and civilians with their train of pack mules clown for the camera in 1909 in Yosemite Valley. At that time, the U.S. Army was headquartered where the Yosemite Valley Lodge is today. The search for F. P. Shepherd took place about this same time and on the cliffs almost directly above them. Life for these men was tougher than this photo would indicate.

There was always the faint hope that should Shepherd be found, life might not be extinct, and it was this hope that spurred on the brave cavalrymen. . . . Every nook and cranny, every clump of brush, not only on the face of the cliffs, but on the upper levels was diligently searched for traces of the unfortunate man.

• • •

MORE QUESTIONS THAN ANSWERS One well-intentioned but ill-informed officer stead-fastly watched a flock of large black birds for hours, thinking they might be carrion-seeking vultures; they weren't. Finally, on June 21, the hunt for the hiker was terminated. What happened? We know nothing of his outdoor skills, nor what he had with him, nor what time of the day he began his hike. The ladies with him turned around—why didn't he? Could being a trans-plant from England and new to terrain like Yosemite have had a bearing? Possibly, probably. Was he disoriented by the heavy fog? Possibly, probably. Within walking distance of his lodging and on several sides are nearly hidden, abrupt cliffs of many hundreds of feet. Did he fall? In the end, as with several dozen other Yosemite visitors who have literally vanished over the years, we may never learn what hap-pened to F. P. Shepherd.

THE TAKEAWAY

There are things for you to consider if going on a hike. This is not intended to be all-inclusive, so see what you can add—and see "Preventive Search and Rescue," page 70:

✚ **Tell someone where you are going** and when to expect you back.

✚ **Take time to consider** your physical conditioning, health, weather, time of day, route, footwear, equipment needed, etc. Ask yourself, "What happens if . . .?"

✚ **Do not rely solely on technology.** Just because you have a cell phone does not mean it will work where you are going, nor can GPS guide you in all cases.

✚ **Stay dry.** Wet is the friend of hypothermia, and that includes sweat, particularly while wearing water-absorbing cotton clothing.

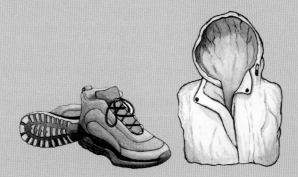

✚ As you hike, **look backward often** in case you need to return that way.

✚ **Cutting switchbacks is never a good idea.**

✚ **If disoriented, do not panic!** Instead, stop and think. When last do you recall a useful landmark, sign, maintained trail, or other people? Before you move on or try to backtrack, consider if doing so will just make matters worse.

VIGILANCE ISN'T ENOUGH

In 1913, there were 13,735 visitors to Yosemite National Park. A front-page article in the February 22, 1913, *Mariposa Gazette* read in part: "Considering the number of visitors and the ruggedness of the country it is gratifying . . . that accidents in Yosemite are very rare. Unceasing vigilance for their prevention is exercised by the park authorities and those . . . serving the tourists who enter the wonderland." While this may indeed have been true, there were two deaths in the park that year, one due to a heart attack. The other was much more dramatic.

A FATAL MISSTEP On May 20th of 1913, Austin Pohli, a popular junior at the University of California, went hiking with three friends from school. The 21-year-old student and his companions hiked up Tenaya Canyon, passed by the Snow Creek Trail, and proceeded to climb and scramble up alongside Snow Creek Falls. That spring, like every other stream and rivulet in the park, Snow Creek was swollen, near overflowing. The fraternity brothers neared the top.

WHAT WENT WRONG As the *San Francisco Chronicle* told it, "Lured on by the rare beauty of the wild, white water, confident of their own skill and judgment they had gained the brink of a dizzy ledge when suddenly young Pohli missed his footing. In an instant the mad torrent seized him and hurled him into the chaos of the cascades and bowlders [*sic*]." He had slipped on the spray-drenched, waterworn granite, disappearing almost immediately, directly down. Despite a valiant effort by his schoolmates to find him, he was gone; in retrospect it might be that his three friends were lucky not to become casualties themselves.

A RECOVERY MISSION Alerted as soon as possible by one of the young men, the park superintendent, Army Major W. T. Littlebrandt, quickly dispatched 15 troopers who, according to the *Chronicle*, "toiled in the midst of the torrents at great personal hazard. . . . Indian guides were sent . . . with ropes and grappling hooks to endeavor to recover the body." A lifeless and battered Austin Pohli was located the second day by First Sergeant Louis Dorn, Troop A, First Cavalry, who had himself lowered by rope to the pool of water beneath the fall and secured the body by diving for it.

VISITATION, THEN AND NOW

In 1918, visitation in Yosemite was 33,527 people. Today, that many people show up on a busy summer weekend. There is no record of accidents or search and rescues for that year, but there is one for deaths, which totaled 18, including two homicides, a suicide, the park's first motor vehicle death, and a drowning.

To compare these statistics to recent years, in 2015 there were 4,150,217 visitors, 124 times as many as in 1918, and only 20 deaths. In 2016—a banner year for parks in part due to the National Park Service Centennial—5,028,868 people visited Yosemite. That's 150 times as many visitors as in 1918, and there were only 16 deaths.

WORLD WAR II

In some ways, the best thing to ever happen to search and rescue was World War II. As war loomed in Europe in the late 1930s, a number of countries activated select soldiers capable of combat in alpine settings using skis, mountaineering, and climbing techniques and equipment. These nations included Germany, Russia, Italy, Austria, Finland, and Norway—but somewhat surprisingly, the United States had no such fighting unit. Charles Minot "Minnie" Dole, the head of the newly formed National Ski Patrol, recognized this and seriously dogged the military and the secretary of war about the need for such warfare capability. Until late in 1941, Dole heard little of consequence.

AMERICA'S MOUNTAIN REGIMENT

Finally, on November 15, 1941, the 1st Battalion, 87th Infantry Mountain Regiment was activated. On December 8th, the day after Pearl Harbor, the first inductee, a young ski racer from Dartmouth, reported for duty. The army wanted men able to pass a night in the winter woods without dying of exposure, meaning outdoorsmen, cowboys, and lumbermen. Dozens came from the National Park Service, including rangers such as Dick and Doug McLaren, Ernie Field, Bob Frauson, Bob Weldon, Laury Brown, Pat Patterson, and Bob Bendt. This expertise was consolidated into the fabled 10th Mountain Division in 1943.

ALL TIED UP

By far the greatest single contribution to mountain rescue during World War II was the development of nylon rope. The war halted overseas hemp manufacturing and importation, necessitating an emergency substitute for the manila line. Plymouth Cordage Company tested the new synthetic; it stretched 39% before breaking. Ultimately, 120-foot lengths of $7/16$-inch-diameter rope, were adopted for climbing and rescue work. Today, standard climbing lengths are 50 to 70 meters, but rescue ropes vary, even up to the 1,200-foot ropes YOSAR uses.

◀ During World War II, the army often used Yosemite for R and R, with the Valley's Upper Pines Campground set aside for it. In 1944 alone, 43 units, with a total of over 32,000 men, enjoyed the park. In this staged photo, El Capitan and Half Dome are being kept safe.

THE RIGHT TOOLS FOR THE JOB Outdoor gear that still defines the standard for SAR was developed and streamlined during this period. Led by the army's famed 10th, there were great advancements in this equipment. Old-style wooden planks were replaced by laminated skis, and quick-release bindings were perfected. New rucksacks, down sleeping bags, and real tents evolved—prototypes for today's lightweight models. Dehydrated food, miniature stoves, and streamlined cook kits arrived. "Bunny Boots," felt-like mukluks developed for winter combat, were still being used well into the 1980s for climbing high peaks like Mount Rainier and Mount McKinley. A novel rubber sole with molded cleats led to a bulky but versatile mountain boot that could also be used for both skiing and rock climbing. Better carabiners, pitons, crampons, and ice axes surfaced and were enhanced.

War Department Field Manual, *FM 70-10—Mountain Operations.* Photo by Butch Farabee.

A PASSION FOR THE MOUNTAINS During the war, ski skills and climbing proficiencies increased, and most importantly, rescue techniques evolved and in many cases were even developed from scratch out of necessity. This body of new knowledge and these fresh ideas and methods were collected in War Department Field Manual *FM 70-10—Mountain Operations,* issued in December 1944. No great surprise, then, that this country's first civilian mountain SAR training (not just in the NPS) was taught by these ranger-soldiers, taking place at Mount Rainier in 1948, with the second in Yosemite in 1955. Fueled by these servicemen coming home to young families, and by the free time and money available to people, the postwar years saw a boom in mountaineering, climbing, and general outdoor adventuring, quite often in the open-space, wild challenges of our parks.

THE HOME FRONT

At the park's many isolated ranger patrol cabins, the first line of defense in handling visitor emergencies was often not the backcountry rangers posted there, but their wives. Long before cell phones and portable radios became common — for at least five or six decades, maybe even into the late 1980s — the women living in these remote areas were the ones to answer that loud knock on the door when their husbands were out in the field.

ON THE FRONT LINES When a campfire got out of control, a car hit a tree, a bear clawed a camper, a Scout chopped open a foot, a freak snowstorm closed a road, or someone drowned or was missing or in need of a rescue, it was often the wife of a ranger who was first to hear of it. Knowing she might be the difference between life and death, she would rise to the occasion, getting on the ranger station's two-way radio and calling for

▲ Eva Cora and Charles McNally at Tuolumne Meadows Ranger Station, 1926.

help or using the landline, if the cabin was lucky enough to have one that was up and running. She'd not only provide key information to first responders, but also often hike or saddle up and ride to the accident scene itself. There, she'd direct, coordinate, and lead, offering much-needed aid and relief and security for many hours if required. Generally, she was not paid a nickel for any of this.

AID AND COMFORT Countless hikers and campers and visitors in distress over the years have been taken in, fed, clothed, equipped, and generally comforted by rangers' wives. There is not one backcountry ranger—or his wife—unable to provide graphic examples of raw, life-saving events. And in great fairness, this readiness to assist also extended to the wives of men stationed in the more established areas of the park, such as the Valley, Wawona, and Tuolumne.

SAFETY FIRST It needs to be added here that for those stationed in these isolated areas, there is a real vulnerability requiring added vigilance and caution. The great majority of park visitors are there to enjoy its beauty and resources, but it only takes one bad apple to bring great harm.

YOU NEVER KNOW

The author taught his new bride how to use the shotgun that stood in the corner behind the front door of Death Valley's very isolated Wildrose Ranger Station. The ranger who'd been stationed there before was the one who caught Charles Manson, ultimately bringing the Manson Family to justice!

HELICOPTERS: THEN AND NOW

This is the first helicopter used for a medevac in the National Park System, in 1949 (see opposite page). It is a Bell 47B-3, open cockpit, two-person ship from Fresno, stripped down to save weight.

Here is the park's contract Bell 205A++ and the 2009 heli-rappel recertification. Rappellers are Jason Ramsdell and Dov Bock, aided from the helicopter by "Boots" Davenport. NPS photo by David Pope.

HELICOPTERS IN YOSEMITE

Few sounds now are more distinctive or even rousing to us than the powerful, pulsing WHUMP-WHUMP-WHUMP of a helicopter. To hear it in Yosemite, possibly even landing in the Valley—with the deep, dramatic reverberations off the granite walls—both the adrenaline and curiosity of anyone within earshot will ramp up. AN EMERGENCY!

THE MILITARY FLIES IN

In March 1958, a helicopter from Fort Ord was used for a multiday rescue from the park's backcountry, heralding an ongoing, nearly six-decade-long relationship with the United States military. In addition to the army, Yosemite has received great support from the Marines, Air Force, and Coast Guard. Particularly noteworthy was the 30-year assistance of crews and craft out of Naval Air Station Lemoore, from 1972 to 2002 (see page 110).

> Only a few helicopter missions were flown in the park during the 1950s, including one to spray chemicals on an invasive tree fungus in Tuolumne Meadows in 1957.

CONTRACTORS ADD AIR POWER In 1961, in an agreement with Sequoia and Kings Canyon National Parks, Yosemite began sharing a Hiller 12-E, furnished by Whirl-Wide Helicopters out of Fresno. Flown by A. P. "Mac" McCloud that first summer, it was used for forest fires and SAR on occasion. Over the next fifty years, at least 10 different models of helicopters, contracted by over a dozen separate companies, have been used by the park. As the performance of park helicopters has evolved and capabilities have increased, so also have Yosemite Helitack crews developed specialized competencies, as well as facilities and equipment, all reflected in a stellar operation. Since 2006, Yosemite's program has been overseen by Kelly Martin, chief of fire and aviation management, the first woman in this position in the park and, as of this writing, the highest-ranking female in NPS Fire.

THE FIRST HELICOPTER MEDEVAC

Who: Terence Hallinan • When: July 31, 1949

The Story: The first medevac ever performed in the National Park System was in Yosemite.

Twelve-year-old Terence Hallinan was on a fishing trip near Yosemite's remote Benson Lake on a July Sunday in 1949 when his horse bucked him off. The boy sustained a possibly life-threatening skull fracture and was still unconscious when guide Pat Campbell rode for the nearest help at White Wolf, some 22 miles away.

THANKS, DAD! At that time no helicopter had made a medevac anywhere in the National Park System. Vincent, the lad's father, was a legendary criminal defense lawyer in San Francisco who had run for President of the United States in 1952. Did this play into Chief Ranger Oscar Sedegren's decision to try using a helicopter, or was it just time for new technology—or possibly both? The boy only needed to be transported about 10 air miles, which would take just minutes, and carrying him by hand could take days. Before the next sunrise, Assistant Chief Ranger Duane Jacobs and local Yosemite Valley Doctor Avery Sturm started by horse toward the accident scene. By that night, the still-unconscious boy's parents had arrived and made the long hike in, and were now also at his side.

HELP ARRIVES Early Tuesday morning, a stripped-down, open-cockpit, Bell 47B-3 left Fresno. Benson Lake is at an elevation of 7,581 feet and the craft's service ceiling was 9,700 feet, making it close to being underpowered for this mission. Knute Flint, a former major in the army recently in charge of a helicopter rescue unit in China, was piloting the ship. Chief Ranger Sedegren, hedging his bets a little, said that should the mission fail, an attempt might be made by seaplane. But there was little room for a plane to maneuver.

THE FIRST TRY Unfortunately Flint barely made it up and out of Yosemite Valley before winds nearly dropped him into the trees in Tuolumne Meadows. Soon he was forced back to the Valley, intent on trying again the next morning. Meanwhile Dr. Sturm, a near-legend in Yosemite emergency medicine, tended to the unconscious boy. The doctor advised against the boy being placed in a seated position, which meant that the operation was delayed until Wednesday as the company tried to locate a casualty litter. Due to tricky winds, a second attempt also failed.

TRY, TRY AGAIN A second helicopter, a more powerful Hiller 360, was trucked in by flatbed from the Bay Area that night, more than three days after Terence had been hurt. Reassembled by lantern light in White Wolf, the ship would leave pre-dawn, flown by Jay Deming, another former army flier. By now, Sedegren had abandoned any idea of a seaplane and said, "If the helicopters fail . . . we will have to carry the boy out." Luckily for Terence, this was unnecessary. Skirting "threatening peaks," Deming took 45 minutes for the trailblazing round trip into and out of Benson Lake. The *San Francisco Chronicle* reported that "Tense moments occurred on the hazardous voyage when Deming who kept his craft low in gasoline to hold down weight, became lost. . . . Rangers and spectators worked furiously to start fires . . . as signals to direct the pilot to a landing spot."

Terence is reported to have said, "My head hurts and my throat is sore. But boy! Was that helicopter nifty."

Terence Hallinan went on to twice serve as the city attorney for San Francisco.

HOW YOSAR CAME TO BE

YOSAR is an acronym for Yosemite Search and Rescue, the park's highly respected, internationally recognized SAR team. But, while search and rescue has gone on in the park for decades, the name, YOSAR, is relatively recent.

HOW IT ALL BEGAN

Pete Thompson, the Yosemite SAR officer from April 1970 until October 1973 had overall responsibility for parkwide SAR. Prior to this time, others had served as SAR officers, but it remains unclear whether they were SAR officers for just the Valley or the whole park. These included Steve Hickman, Lee Shackelton, Rick Anderson, and Dave Huson. Before he became the SAR officer, Ranger Thompson had already toyed several times with the YOSAR abbreviation (the earliest report seems to be the helicopter evacuation of Donna Pritchett with a sprained ankle near Burro Pass on August 28, 1969), but it was not until the fall of 1972 that it was formally accepted. And it was somewhat an afterthought, born of an ugly incident.

That summer, a young man had been employed on a park trail crew led by Jim Snyder (who is now a retired park historian but at the time was a trail crew supervisor). Working near Merced Lake, the younger worker was stung by a bee and quickly went into anaphylactic shock. He was flown out from nearby Merced Lake Ranger Station and, in the process it was discovered that he was only 17 years old, too young for the job. He was immediately let go from his government laborer position.

A TERRIBLE ERROR Just after midnight on August 1, 1972, that recently fired employee set the government's horse barn in the Valley afire. The teen's intent had been to torch the stacked hay and then rush in and rescue the horses, become a hero, and be welcomed back as an NPS employee. The plan backfired, and 17 horses and mules died a horrible death. Additionally, seven other nearby buildings totaling some 20,000 square feet went up in flames. Several of these buildings were among the oldest historic structures still standing in the park, including two that had been built during the Civilian Conservation Corps era and a couple built far earlier by the U.S. Army when they were administering Yosemite.

It was a significant fire, requiring all of the resources available in Yosemite Valley (had it been in a city setting, it might have rated a three-alarm response). That barn was at the same spot where the current horse facility stands; the other buildings were near the site of the present-day SAR cache.

Ironically, the teenager was kicked by an animal he was trying to save from the fire he set and had to be taken to nearby Lewis Memorial Hospital. Luckily, this was the only injury to a human during the catastrophic fire.

UP IN FLAMES In addition to the barn, buildings, and animals, this disaster also consumed virtually all of the Valley's mountain and water rescue equipment. Just as today, the Valley had the largest SAR cache in the entire National Park System and one of the larger rural SAR caches in the country. Within days of the destruction of the cache, Pete Thompson inventoried equipment existing in the park's outlying ranger districts and began to assemble piecemeal the items that he believed essential for routine SARs in the Valley. The park also began requesting assistance from the National Park Service's Western Regional Office for replacement of major capital items such as the horses, barn, and other buildings.

REBUILDING FROM THE ASHES

The fact that the park's Big Wall rescues (and small wall rescues) were becoming more prevalent, complex, and certainly more visible was not lost on the National Park Service's Regional Office. Thompson was soon given limited funds to begin replacing ropes, climbing hardware, sleeping bags, clothing, dry food, stoves, rain gear, tents, and the like. Specially ordered carabiners in a highly distinctive anodized orange coating arrived by the hundreds, and the park's procurement staff insisted Pete keep these coveted items from wandering off and ending up in someone's climbing equipment bag or hanging from a belt loop. As a result, Pete formally adopted the term YOSAR, which was then stamped or inscribed onto anything and everything (especially the carabiners) that would take those five capital letters.

The name, YOSAR, which began as a simple, efficient way to identify gear, evolved into a program synonymous with professional, cutting-edge search and rescue. In the mid-1980s, Joshua Tree National Monument adopted the term JOSAR for its SAR team, and down through the years several other parks have made use of this play on their park names. Photo by Butch Farabee.

▶ Here, Ranger Dov Bock helps prepare an anchor to lower an injured climber off The Prow on Washington Column in the Valley District, June 14, 2010. NPS photo by David Pope.

The home of the SAR cache starting in 1972 had been the park's second jail from September of 1927 until May 30, 1971. It had four cells, one on each end and two in the middle, with at least four beds accompanied by a metal toilet and sink in each. The facility could hold at least 16 prisoners, but on occasion in the 1960s and very early 1970s often held more. It was not well staffed, and the prisoners often went unsupervised. On that May day in 1971, one of the prisoners set fire to a mattress, injuring other prisoners and damaging the building. Staff Park Ranger Dick Marks contended the young man was given matches through the cell window, but no one really knows how the fire began. Regardless, the decision was made to stop keeping prisoners there due to the real potential of injury. Following the incident, prisoners were transported to Mariposa and housed in the county jail.

▶ About 1995, the cache, a portion of which is shown here, was moved to the present location, an old warehouse. This is probably the largest mountain SAR cache in the NPS, with enough gear to handle more than one Big Wall rescue at the same time and 17 water rescue wetsuits. NPS photo by Keith Lober.

THE PIECES COME TOGETHER Probably the September 23, 1972, Neal Olsen rescue from the The Nose route on El Capitan proved the frosting on the cake when it came to the final purchasing of the still-missing equipment. This nationally visible Big Wall SAR was an 1,800-foot stretcher lowering, requiring two full days of great expertise, most of which was furnished by the local Camp 4 climbers. For more on this rescue, see page 118.

A NEW CACHE Since the wooden building housing the Valley SAR cache was destroyed in the 1972 fire, a replacement was needed; it was found less than 100 yards away, ironically sitting vacant due to a different fire (see sidebar). Led by SAR Officer Pete Thompson, rangers and volunteers jumped in and ripped out the sinks and toilets as well as cell bars. And over the next several months, a new SAR cache appeared from the then-unused jail.

▲ Yosemite's primary SAR cache began in the Valley Fire House, at least back into the 1940s, then moved into what had been the park's second jail in 1972. In the 1970s, two of the park's many ropes were each over 4,000 feet long. They were obtained during the Neal Olsen rescue in 1972, but were never used. This is the cache c. 1975. NPS photo.

PETE THOMPSON REMEMBERS

Yosemite Search and Rescue Officer, April 1970 to October 1973

" When I look back at Yosemite rescue history, four operations come to mind:

- Warren Harding and Galen Rowell (SW Face of Half Dome—November 1968)
- Roy Naasz (Arrow Direct, broken leg—April 1970)
- Warren Harding and Dean Caldwell (Dawn Wall first ascent—November 1970)
- Neal Olsen (The Nose, broken leg, long lowering—September 1972)

Of course there has been search and rescue as long as there have been people hiking, climbing, kayaking, or otherwise using the backcountry, but until about 1970 nobody had as much consolidated support doing it as I (we) did. Prior to then, SAR was the poor stepchild to more major aspects of land management: underfunded, and often performed by guys who had little training and who sometimes (understandably) were in over their heads, who hadn't really trained for it, and who were not encouraged by the agency to get good at this stuff. Despite the lack of institutional support, there were individuals and teams in Yosemite, Grand Tetons, Rocky Mountain, and Mount Rainier who pulled it off when it was called for. Dick and Doug McLaren, Richard Reese, Ralph Tingey, and Bill Butler jump to mind, but there were many others.

I got into it because as a young ranger I wanted to develop all the skills necessary to fulfill what I believe is the park ranger's mandate: to uphold the Organic Act of 1916 by doing (or being able to do) whatever is necessary to protect life and property in the national parks. This varies from park to park, of course, but in areas like Yosemite where there is no shared jurisdiction with other agencies, one of the skills required of some rangers has to be the ability to perform, lead, and execute evacuations from places that not many people get to recreationally or otherwise—the faces of exceptionally exposed granite walls.

When the full-time Yosemite SAR officer position was established, I was asked to take the job. Happily, I did. And I could devote full time to professionalizing our training and responses. This included formalizing the agency's relationship with professional climbers (many of them did not have much income). We needed their skills for ongoing operations and working with other cooperating agencies.

The SAR officer pretty soon found himself out of a job except for staff functions and really complicated missions. I recognized that once trained and capable, it made sense for field rangers to lead operations in their areas of expertise. "

▾ Looking down the Half Dome cables at the subdome in fog. NPS photo by Jack Hoeflich.

YOSEMITE'S SAR OFFICERS

A FLEXIBLE ORGANIZATION

In smaller, less busy areas, oversight of search and rescue generally rests with the chief ranger, although it is often delegated out. He or she will ensure a timely, skilled response, hopefully reflecting appropriate training and adequate equipment, followed up by paperwork. And even in the busier parks, an able, practiced SAR response is certainly crucial, but SAR is always just one of several other equally important assignments for the rangers.

A FEDERAL CHANGE In 1965 all federal agencies were tasked with reviewing their job classifications. NPS appointed a Field Operations Study Task Force (FOST). The task force ultimately recommended a number of fairly radical changes in structure for work and positions throughout the NPS, including Yosemite.

A HISTORY OF EXCELLENCE Between 1955 and 1970, Yosemite had many rangers who were rescue standouts; to name but a very few: Frank Betts, Harry During, Buck Evans, John Henneberger, Dick McLaren, Wayne Merry, Jack Morehead, and Dick Stenmark. Several of these men were even assigned as the Valley SAR officer, including Rick Anderson, Lee Shackelton, Dave Huson, and Steve Hickman. But in April of 1970, partially as a result of the FOST task force, Pete Thompson was officially appointed Yosemite's parkwide SAR officer by then Park Staff Ranger Dick Marks. For the next year Thompson would perform this function as a collateral assignment while remaining the park's assistant Valley district ranger to District Ranger Bill Worthington, until March 8, 1972. He then became the first full-time SAR officer in the National Park System. He was responsible for training, policy, and overall oversight for SAR in the entire park, not just Yosemite Valley. He was a senior protection ranger, head of the park's elite Horse Patrol as well as a seasoned, talented all-around outdoorsman.

"I came to the Big Wall rescue business just as a product of timing. When I was selected to be the assistant Valley District ranger (fall of 1968), I had done very little rock climbing, but had been extensively trained by Yellowstone Park Ranger Gerry Mernin out of Canyon Ranger Station in low-angle operations with both tragsitz (Austrian leather and canvas device for a cable raising and lowering system) and less technical long-rope techniques. I believe I was hired because the Valley was getting more complicated and required leadership and direction in several skills: law enforcement, rescue, and communications."
—Pete Thompson, 2015

▲ In this photo of a training, YOSAR techs in Tuolumne Meadows tie a "victim" into a litter, readying to lower him down a cliff. There are fewer SAR incidents in this area, but there are fewer rescuers to respond, so this team is very busy. NPS photo.

Yosemite was the only park in the National Park System to have a full-time SAR officer until February 2003, when Ken Phillips, a ranger at Grand Canyon, took a similar position there. Since then, several other parks have added a full-time emergency operations manager, including Big Bend, Glen Canyon, and Rocky Mountain.

YOSEMITE'S EMERGENCY MEDICAL PROGRAM

▲ Here are rangers in 1915. Beginning on June 24, 1898, 11 men were sworn in as forest agents for Yosemite. They received either $3 or $4 a day, depending on where they patrolled.

Dr. Henry F. Pipes ministered to fellow soldiers in Wawona in 1904; the first lieutenant was then the only trained medical talent in what is today Yosemite National Park. Six years after moving to the Valley in 1906 and creating Camp Yosemite, the army built a temporary two-story hospital in 1912. During the summer of 1914, H. H. Sheffield became the first civilian physician to practice medicine in the park. That same year, the War Department granted the park the use of its hospital as the troops finally left Yosemite for good.

THE EARLY DAYS OF EMERGENCY CARE

For decades, Yosemite rangers did the best they could while routinely dealing with heart attacks, broken backs, diabetic comas, near-drownings, frostbite, skull fractures, pulmonary edema, and dozens of other illnesses and injuries. Rangers handled these with first aid; without question, it was inadequate for the complexities at hand, but it was the best option then available. If lucky, these misfortunes happened near Lewis Memorial Hospital and its staff, but all too often the victims were out scrambling on mountaintops or camping along isolated lakeshores.

FIRST AID FOR ALL In 1910, the American Red Cross First Aid Manual was first published, essentially establishing first aid as a national program. Over the next two decades, bolstered by the cruel lessons of World War I, these basic principles and techniques gradually found their way into the national forests and parks. These early tenets of first aid were terribly modest by today's standards. Yet for nearly 60 years, they were the norm for policemen, firefighters, park rangers, and those others we now call first responders.

LEWIS MEMORIAL HOSPITAL In 1928, Congress granted money for a new hospital for the Valley; on February 19, 1930, after spending $36,000, it opened. Soon named after a beloved, recently deceased former park superintendent, the W. B. Lewis Memorial Hospital quickly became LMH for short. For 45 years, LMH routinely (and somewhat uniquely) doubled as both a small-town, family-oriented medical and dental practice and a full-service, 20-bed hospital—its matchless staff of doctors, nurses, and technicians earning love, trust, and admiration as only a caring, close-knit facility can. Hundreds of thousands of visitors and residents, embodying several generations, passed through its doors—many beginning life there, more ending. In October of 1975, LMH quit functioning as an inpatient hospital facility, precipitated by drastic increases in liability insurance, operating and administrative expenses, and a change in the nature of the medical practice. Since then, it has served as a clinic and urgent care center.

INTO THE MODERN ERA

The 1970s saw many factors come together to help advance and improve emergency prehospital care for the country's first responders. As the decade began, the American Red Cross (and therefore, the NPS) had two courses of first aid. The Basic Course was eight hours in length, and the Advanced was 24; there was also a relatively new four-hour course in cardiopulmonary resuscitation (CPR) offered under the auspices of the American Heart Association.

THE RISE OF EMS MAST, the Military Aid to Safety and Transportation Act, began in 1970. This was a collaboration between the Departments of Defense, Transportation, and Health and Human Services, and provided much-needed assistance to rural areas, principally with flight-medic-staffed military helicopters. Paramedics—generally firefighters—were now busy in cities such as Los Angeles and Miami. A few 80-hour EMT classes began to spring up around the country.

In 1971, the American Academy of Orthopaedic Surgeons published a report titled *Emergency Care and Transportation of the Sick and Injured*. With 84 expert medical and rescue contributors, these nearly 300 pages became the first textbook for the Emergency Medical Technician (EMT) level. The 80-plus hours of this additional, more advanced pre-hospital care course gave first responders, including park rangers, a new, higher standard of performance. EMT is now called Advanced Emergency Medical Technician (AEMT).

◀ First responders carefully transfer an injured person from the rescue litter to the park's ambulance. An officer with the California Highway Patrol's helicopter, just used to hoist the victim from the accident scene, stands on the left, and Ralph Groves of the U.S. Public Health Service, the park's physician, faces the camera. NPS photo by David Pope.

MEDICAL RESOURCES TODAY

In the Valley today, there is a U.S. Public Health Service doctor, a physician's assistant, two nurses, and at least five paramedics solely dedicated to staffing the Yosemite Medical Clinic, in what was historically the Lewis Memorial Hospital. Throughout the park—in both more-developed and wilderness areas—you'll find medical responders, dedicated men and women armed with electronic and digital tools, cell phones, state-of-the-art communication centers, and related technological refinements. Medical responders are in almost constant contact with advanced medical control, including several large health centers for consultation. In 2015, Yosemite first responders managed 1,092 emergency medical incidents.

The background of all of this creative energy was the Vietnam War. Every night at suppertime America tuned into the national news and watched as "Dust Off" rescue helicopters and military corpsmen provided demanding emergency medical care and life-saving transport to wounded soldiers from dangerous jungles and remote rice paddies.

TRAINING FOR RANGERS Between November 6 and 18, 1972, the U.S. Marine Corps' Field Medical Service School in Camp Lejeune, North Carolina, hosted 22 park rangers, including two from Yosemite, at the NPS's first EMT school. Childbirth, unconscious states, cardiac care, advanced fractures, IV therapy, and dislocation reductions were made real by the navy corpsmen who led the training sessions, recently returned from the horrors in Southeast Asia. For several years, Camp Lejeune was the only EMT school utilized by the NPS, but as this level of care spread nationwide, local doctors including Jim Wurgler and Jeff Fokens began teaching it. By 1977, the standard of advanced, pre-hospital care in Yosemite was EMT, a giant improvement over even five years before. It got better.

▲ While hiking, a 53-year-old woman fell 90 feet off the trail near Clouds Rest, on August 14, 2009. Here, a ranger confers with clinic and air ambulance staff while awaiting arrival of the patient by short-haul from the accident scene. She was pronounced dead shortly after arrival. NPS photo by Keith Lober.

WHERE WE ARE TODAY

Yosemite and Sequoia and Kings Canyon National Parks have essentially exclusive federal jurisdiction, which means that living and working in them is loosely analogous to living on a military base or an Indian reservation where some state laws may not (or do not) apply. Given this unique federal status and a need for even more improved care in the isolated wilderness environment, two rangers—John Chew and the author—from the three parks conceived a new level of training.

A NEW IDEA In late 1977, the three parks' medical controls, Dr. Jim Wurgler and Dr. Tom Webster, facilitated a program of increased pre-hospital care, the Parkmedic. An additional 80 hours of training was added to the basic EMT courses, gambling that it would pay off and that these ranger practitioners would be pragmatic and judicious. On June 6, 1978, some 20 parkmedics graduated from the host training site, Valley Medical Center (now merged with Community Regional Medical Center) in Fresno, California. Yosemite now had a dozen or so rangers trained to a level between EMT and paramedic. Because of the parks' jurisdiction, parkmedics could provide far more advanced care—such as starting IVs and administering painkillers—than would be allowed outside the three parks. Since this innovation in 1978, the degree of training and sophistication in Yosemite's pre-hospital care has grown even greater.

THE MAKING OF A PARKMEDIC To become a Yosemite parkmedic today, a ranger first needs to be a nationally certified EMT. He or she will then attend a course available every two years at the Community Regional Medical Center, a Level 1 Trauma Center reputed to be the second busiest trauma hospital in California. The 150 hours of classroom instruction are augmented by nearly 50 hours of clinical time as well as 40 hours of field internship with an ambulance service. Emphasis is on advanced life support in medical, trauma, and cardiac settings. Yosemite currently has approximately 20 parkmedics.

PARAMEDICS IN THE PARK A nationally certified paramedic is generally a graduate of a six-month to two-year program, often as part of a junior college curriculum and always with a greater degree of advanced, street-level pre-hospital training than an EMT or parkmedic, including cardiac care. Currently the NPS has over 80 paramedics, with approximately 10 working in Yosemite. While most Yosemite paramedics are in non-law-enforcement positions, a few are also law-enforcement officers. The park's EMTs, parkmedics, and paramedics provide much of the first line of defense for medical emergencies, staffing the park's six ambulances.

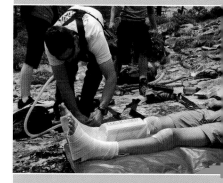

▲ On May 16, 2010, Ranger Matt Stark administers medical care to a 21-year-old man who took a 30-foot sliding fall on wet rocks near Bunnell Cascade. He injured both ankles and his lower back. He was moved 2 miles by wheeled litter to a helicopter and then flown out. NPS photo by Dov Bock.

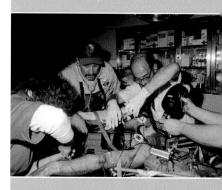

▲ The Valley Clinic's Dr. Flashner checks for breath and lung sounds while others administer to this intubated victim of a fall, still in a Stokes litter, c. 1985. Ranger/Parkmedic Dan Horner (in hat) is still in his rescue gear and chest radio harness. NPS photo.

WORKING TOGETHER TO SAVE LIVES

One of the most impressive things about medical operations in the park is the way that so many people and agencies work together smoothly. Here's an example of that expertise and cooperation, which was laid out in a series of emails with Ranger Heidi Schlichting in 2016.

THE STORY BEGINS The blizzard that began that Friday night in 2011, although not unprecedented for March, was still exceptional by Sierra standards. By Monday morning, Wawona and the nearby Mariposa County village of Fish Camp had upwards of 3 feet of new, water-filled snow. Highway 41, the only outside road into the park's South Entrance was completely closed by numerous fallen trees and downed power lines, leaving Fish Camp and neighboring Tenaya Lodge with its many guests totally stranded. At 11:08 a.m., the park's radio center received a 911 call from the Lodge—while shoveling heavy snow off his car, a 61-year-old visitor with a history of heart problems had begun suffering acute chest pain. County first responders could not get there, so Yosemite Ranger-Paramedic Heidi Schlichting was dispatched. With all tires of her Ford Expedition chained up and in low, four-wheel drive, she began skidding and crunching her way toward the Lodge.

RANGERS TO THE RESCUE Despite the bumper-deep white stuff, Ranger Schlichting somehow reached the stricken man 15 minutes later, along with a Cal Fire paramedic from Fish Camp, Mark Spencer. The victim was taking aspirin and nitroglycerin borrowed from other guests. Because they did not think they were going to get any outside help, the hotel staff and patrons were developing a long-term care plan using doctors staying there, random people's medicines, and phone calls to a hospital in Fresno. As reported in the National Park Service's Morning Report of April 5, 2011, Heidi "gave nitro and morphine before transporting, which was critical." Given miserable flying weather and road conditions, getting very far in any direction, including up, became a highly iffy option. The two on-scene paramedics went to Plan B.

CALLING FOR AIR SUPPORT Heidi Schlichting and Mark Spencer transported the failing man in her patrol car. An air evac was asked for, and before long, a California Highway Patrol chopper was dodging low-lying clouds overhead. The victim sat upright in the passenger seat while Mark kept an eye on him through the window of the rear prisoner cage. Heidi, maneuvering around several vehicles abandoned overnight due to the nearly 3 feet of snow, drove until she

▲ A class of high-school kids was hiking up the Mist Trail below Vernal Fall on March 13, 1974. A small avalanche of blocks of ice fell onto them from 400 feet up, killing one person outright and injuring several others. Rescuers responded as they were dressed before the call. When this incident was reported to the park's communications center, the number of injuries was unknown although thought to be significant. This SAR was in March, before seasonal rangers were hired, and SAR assistance was minimal. The Valley's fire alarm was sounded to attract rangers' attention to the severity of the incident, which was unusual, as this loud siren was generally used only for structural fires. NPS photo.

encountered the first of many trees across the road. Using hands and a chain saw to clear this and other debris, they slowly plowed their way down the road. All the while the two paramedics maintained crucial, hands-on patient care, which included administration of emergency cardiac medications. Not surprisingly, the CHP helicopter was unable to land anywhere close.

THROUGH THE TREES Along the way Heidi and Mark were joined by three NPS forestry and fire technicians, whose sawyer expertise under these trying conditions was invaluable in cutting a path through some 15 trees. It took 75 minutes for the party to go just 2 miles before, as Heidi notes in her log book, "we were halted by power lines." Stopped dead in their tracks, their race with time now became a waiting game. For almost two hours they sat, "because we couldn't get past the power lines." Heidi's log seems to reflect frustration: "helicopter still unable to land due to weather" and "wait for crews to move in from the south and continue attempts for helicopter evacuations from the north."

WHEN PLANS A AND B FAIL Plan C was already in motion—extricate the patient over the snow. "Brian Mattos [NPS forestry] started snowshoeing a trail under the power lines with the plan of carrying/assisting the patient . . . to whatever first vehicle reached us from the south." Alerted previously by the park's radio dispatchers, a Madera County Search and Rescue snow cat arrived on the opposite side of the fallen lines and assisted the desperately sick man to a waiting ambulance. It had taken over three hours for the patient to get to the ambulance and another hour before he reached the CHP helicopter and was flown to Fresno, where he subsequently underwent successful triple bypass surgery.

A CLASS ACT This response by Heidi Schlichting and Mark Spencer was truly a display of emergency professionalism under challenging conditions. It was also an excellent team effort of tenacity and ingenuity by everyone involved: paramedics, dispatchers, sawyers, CHP, CAL Fire, CAL Trans, Sierra National Forest, Mariposa County, Madera County, as well as the hospital medical staff. We are told the man would not have survived otherwise. In many ways, saving this life was business as usual for all involved.

▲ On February 7, 2010, rescuers were faced with a difficult albeit interesting over-snow evacuation, similar to what Ranger Heidi Schlichting had to do in the SAR on these pages. A 48-year-old man who had cross-country skied six miles to isolated Ostrander Hut began experiencing serious symptoms related to altitude. Despite the best of efforts, neither a California Highway Patrol helicopter nor a second helicopter could land due to fog and wind. Finally, rangers and rescuers, including volunteer campers at Ostrander Hut, brought him out by way of a rescue sled, requiring about 10 hours to do so. NPS photo by Keith Lober.

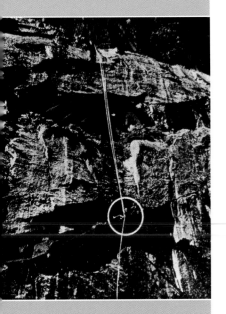

▲ Ranger Frank Betts rappels down Glacier Point for a 17-year-old boy stranded on a ledge above Curry Village.

A HISTORIC TEAM

Late in the summer of 1958, Wayne Merry's former climbing partner, Warren Harding, asked Wayne if he could join the team that also included George Whitmore, Merry's fellow Sierra Club Climbing Section devotee. With major help from Mark Powell, Bill Feuerer, Allen Steck, and Wally Reed, the three went on that fall to make the first ascent of El Capitan, via The Nose.

THE YOSEMITE MOUNTAINEERING SCHOOL

Founded in 1968, the Yosemite Mountaineering School and Guide Service (as it was then called) was the backbone of Big Wall rescues in the park for at least three decades. When the SAR team lacked rangers with sufficient climbing skills, they'd ask the climbers in the YMS to lend their leadership and talents to a rescue emergency. The school popularized the sport of rock climbing, helping it gain legitimacy in the public eye as well as making it safer and easier to learn.

THE WRITING ON THE WALL

By the late 1950s, park managers and rangers were well aware of the public's ever-increasing interest in climbing and in tackling not just small stuff but larger climbs as well. The writing was on the wall—the parks needed rangers who were also skilled climbers. Upon his 1959 graduation from San Jose State University with a degree in conservation, Wayne Merry was hired by Chief Ranger Elmer Fladmark as a permanent ranger. Wayne worked in Yosemite until 1964, mostly in the Valley, with the last several summers serving as the assistant district ranger in Tuolumne Meadows. He then went on to work for the NPS in Olympic National Park and what was then known as Mount McKinley National Park (now renamed Denali). Wayne was the only ranger there with climbing experience and was given the rather informal position of climbing ranger. Within another year, however, he was offered a job he couldn't refuse back in California beneath Yosemite's granite walls.

FOUNDING THE SCHOOL Bob Maynard, the vice president of the Yosemite Park and Curry Company (YPCC) asked Wayne Merry to return and start the Yosemite Mountaineering School and Guide Service, and become its first director. It began the summer of 1968. "Bob saw it as a business move, with the increasing visibility of climbing as a sport," Wayne recalls. "He wouldn't have done it otherwise. Bob was great and I got incredible support—gave me pretty much a free hand." His first hire was Loyd Price, a pantry man at the then Ahwahnee Hotel. Loyd was a rising star in the Valley climbing scene and had very good credentials, including the fifth ascent of the Salathé Wall.

THE FIRST GUIDES That first summer Wayne also hired Jack Miller and Gary Colliver as the next two guides. Colliver ended up serving as a ranger for 14 years, and would earn a Department of the Interior Valor Award in 1983 for a dangerous river rescue (see pages 142–3). Merry also tried hiring climbing-great Warren Harding as a part-time guide, but "Warren did not have the patience for it."

Colliver told the author in a September 23, 2015, interview, "I was a climbing guide for the Curry Company for only one year, but I thought the Mountaineering School was a dramatic shift for climbing and for the better. A sea change of sorts. In my eyes it very much helped to legitimize the sport, brought it 'into the light and out of the rocks,' if you will. Not only in Yosemite but at a national level, as well. It was very controversial within the climbing community in the park. Some of my friends liked it and others thought it brought too much attention to them. To that point, climbers were considered on the fringe."

WAYNE MERRY REMEMBERS

" The first climbing and guide store and office was in the dress shop at the Yosemite Lodge, where the souvenir shop is now. I wrangled a couple of shelves for carabiners, pins, and webbing, urging that prices be kept competitive with The Ski Hut in Berkeley or there would be no business. The cross-country ski shop started there too. Things went so well that we moved to the little building between the Ansel Adams Gallery and the Post Office. We quickly outgrew that too, and moved to bigger quarters at Curry Village.

Loyd and I scouted a basic training area. He found Swan Slab, which worked out very well. Rather shortly the permanent guides were given tent cabins at Curry Village. I had to work pretty hard to convince the YPCC overhead that guides could have facial hair and that they shouldn't be required to wear a fancy uniform. I also convinced the company to have guides paid 50% of the guide fees. Our early basic classes were usually about 10 people and at $10, a $50 day was considered good money by the guides of the time. Initially there were only basic courses. Once we got to Tuolumne Meadows we started doing quite a few intermediate classes—meaning second day—and a little actual guiding, mostly on things like the Great White Book, Tenaya Peak, and the domes. The Mono County Sheriff's Office sent their officers to Tuolumne Meadows to be trained for basic rescue.

▲ Wayne Merry after an epic cross-country ski trip in Alaska in 1972. Photo: Wayne Merry Collection.

Our original 'Go Climb a Rock' T-shirt, although they are no longer sold today, ended up being one of the best advertising and publicity tools the YPCC ever had. These brightly colored shirts could be spotted all over the world. Henry Berry, who at the time worked in marketing for the company, came up with the idea. "

YOSEMITE'S FIRST CLIMBING DEATH

Who: Charles A. Bailey • **When: June 5, 1905**

The Story: El Capitan claims its first experienced mountaineer.

According to an article titled "Fell from El Capitan" in the June 10, 1905, issue of the local *Gazette Mariposan*, Charles A. Bailey was "dashed to death" on June 5, 1905, while trying to make a "record climb up a cliff west of El Capitan." This is the first reported climbing and/or scrambling death in Yosemite, and all quotes below are from this article. Bailey, 50, a real estate dealer from Oakland, was no stranger to the park, having spent 16 summers in the area, nor was he a novice outdoorsman. In fact, he'd just returned from a 14-month trip around the world during which he climbed the Matterhorn, as well as other notable mountains in Europe.

A CLIMB GOES WRONG

On that fateful summer day in 1905, Bailey and his 22-year-old climbing partner J. C. Staats started clambering up the "almost perpendicular face of the cliff where there is no trail and where man has never placed foot before." In the midafternoon the two stopped for a breather nearly halfway up the approximately 3,000 feet of broken cliffs. "Bailey was sitting on a narrow shelf and Staats was clinging to the face of the rock below. Suddenly, Bailey began to slide. He shot downward a few feet to Staats's left and fell headlong out of sight, striking his head several times before he disappeared."

GOING FOR HELP Marshalling his courage although "horror-stricken," Staats gingerly worked his way down to where he found a hat and blood-spattered rock. Unable to go farther and with "almost super human efforts," he struggled up the ledge systems to the top of El Capitan and worked his way back to the village. "Staats was almost prostrated by the physical and mental strain."

The newspaper article continues, "The party searching for the

▲ Galen Clark was the first guardian of the Yosemite Valley and the Mariposa Grove of Big Trees, serving from 1866 to '80 and 1889 to '97. At the time of Bailey's demise, Clark, age 91, was working as a camp manager and guide.

body of Baily [*sic*] located it at 11 o'clock to-day [June 6]. J. A. Snell of Calistoga and H. Spaulding and F. Curry of Palo Alto were lowered by rope 600 feet and by 1 o'clock had brought the corpse to a point where it could be taken by others. The body was badly mangled and most of the bones were broken." Climbing historian Steve Roper has identified this climb as the El Cap Gully. On the very western edge of El Capitan, it's rated as a Grade II Class 4 route. For most of us, a Class 4 rating indicates that the route will require a rope for even basic assistance while ascending or descending.

CLIMB OR SCRAMBLE?

There is no mention of ropes or other mountaineering or climbing equipment in the single news article on Bailey's death. This makes it pretty clear that this was not a climb as we use the term today, but rather a serious scramble. The men's effort and sense of adventure should be admired, and indeed, for his time, Bailey seems to have been very experienced and capable. As we know all too well, life is full of risks and I think it is too easy and a little unfair to say, "They should not have tried this!" Since Staats made it, the climb was obviously doable, albeit with no small amount of physical and mental strain. This is not hyperbole on the part of reporters—the young man just witnessed his partner's ugly death, and no doubt feared suffering the same fate himself. There are a few things we can learn from this fatality; see The Takeaway.

EARLY ACCIDENTS

There is no way to accurately measure the number of search and rescue missions that historically took place in Yosemite, at least until the 1950s. Some accidents did make their way into the newspapers, park archives, and other sources available to us—but only the really impressive ones and, even then, reporting seems to be hit or miss. We do know that between 1900 and 1950, 4 people died while climbing, 40 drowned, and another 20 perished while hiking and/or scrambling. Which raises the question: when does a hike turn into scrambling and then into climbing? Obviously, both ends of the spectrum are clear cut, but defining the middle is often confusing. Witness the Bailey fatality detailed here.

THE TAKEAWAY

Can Mr. Bailey's accident be traced back to at least one definite, final mistake? The pair intentionally chose not to follow a trail, so I cannot speak to that. Weather was not a factor nor was time of day. He was with someone, which is often important although in this case didn't save him. He was experienced, with years of hiking and scrambling in the park, so I will assume his preparations and familiarity with the quirks of the area were adequate.

+ Maybe, however, **he was too complacent,** too cavalier, too casual with his knowledge of what to expect. A sense of overconfidence has spelled disaster for hundreds of others . . . and caused the occasional death.

+ **The pair may have been in too great a hurry,** with Bailey just a little too comfortable with the success of their climb to that point.

+ **His footwear may have been the best money could buy at the time, but it is highly likely that it contributed to his fall.** Even today's state-of-the-art footwear is no match for sloping rocky ledges with even just a hint of gravel or twigs or leaves on them acting as ball bearings. There is no hiking footwear that will give you a 100% sure grip.

+ **It seems that Bailey was in excellent physical condition— perhaps.** The records are filled with men (but only a few women) who needed rescue—or even died—while hiking, due to medical causes, e.g., heart disease, many of them in their 40s and 50s and even a few in their late 30s.

+ We will never know why Bailey began to slide. **You can never be too cautious while hiking and playing in Yosemite or anyplace in the great outdoors.** The more you scramble and climb without adequate protection, the greater the chances of getting hurt.

CALL IN THE ROCK STARS

The Yosemite Search and Rescue Team relies on SAR-Siters to augment the ranger ranks. SAR-Siters are skilled climbers and rescuers. They live for free in SAR campsites in the Valley's Camp 4 and the Tuolumne Meadows campground, spring through fall. Hence the mysterious name, SAR-Siter. These young(er) men and women are used for carry-outs, cliff evacuations, searches, and swift-water rescues, as well as support for the park's firefighting program. Perhaps most importantly, YOSAR can call on their high-angle, Big Wall prowess. At summer's end in 2016, there were eight SAR-Siters in each of the two campgrounds. Yosemite is the only national park with SAR-Siters.

THE MAKING OF A SITER

For several years, the sole qualification for a SAR-Siter was to be a climber with demonstrated skills on the demanding Yosemite Big Walls. Today, these expert climbers must also complete a formal, written application to compete for a SAR-Siter position. In addition to proven climbing skills, the candidate is interviewed and assessed as to leadership ability, dedication to teamwork, field medical skills, and organizational talents. SAR-Siters are formal NPS Volunteers-In-Parks (VIPs). They carry pagers and are expected to respond according to certain parameters. Their time spent may take the form of training, rescue missions, or some other method of earning their keep.

ON THE JOB Once off and running—sometimes literally—SAR-Siters are on the government's payroll intermittently. The job they were hired for on a given incident dictates their pay rate. This policy is known as Administratively Determined Pay Plan for Emergency Workers (AD) and in 2016, there were over 200 separate functions SAR-Siters could fall under, including canine handler, basic search and rescue technician, technical mountain-rescue leader, traffic-control aid, and all-hazard swift-water rescue technician, just to give a few examples. The pay in 2016 ranged from $14.68 to $55.36 per hour.

VOLUNTEERS -IN-PARKS (VIPS)

Any individual, as well as organized groups, can volunteer for a great many jobs and activities in most of the national parks. Those under 18 can be VIPs with the signed permission of a parent or guardian. Yosemite has a VIP coordinator. For further information, visit nps.gov/getinvolved. The written process is simple and straightforward.

▶ Volunteers-In-Parks patch. NPS photo.

WHAT IT TAKES A great Yosemite climber is not automatically a competent Yosemite rescuer. So to that end, SAR-Siters are provided classes in rescue techniques, EMT, fire fighting, helicopter ops, and SAR management, and must attend three days of swift-water rescue training. In addition, informal mentoring and on-the-job training are constants. SAR-Siters come from a number of professions, including engineering, paramedicine, nursing, and law. By the end of their first season, SAR-Siters have become a great addition to the well-oiled YOSAR machine, and many return year after year. For more information on becoming a SAR-Siter, go to the Friends of YOSAR website at friendsofyosar.org (see page 209).

(see page 209).

▲ On August 21, 2007, rescuers top out on Half Dome with a 31-year-old climber with fractures in his back. NPS photo by David Pope.

BENDING THE RULES

When Yosemite SAR Officer Pete Thompson first launched the Camp 4 Rescue Sites in 1970, there were no provisions in place for someone not already on the government payroll to be paid for a SAR. There were, however, guidelines for hiring "administratively determined emergency hires," known as ADs. At that time, the Department of the Interior only allowed wildland firefighters to be hired as ADs, but Pete found a way to work around that. The logic to Pete and the few others who quietly sanctioned this minor violation was the increasing—often life or death—need for this rescue expertise. And the only precedent to go by was with firefighters. It was one of those "it seemed like a good idea at the time" concepts. For years this hiring practice was problematic, although it was eventually endorsed at the highest levels.

MICHAEL A. NASH REMEMBERS

Yosemite Search and Rescue Officer, April 2001 to February 2002

▲ A canvas tent in the Camp 4 SAR Site. NPS photo.

" The amazing part of the job was you never knew what a given day would bring: who would walk into the SAR cache or what might come over the radio. But the one thing you could count on was that when the SAR alert-tone came on some of the most dedicated rangers and volunteers would answer the call.

Managing the program certainly was less glamorous than getting out on the actual rescues. I spent much of my year working to clean up the program to include a massive overhaul of the SAR Site in Camp 4, one of the most famous campgrounds in the NPS. Historically, tent cabins were sold from one SAR-Siter to another with very little oversight. The camp was in poor condition, and there was a lot of nonsanctioned camping and subletting. I made a concerted effort to clean up the site and to rebuild all the tent cabins and raise the expectation of what it meant to have the privilege of living in Camp 4 as a member of YOSAR. There was significant controversy surrounding all of this. One of the SAR tents even had a false wall built into it, concealing a single bed (once the hiding place of a few illegal campers). At the overhaul's completion, some volunteers were gone, all the tents in the SAR Site had been rebuilt, and more than two 20-yard dumpsters of trash and abandoned property and gear were removed, an accumulation of more than 30 years.

My most memorable rescue was on August 4, 2001, and involved five Korean climbers, none speaking English. One had broken his right leg in a fall on the Northwest Face of Half Dome the day before. An open fracture at the ankle, it had bled heavily for a time. He was moved to a larger ledge and then two of them rappelled down. At 8:00 a.m., they luckily reported the accident to Ranger Steve Yu, whose father in Wisconsin was fluent in Korean. Steve, an accomplished climber himself, then became the incident commander. He paged out the YOSAR team for a rope rescue, as well as the park's ship and a hoist-equipped Huey from Lemoore. Clouds were building, so the faster we could do this, the less likely a lightning storm would come near us.

With about 15 feet of rotor blade clearance, Park Pilot Dana Morris and Helitack Crew Chief Karen Kufta put us over the injured climber. Paramedic/Ranger Keith Lober and I then rappelled onto a 2-foot-wide ramp, 25 feet below our man. When Keith reached the climbers, he found all three attached to just a single, $1/4$-inch bolt. The victim was stable and he still had his blood-soaked shoe on, which helped when we put him into the stretcher. H-551 had no problem short-hauling the patient, and he was at the clinic by 12:30 p.m.

Meanwhile, Lemoore's Rescue Six made two flights to hoist out the four of us on the wall. Lober and I were the last two pulled off the cliff, and as we clipped to the hoist line and unclipped from the wall, the 'King Swing' from our stance out over the Valley was one experience I will never forget! Then the hail storm began. "

HOW YOSAR FITS INTO YOSEMITE

With more than four million visitors per year, and 1,200 employees and volunteers as summer staff, Yosemite is a busy park.

PARK OPERATIONS

Under the park superintendent, eight divisions manage distinct aspects of park operations, e.g., Facilities Management and Interpretation. The Division of Visitor and Resource Protection (Protection) is led by the chief park ranger. Protection includes law enforcement (LE), fire (see page 102), aviation, emergency medical services (EMS, see page 46), and search and rescue (SAR). As the old saying goes, their challenge is to: "Protect the park from the people, the people from the park, the people from the people."

For some administrative purposes, the park is currently divided into three geographic districts, each led by a district ranger: Wawona District (south of the Valley), Mather District (north of the Valley), which includes Tuolumne Meadows, and the Valley District (see map on page 6). Districts run their own LE, SAR, and EMS operations, but they often draw on resources from elsewhere.

The districts are supported by specialty branches in Protection including fire, aviation, EMS, and the SAR Office. The park SAR officer oversees parkwide SAR policies, training, budgets, quality control, and other SAR functions. The park-wide SAR office also operates the Preventive Search and Rescue (PSAR) program—the education component of SAR (see page 70).

SO WHERE DOES YOSAR FIT IN?

There is no specific team or separate organization named YOSAR; it is only shorthand for the SAR function in the park. The core of the team are the LE rangers, but other essential components include the SAR-Siters (see page 56), YODOGS (see page 96), PSAR volunteers, Communications Center, and other NPS employees.

▲ Yosemite is a 1,169-square-mile World Heritage Site, with 95% formally designated as wilderness. On August 21, 2007, en route to an emergency near the eastern boundary, Helitack crewmember John DeMay looks down on a remote lake in the big park. NPS photo by David Pope.

WHEN RESCUER BECOMES VICTIM

Down through the years and around the country, far too many expert, well-trained first responders have perished on cliffs and in rivers, or traveling in boats, planes, or helicopters. Many have died rushing to an accident in a patrol car or ambulance. In fact, one of the very first things police, firefighters, EMTs, and others are taught is, "If I don't get there, I'm no help to anyone!"

THE ULTIMATE SACRIFICE

Only two SAR professionals have died on the job in Yosemite, but this is not the whole picture. Ending the story there would be a pronounced disservice to the other 17 or so people who have made the ultimate sacrifice trying to save a friend or family member, sometimes even a complete stranger, from drowning or from going over a waterfall. These brave souls were not on any organized SAR mission. Rather, they spontaneously, probably without even thinking about it, leapt a fence, or bolted down an embankment, or grabbed frantically at an arm or shirttail. This failing, they then entered the water.

Ever since the first recorded drowning in 1870, drowning has been historically second only to motor vehicle accidents as the most common way to meet a traumatic end in Yosemite. As of 2017, at least 174 people have drowned, 13 of them while attempting to save another person from drowning. Out of those 13 rescue attempts, only three people were actually saved! The records are full of helpful people who did successfully save other visitors' lives, but these rescues were generally on dry land. In the water, would-be rescuers have all too often sacrificed themselves in vain.

VERNAL FALL CLAIMS A HERO

At least five people have died helping someone who was only seconds away from going over a Yosemite waterfall, and four of those deaths occurred at Vernal Fall. Vernal has claimed 16 victims since the first recorded death in 1924. One of these would-be rescuers, 21-year-old navy veteran Orville Loos, did not even know the young victim. On July 9, 1946, 11-year-old Keen Freeman of Washington, DC, tried to fill his canteen 60 feet upstream of the 317-foot-high waterfall. He dropped it and tried to retrieve it, but instead slipped into the river. Witnessing the unfolding drama, Loos plunged in and caught the

▲ On September 29, 2006, a 26-year-old male disappeared from Tamarack Flat Campground. A major search ensued for the barefoot man. Thirteen days after disappearing, his body was found in The Cascades. Here two members of YOSAR are placing him in a body bag. Suicide was suspected but undetermined. NPS photo by Keith Lober.

boy 15 feet from the brink. As he frantically fought for the shore, the current yanked at them and carried him, holding Keen, over the lip.

A TRIPLE TRAGEDY On July 19, 2011, Vernal Fall took two rescuers at the same time. Twelve members of a church group from Ceres, California, chose to ignore warning signs and climbed over the safety railings at the top of the fall. Several onlookers tried to warn them of the danger, and they, too, were ignored. The group settled on the lip of the waterfall, a few feet from dozens of other visitors who were obeying the safety restrictions.

For a half hour the group sat on the smooth and gently sloping granite near the river, which, due to a snowpack twice as great as normal, was flowing very high. Finally, Hormiz David, 22, stood to leave, lost his footing, and fell in. Ramina Badal, 21, reached out to him. He grabbed her hand, and she too stumbled and toppled in. For a few brief moments they hugged each other. Then 27-year-old Ninos Yacoub jumped in, probably following the instinctive urge to rescue them. As onlookers screamed in horror, all three shot over the edge and died within moments.

PERIL AT NEVADA FALL One of the would-be rescuers was a 30-year-old mother trying to save her 9-year-old daughter in 1970. The girl's family had scrambled off the trail and climbed the safety railing to sit on the rocks, wade in the river, and pose for photos less than 75 feet from the brink of the 600-foot Nevada Fall. The youngster dropped her hat and lost her footing trying to retrieve it. The mother jumped in to save her daughter. Both went over, and the little girl's body was never found.

UNDERSTAND THE RISK Please do not interpret these thoughts to mean you should never consider rescuing a person in the water. But you must remember that most people who have attempted this in Yosemite have died for their efforts. Drowning people are notorious for unintentionally killing their rescuers. If you are entering water to help, you need to understand your risk and how to minimize and survive it. All courses in life-saving stress using every conceivable on-shore technique first before entering the water. Reach—Throw—Row—Go. If it comes down to "Go," it is then also advised to keep out of reach of the person in trouble. Toss the victim something rope-like and tow them to safety.

A WARNING ABOUT WATERFALLS

Always obey the warning signs and keep on the proper side of all railings and fences. These safety measures and warnings are installed based on the area's history and potential for tragedy. In fact, **the lack of a sign or railing does *not* mean an area is safe.** Treat these signs as lessons to follow elsewhere.

Few things are as noble, yet as totally futile, as jumping into the water above a waterfall in an attempt to save someone. The edge of any body of moving water—river, stream, rivulet, waterfall—in the Sierra can be lethal, despite your level of comfort in the water. Rocks are waterworn and smooth, maybe even polished by glaciers. These edges, ledges, and boulders will have ball bearing–like granite sands and invisible-to-the-eye algae on them, which when moistened may even be too slippery to stand upright on. Your feet can come out from under you in the blink of an eye. For more on waterfalls and SAR, see page 144.

Just before 6:00 a.m. on May 25, 1991, 44-year-old Elaine Watson of Compton, California, was driving up Southside Drive, 300 yards east of the Bridalveil Fall Road Junction. Along this stretch, the road passes within a dozen feet of the Merced River. That morning it was in near-flood stage, flowing deep and fast. This road, particularly in this spot, is not very forgiving. In the Toyota Camry with Watson that morning were her 62-year-old mother, Pearl, her two nephews, 3-year-old Mario and 5-year-old Lance, and her 7-year-old niece, Sequoia. As she headed east into the Valley, the rising sunlight and shadows may have flickered in front of her in a mesmerizing manner, and perhaps she nodded off at the wheel.

A TERRIBLE PLUNGE

The car left the road and quickly bounced down the boulder-strewn riverbank, splashing into the water at the head of a long, whitecapped rapid. It floated for 60 feet, finally becoming lodged facing upstream against a log jam, 25 feet from shore. The frigid waters now boiled up over the submerged engine compartment, pushing the vehicle deeper into the river. A man who had been driving immediately behind them stopped. As he watched the family of five clamber out of the rapidly filling car onto the rooftop, he yelled to them to stay put while he went for help. Moments later, four more tourists stopped. One threw Watson a rope, and these Good Samaritans yelled and signaled they would pull them all to shore, one by one. This was a mistake.

RESCUE ATTEMPTED Watson, now wide awake, hurriedly knotted the line around her niece Sequoia. The seven-year-old jumped into the river and was safely pulled to shore. But Mario and Lance, seeing their older sister leap into the water, immediately followed suit without waiting for the rescue rope. Both tiny boys quickly bobbed out of sight downstream on the two-foot-high waves of the swollen Merced. With little hesitation or regard for her own safety, Watson plunged into the river to save her two young nephews.

RANGER ON THE SCENE

As luck would have it, Ranger Dave Panebaker heard the call come in: "CAR IN THE RIVER." Within 13 minutes of hearing the radio report, Dave was on scene. The senior park ranger was a veteran white-water rescuer and had his life-saving gear with him.

TWISTS OF FATE Watson's mother, Pearl, was still immersed to midthigh in the river, becoming hypothermic but otherwise unhurt. Fortunately for her, the force of the rushing water had pinned her legs tightly between the car body and its open front

▲ Ranger Dave Panebaker rescuing Elaine Watson's mother, Pearl, on May 25, 1991. Three people died in this car accident. NPS photo.

door, keeping her from being swept away. Quickly wiggling into his wetsuit and dragging a safety rope behind him, Dave swam out to the terrified woman. With time critical, he could not wait for backup. Dave cradled Pearl to warm her while shielding her from the unrelenting current until more rescuers could arrive. Once they did, Pearl was quickly hauled to shore. And when it was learned the two boys and their aunt were in the river, searchers were soon in the rushing water as well as combing the shore for the missing trio.

Two hours after Elaine Watson possibly had dozed off, she was found. But despite CPR by rangers, Watson—the would-be rescuer—was pronounced dead. First responders dread nothing more than the death of a child, and a huge search was mounted for the little boys. Two weeks after five-year-old Lance bobbed downstream, his body was found. Three long months later, the skull of seven-year-old Mario was discovered lodged in some driftwood among the boulders.

THE TAKEAWAY

There's no need to belabor the danger of drowsy driving; most readers are only too aware of it. After that, though, this is not an easy incident to analyze due to factors including the sudden surprise of plunging into the river, the ages of the boys, and the specific skills of the adults in the car. But here are some things to consider.

+ **Most people consistently underestimate the power of ocean waves, river currents, and falling water.** The more training you have in these environments, the more respectful you become of water's strength and capability for surprises.

+ **Unless the body of water you are in is warmer than your core body temperature, you will instantly begin to chill and slip toward hypothermia.** In the rushing, snow-fed Merced River that morning, hypothermia was inevitable, and its onset would have been quick. If you find yourself in a similar situation, climbing to the roof of the vehicle or onto a rock that is even partially out of the water might save your life.

+ It is impossible to criticize Elaine Watson for jumping in to try to save her nephews; I probably would have done the same thing. But even for a strong swimmer, **the dangers from sunken boulders and logs and other hidden and unavoidable life-threatening traps are extreme and success is unlikely.**

+ **In this situation, you should float on your back with your feet downstream, as much as possible.** This allows you to see obstacles and push off when necessary. Entrapment by boulders, logs, and trees is the greatest danger for you at this point. This feet-first position also permits you to keep an eye on the person you went in for. But your first obligation is to yourself—the person you are saving becomes secondary.

WHEN A SAR TURNS DEADLY

Above, it is noted that only two people working on a SAR have died on the job in Yosemite. These are their stories. The first instance was in 1968, when Jim Madsen lost his life attempting a rescue on El Capitan.

James Madsen, just 20 years old, was a sturdy University of Washington engineering student and football player. Wayne Merry, former Yosemite National Park ranger, had been in the first group to climb El Cap and in 1968 was the new director of the Yosemite Mountaineering School. He recalls that Madsen "was certainly one of if not the best and fastest climbers this country had produced."

▲ On October 4, 1977, rescuers on top of El Capitan raise a climber with a possible broken ankle. This would have been on a route close to where Pratt and Fredericks were climbing and near where Jim Madsen fell. NPS photo by Tim Setnicka.

A BROTHERHOOD OF CLIMBERS In the late 1960s, the Yosemite climbing community was minuscule compared to today's numbers, and perhaps for that reason it was a tightly knit brotherhood. Many historians of park climbing describe it as the Golden Era, those years when only an elite few were climbing El Capitan, Half Dome, and the other Big Walls that Yosemite is world-famous for. The loyalties and friendships among the climbers were powerful, and they looked out for each other, keeping track of who was climbing what, maybe even second-guessing the climbers' likely schedules. And so it was in the middle of October 1968.

ASCENDING THE DIHEDRAL WALL Chuck Pratt and Chris Fredericks, both among the very best climbers and veterans of previous, serious Big Wall climbs, were inching their way up El Capitan's Dihedral Wall. When it was first scaled six years before, the ascent of the nearly 3,000-foot rock face had taken 38 days. At that time it was rated as a Grade VI, 5.9 A3 climb (see page 117), making it among the most difficult routes anyplace in the world. By 1968, three to five days had become the norm, and Pratt and Fredericks expected to do the giant in five. Neither, however, had predicted an unseasonably early storm, or that a good friend might die trying to save them.

UNEXPECTED WEATHER On Saturday, the fourth day of the climb, the unexpected weather settled in and quickly soured; nearly 3 inches of rain fell, followed by wet, heavy snow. The temperature dropped to

24 degrees at Crane Flat, the park's 5,000-foot level, that night—and the two men were more than 1,500 feet higher. With frigid water cascading down the rock face, they were forced to stand in their painfully narrow nylon web slings all night, pressed vainly against the freezing rock to try to find shelter from the torrent. Barely moving, their progress that morning was halting and slow. Their friends watched, peering from below through the increasing puffs of mist blowing across the immense granite wall. Some grew anxious, including Jim Madsen.

MADSEN MAKES HIS MOVE With Kim Schmitz, Madsen had made this same exacting climb that spring in a very fast two and a half days. Alarmed by the storm, he had been monitoring Chuck and Chris's progress. He understood the demands they faced and wanted to help in any way he could. Armed with great skill and an intimate knowledge of the route, the young man pressed the park rangers to mount a possible rescue, even though Chuck and Chris had not indicated they needed one.

▲ This upward view of granite is what climbers on Yosemite Big Walls see and experience. NPS photo.

He led a team loaded with ropes, climbing tackle, shelters, sleeping bags, food, and stoves to the top of El Cap long after dark. They were drenched when they finished the 9-mile hike in, from rain, snow, and certainly sweat.

DISASTER STRIKES At first light, with little sleep, Jim Madsen prepared to rappel down and make voice contact with the pair far below. If they asked for help or sounded too weak to ascend, he would continue down the 600 more feet to their tiny ledge. He tied a 150-foot rope to a 3-foot-thick pine tree a few feet from the edge of the cliff, threw the rope over, and started down with 45 pounds of survival and climbing gear fastened to his back. Within minutes, the unthinkable happened.

Loyd Price, chief guide of the Yosemite Mountaineering School, was the closest witness. Other rescuers saw Price scramble up from the edge with a look of horror on his face while he said simply, "Madsen fell." He had heard Madsen say, "What the f—," and then yell. The rope then snapped upward and Price heard Madsen hit twice on the way down.

Incredibly, on October 15, 1968, experienced, talented young Jim Madsen had somehow slipped off the very end of his rope, despite having tied a small safety knot in it. He was the fourth climber to die in Yosemite Valley to that point in time. Ironically, Chuck Pratt and Chris Fredericks completed their climb without needing the assistance Jim and the others felt might be so crucial.

▲ Ranger Jim Reilly hangs off the Mescalito route on El Capitan on June 2, 1981. He is administering to a climber with a broken collar bone, about 300 feet from the top. NPS photo by John Dill.

A RESCUER VANISHES

This second story is one that I was directly involved in. Just past 10:00 p.m. on a cool night in May of 1977, my wife, Anne, and I were getting ready for bed when I sensed something below the level of actual hearing. Our open bedroom window was directly beneath the Yosemite Point Buttress, or YPB as it is called, and I strained to hear the muffled cries, unsure. Finally, Anne said, "*Yes, I hear them!*" A chill ran down my spine. Within moments I radioed it into our dispatch center. I didn't know it then, but the yells for help were coming from the YPB. And so, I was the acting search and rescue officer the night Jack Dorn died.

FINDING THE CLIMBERS Ginny Rousseau and Bruce McKeeman were on road patrol that night. Ginny took the call and set her vehicle up on the road between the Village Store and Yosemite Lodge to try to contact whomever was yelling, using the car's loudspeaker. Asking simple yes or no questions, it took a good two hours to determine the person's rough location and ascertain the nature of the problem. By 1:00 a.m., a six-person team from the rescue site in Camp 4 was rousted out of a comfortable sleep; team leader duties fell to Craig Patterson, a seasonal ranger.

A TEAM SETS OUT It was still a few hours till dawn when the team started up the Yosemite Falls Trail. All were accomplished Big Wall climbers, and most had likely done the YPB. Their mood was relaxed and very confident as they started up what, by many standards, is a broad highway of a path. Zig-zagging their way up, they moved easily, the beams from their orange rescue headlamps bobbing eerily in the swirling mist. A gentle rain fell, and the wind and water trickling over nearby rocks mingled with the fading sound of an occasional car from below.

Like everyone else in Camp 4—a historic campground for climbers—30-year-old Jack Dorn from Utica, New York, lived for the challenge of the Yosemite walls. A veteran of the Valley's granite, he was also on the park's climber-rescue team; in exchange for a free tent spot and long-term camping, he was to be available for SAR missions whenever possible. Thirty minutes into their fast-paced hike, just east of Columbia Point, Jack was last in line.

A TERRIBLE FALL It was several minutes before Ranger Patterson and his team realized Dorn was no longer with them. Initially they didn't worry too much, as Jack was a seasoned, very qualified outdoorsman, capable of taking care of himself. However, when they backtracked to look for him, they soon found a recently scuffed basketball-sized

▲ Jack Dorn climbing not long before his death in 1977. NPS photo, Keith Lober collection.

hole in the trail's rock-lined retaining shoulder. Jim Pettigrew quickly rappelled down a couple of hundred feet until he could just make out a body some 600 feet below. Jack lay at the bottom of the cliff, and Jim felt certain he was dead.

How did it happen? Perhaps he was lost in the music he'd been listening to on his headphones. Maybe he had climbed too hard the day before or had stepped off the trail to relieve himself, or didn't notice the slight turn in the trail. Why Jack Dorn, responding to pleas for help that night, walked off the well-worn trail and plunged to an almost instant—and certainly needless—death, no one will ever know. Like with Jim Madsen, however, it is surely fair to say he was not paying attention.

THE SAR CONTINUES Once Jack's death was established and relayed to Rangers Rousseau and McKeeman, the five team members proceeded with their initial rescue, their mood far more somber. It was not until after daylight that they reached the rim above the Yosemite Point Buttress and located the trapped men. Don, a 22-year-old from Florida, and 26-year-old Larry from Kentucky were wet, cold, and stranded. Patterson was lowered down several hundred feet to their location. Don, in an intermediate level of hypothermia, was unable to climb out on his own, but both were rescued safely.

▲ Ranger Jim Lee is lowered with the body of Jack Dorn in the litter. Would-be rescuer Dorn fell to his death on May 23, 1977. NPS photo by Butch Farabee.

HEARSAY

Jack Dorn was rumored to be one of the many Valley entrepreneurs who struck it rich from the sizeable load of marijuana aboard an ill-fated twin-engine plane lost in Lower Merced Pass Lake the previous December (for more on that story, see page 154) and, based on this, conspiracy theories arose about his death.

It is true he somehow found a personal address book from one of the pilots on that plane.

But it is also true that he ripped it up and threw it into a snowy field. He soon came forth and admitted this and was able to take Ranger Fred Hemphill back to the spot. The book was found and reconstructed like a soggy jigsaw puzzle. It ended up proving valuable to the criminal investigation in the attempts to determine who owned the aircraft. To add to the mystery, no one knows the whereabouts of that book today.

Did Jack get rich from either the marijuana or some stash of money carried by one of those two pilots? You definitely could not prove it by his lifestyle. Might he have been the victim of foul play? It seems entirely unlikely. How would you engineer this scenario? The stranded climbers, the rain, the spot where he fell. And for what reason? As tempting as it is to weave a tale of treachery and intrigue, this was merely a wretched, heartbreaking, needless accident.

PART 2
IN THE FIELD

Ranger David Pope searches for 22-year-old Rachael Neil who fell into the rapids upstream of Nevada Fall on August 19, 2005. Despite an intensive effort by YOSAR over the next three weeks, she was not recovered until September 11. NPS photo by Jack Hoeflich.

"You have a permit, but how much water do you have? It's a 16-mile round trip."

★

"Yes, I do think it is a bad idea to hike to Nevada Fall in flip-flops!"

★

"A thunderstorm is forecast this afternoon; Half Dome is very dangerous then!"

★

"The sun on this trail can be brutal: you need a hat, preferably one with a broad brim."

★

"Yes they are cute, but please don't feed the ground squirrels at Vernal Fall."

★

"I'm sorry, but dogs are not permitted on any of the trails in the park."

▶ Bear near caution sign.
▶▶ A climber's potentially broken ankle is stabilized in a metal "ladder" splint in 1977. NPS photo by Tim Setnicka.

PREVENTIVE SEARCH AND RESCUE

"The Mountains Do Not Care" has been a mantra of SAR groups for decades. This refrain is certainly true for Yosemite. Make no mistake; behind the breathtaking allure, the park is deceptively hazardous, sometimes even lethal—cliffs, waters, and trails are unforgiving. Inexperience, haste, complacency, and/or being ill-prepared trigger most of Yosemite's accidents, for tenderfeet and old hands alike. Preventive Search and Rescue (PSAR), strives to make park visits—your visit—safe and rewarding through education, information, and support.

THE MOST SAR INCIDENTS

Records show that two-thirds of Yosemite SAR incidents involve day hikers, most along just a few main trails. These routinely include sprained and broken ankles, heat exhaustion and dehydration, heart attacks, and separated parties. To help stop these occurrences, one full-time employee and more than 40 trained PSAR volunteers and interns oversee the busiest trails, mostly those going up and out of the Valley. On any given day in the summer, these men and women wearing distinctive yellow "Hike Smart" T-shirts dispense information and advice about vital topics including the length of any given hike, trail conditions, health and safety considerations, what to wear and bring along on your hike, weather reports, how to deal with wild animals, and much more.

PSAR is nothing new; park areas worldwide have focused on these problems for years. Grand Canyon National Park has been doing this even longer than Yosemite, with even more volunteers assisting.

▲ At this trailhead, Ranger Stephanie Hance conveys the park's PSAR message. It's good for all ages but especially important for children. NPS photo.

2006–2015 YOSEMITE DEATH STATISTICS

Falls on trails, scrambling, and Half Dome cables: 22

Water-related: 15

Rock climbing: 14

Motor vehicle accidents: 7

Miscellaneous accidents: 14

Suicide: 12

Cardiac: 46

Other natural causes: 17

TOTAL: 147

Source: National Park Service, 2016

DON'T BE A STATISTIC

So, what does PSAR want park visitors to know? Here are suggestions for staying safe in a range of conditions.

+ First and foremost, you are responsible for your own safety and for that of anyone under your care. This is a rugged natural area, and will be totally unforgiving of any missteps.

+ Before setting off, ask yourself "What if . . . ?", and expect the unexpected; do some reading on the area.

+ Park animals are wild, so keep your distance and do not feed them.

+ Never rely only on cell phones or GPS to keep you safe. They won't.

▶ Rangers David Pope and SAR-Siter John Gleason bring a four-year-old to safety, July 23, 2006. Four adults and the child were rafting in a closed area near Happy Isles. NPS photo by Jeff Sullivan.

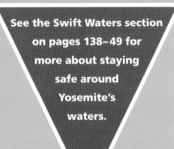

See the Swift Waters section on pages 138–49 for more about staying safe around Yosemite's waters.

BE SMART AROUND WATER Many accidental deaths in Yosemite have resulted from water-related incidents. Being around moving water is one of the most dangerous things you will do in the park. Most drowning victims were not trying to swim but merely wade, soak their feet, or take a picture. Here are the keys to staying safe around water:

✚ Unless very experienced, stay on the trail whenever practical.

✚ Never cross a protective railing or a fence.

✚ Carry enough drinking water so that you won't be tempted to approach a stream to fill a canteen.

✚ Be extra cautious when near or above moving water. Both dry and wet polished rocks are much slicker than they look.

✚ Avoid letting that great photo entice you into doing something stupid.

✚ Some areas, for example Emerald Pool and Hetch Hetchy Reservoir, are off limits to swimming and wading.

HIKE SMART The cliffs and rugged scenery that make Yosemite so beautiful also make it downright dangerous. Simply put, know before you go. Ask yourself, how much effort will this hike take, is it within my limits, and what will I need to safely enjoy it? Remember, the more you prepare, even for a short hike, the more enjoyable and safer the adventure will be. Here are some basics to keep in mind:

✚ Tell someone your plan, and when you expect to return, and stick to it. If no one knows you are overdue, there will be no search.

✚ Check the weather forecast and be prepared for unexpected changes.

✚ Wear substantial, appropriate footwear.

+ A rule of thumb is to drink a quart of water for each two hours of hiking, but variables such as heat, elevation gain, and physical condition can influence this. Halfway through your water, consider turning back.

+ Watch for signs of dehydration, even when it is cold out: thirst, dry mouth, extreme fatigue, decreased and/or dark urine, dry skin, and headaches.

+ Bring a detailed map, a compass (and the knowledge of how to use it), whistle, and headlamp.

+ Frequently snack on slightly salty foods to replace salts lost during hiking.

+ Stay on the trail or other developed areas. Avoid shortcuts and cutting switchbacks. Always be able to turn around and go back the way you came.

+ Avoid ridgetops and other exposed places during a lightning storm.

+ Never cross a protective railing or a fence.

+ Always keep young children in sight.

▲ In October—an often misty or rainy month—of 2006, a 21-year-old in dangerous footwear (sneakers) was backing down the cables on Half Dome and slipped on wet granite. He slid 150 feet until his clothing bunched up and caught in a crack, stopping him from falling 800 more feet (see arrow). SAR-Siter Scott Ring and Ranger David Pope responded, and Pope recalls, "It took us less than 10 minutes to retrieve him, but this is one of the few rescues each year where YOSAR's intervention clearly resulted in saving a life." NPS photo by David Pope.

THE MORE YOU KNOW

In addition to talking to the eager, yellow-shirted PSAR volunteers who are dedicated to making your trip safer and more enjoyable, you can search for information online: nps.gov/yose and hikesmartyosemite.com. And if you have any doubts once in the park, uniformed ranger and maintenance staff stand ready to provide assistance.

For take-along tips for enjoying Yosemite safely, copy or photograph pages 202–5 in the back of this book.

HIKING ESSENTIALS

Consider all of these items and see page 202 for more information.

Sturdy footwear

Water (1 quart per two hours)

Emergency shelter

Sun protection (sunglasses, sunscreen, and hat)

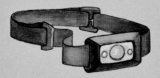

Illumination (headlamp/flashlight)

Knife/utiltiy tool

Whistle and fire (lighter/waterproof matches/candles)

Food (eat regularly and/or more than you normally would)

Insulation (wind/rain protection)

First aid supplies (and know how to use)

Know your limits! Make an emergency plan and tell someone where you're going before you go. Check the weather forecast.

Navigation (map and compass)

ROBIN'S WINTER HIKE

Who: A hiker we'll call Robin • When: January 14, 1973

The Story: Why you should never, ever ignore a "Trail Closed" sign.

On a cold January day, 20-year-old Robin set out on what was supposed to be a simple winter hike. He was wearing a long-sleeved turtleneck, a wool sweater, cotton jeans, and tight, slick-soled cowboy boots. For energy he had a carrot, a bag of nuts, a bag of dates, and a small can of pineapple juice. He did have a waterproof nylon poncho, which he took after a nearby camper who was just leaving the park suggested it upon learning he was going up the Mist Trail. Robin was fortunate to have it in his daypack, as it would probably save his life. No one really knew where he was going on this solo hike.

THE DEEP FREEZE Robin intentionally walked around a "Trail Closed" sign, saying later, "There were no prints on the trail, which was one of the reasons I took it." It wound through a narrow canyon with high granite walls—so narrow that the sun hadn't touched the snow all winter.

The way up toward Nevada Fall by way of Clark Point followed a zig-zagging trail that kept Robin in the subfreezing shade. After maybe 90 minutes, he rounded a corner and saw the nearly 600-foot-high waterfall, spray partially frozen on the edges, in the near distance. Under him the path soon turned from crunchy snow to a sheet of hard, clear ice, in places many inches thick—the reason that the trail had been closed in the first place.

A CRITICAL ERROR When the way morphed from snow to ice, Robin should have turned around. On one side of the 5-foot-wide pathway was an overhanging 10-foot-high wall of granite covered by icicles, and on the other, a drop of 40 feet into a brush-hidden rock pile. Instead of turning back, Robin made the worst mistake of his young life. He chose the trail's ice-covered outer edge and, in his slick-soled cowboy boots, proceeded to gingerly scoot along, sliding his feet up the gently sloping trail. "I actually did consider turning back," he recalls, "but I was just a few feet from the short retaining wall that runs along the trail before the fall and thought I would be safe, if I made it. Didn't happen."

Before he knew it, he was falling. He recalled, "I free fell, landing feet first on a frozen snow slope, which no doubt covered underlying rocks, then hard on my butt and rolled forward." He had dislocated his left ankle, crushed

▲ The Mist Trail corridor is shown here in warmer weather than when Robin took his hike, with Vernal Fall (bottom) and Nevada Fall. Just out of sight, Clark Point is above Vernal Fall at the photo's right edge. NPS photo.

four vertebrae, and broken several ribs.

He lay twisted beneath the brush, out of sight of the trail above him. His sweaty cotton clothing was covered in dirt and snow, and his soaking-wet cowboy boots soon grew tighter, offering no protection from the cold. Startled by the fall and already seriously chilled, he was not immediately aware of the extent of his injuries.

It began to rain that night and was snowing by morning—and it snowed off and on the entire week Robin lay there. The young man quickly grew bone-numbingly wet and teeth-rattlingly chilled. "I gathered what I could of my torn daypack," he said, "which, luckily, included the food and poncho. I lost my straw cowboy hat and ski pole hiking stick." He whistled and yelled for days, but nobody heard. "In order to conserve energy I never called out when the weather was really bad. I did call most of Wednesday, but without response. Believe it or not, I slept soundly every night except the first one." He rationed his dates and sucked on snow and ice. He "picked at scabs from existing cuts and sucked at the blood." And, as darkness fell that last night, Robin considered that if his shouts weren't answered the coming day, he might try to end his life by slashing his wrists.

AGAINST ALL ODDS Another group of hikers, also ignoring the very same warning sign at the bottom of the trail, had made it up the other trail to Nevada Fall and were on their way down. "They were about to turn around, realizing it was dangerous," Robin said, "when Skip Stahmer heard me. Alan Potter stayed up on the trail where he could hear me, while Charles Vertrees and Skip backtracked. Skip went for help while Charles located me using my voice and Alan's directions. He did reach me and then Alan went back around and followed Charles's path to me. I distinctly remember him getting to me. Charles later

told me in our reunion in 2012 that he wasn't sure I would make it until SAR showed up, as I was in and out of consciousness."

SAR ON SCENE Fellow ranger Joe Abrell and I (the author) were the first rangers on scene. We had a sleeping bag, first aid equipment, and maybe most importantly to Robin, a thermos of deliciously hot, thick pea soup my wife had thrust into my hand as I rushed out the door. Robin would later recount, "I remember a Snickers bar, and I love frozen Snickers to this day." After lying for seven miserably long days and longer nights in the rain, snow, and subfreezing cold, Robin was elated, almost deceivingly light-hearted, at seeing us. Despite the pain from his broken back and after crying some, he joked amazingly soon and maybe even laughed a little.

We were quickly joined by others, including my good friend and fellow ranger Paul Henry. Infamous for never mincing words, Paul was thrown off by Robin's cheeriness. He initially felt "this guy is full of bull——." This soon changed; you could see

THE TAKEAWAY

Robin was young, healthy, and had a great will to live. By most metrics, however, he should have died. It is easy to identify some things he did wrong.

+ **He did not ask himself, "What happens if . . . ?"**

+ **No one knew he was going** for a solo hike, nor his destination, route, or when he'd return. Nobody was looking for him.

+ **He disobeyed a warning sign.**

+ **He wore the wrong boots** for hiking in snow and ice. In fact, there may be no right boots in this situation, without traction devices.

+ **Cotton clothing was wrong** for even a short hike in the snow in January.

+ **He did not have other basic emergency equipment.** Robin says, "There is a loud whistle in my pack now!"

+ He did have a waterproof poncho, which probably saved him. **Remember to carry some form of waterproof covering**, even if it is just a large garbage bag.

+ Had he fallen in another spot where sun would have actually hit him, a signal mirror (and knowing how to use it) might have been useful.

him quickly, outwardly cringe. Paul paid more attention to the young man's feet—they were ice-cold and rock solid. Robin, unable to remove his tight boots due to his badly swollen ankles and with greatly impaired circulation, had frozen both of his feet. One eventually had to be amputated.

A HAPPY ENDING Robin went on to carve out a nice career for himself, leading environmental excursions in the Southwest. In 2012, he orchestrated a mini-reunion of those who had assisted in his rescue.

EVEN A SIMPLE HIKE CAN GO WRONG

Who: John H. • **When: August 23, 1989**

The Story: A moment of inattention leads a hiker into peril.

On the crest of Clouds Rest, one of the largest granite cliffs in the world, the trail offers hikers staggering views of nearby Half Dome as well as unparalleled panoramas of the whitish peaks of the Sierra, far in the distance. Nearly 5,000 vertical feet below courses Tenaya Creek, a thin, greenish-blue ribbon of water winding down toward Mirror Lake. The smells of pine and chaparral mingle sharply. Softened by up-canyon afternoon breezes, the late-summer heat of Yosemite Valley is always welcome on the 9,926-foot summit.

A MOMENTARY LAPSE On his second day of hiking, John H., a 20-year-old from England, let his mind wander while his feet did the same. He was roused from his daydream when he found himself going down a fairly minor, water-carved hollow, having mistaken it for the same colored and textured trail that he had been on for hours. Trying to cross a short, sloping section of bare, smooth granite, he slipped on the ever-present gravel and sand known as DG, or decomposed granite. He hit his head in the fall, and was knocked unconscious.

John is not sure how long he was out. When he came to, he was racked with pain. He knew his right femur was shattered. Luckily, there was no break in the skin nor blood showing, which meant that at least he didn't have to worry about infection going deep into his injured leg. John attempted,

unsuccessfully, to stand. Soon, fatigue drove him into his sleeping bag. He began yelling for help, but nobody heard him.

STRUGGLE TO SURVIVE As storms threatened, John spent the first two difficult days in his sleeping bag, eventually succeeding in putting up his tent. Luckily, he was also near a small water source, and although it was very painful, he was able to fill his water bottle by dragging himself over to the trickle. Managing to drink at least a quart of water each day may have been a life-saver for him. He stretched his food out for 14 days as well. Intermittently he would scream out for someone to help; at night he knew to save his energy. Two attempts at dragging himself up the loose, boulder-filled ravine failed. But he understood that survival lay in getting to the path above, so he tried again. Fifteen very long days after falling and smashing his leg, he took seven hours to inch his way up a ragged gully to reach the trail—and help.

◀ Not all hazardous spots are marked by "Danger" signs, like the site identified here by Yosemite PSAR. NPS photo.

THE TAKEAWAY

+ Leave word of your plans. It's likely no one even knew John was in Yosemite, as he was on an extended trip in the United States. Even if someone did know, they surely did not know of his itinerary, i.e., where he was going and when to expect him back. No one missed him. While a cell phone might work in that spot today, a phone will not assure a gentle landing if you fall. **Never assume technology will keep you safe.**

+ Stay aware of the trail. Every hiker loses the trail sometimes, with most finding it again quickly. In John's case it was because of the water bar (also called a "water break," a rock, log, or mound of dirt that serves to divert water off the trail in order to prevent erosion). **The off-trail side may look like the correct way, with the same colors and qualities as the real trail.** These features are common at switchbacks, where the trail makes a sharp turn, and it's easy to continue straight in error. These spots are confusing on granite soil as well as the duff of the forest floor. In John's case, they proved life-threatening. See page 203 for tips on how to find the trail again.

+ Carry survival supplies. John landed near a trickle of a water source and had matches as well. **Had he carried a signaling device such as a loud whistle or signal mirror, he might have been out of jeopardy far more quickly.** He was just lucky that the broken leg was not an open fracture, which might well have proved fatal. It seems he built a fire, but it is unclear if it was used in any way to try to summon help. He may not have been mobile enough to gather fuel.

A YOSEMITE SAR FROM START TO FINISH

 LOCATION UNKNOWN

This flowchart outlines the steps and some of the factors considered during a SAR; some have been excluded due to space limitations.

INITIAL REPORT

REPORTING PARTY
Victim (Subject)
Witness at scene or remote
Friends/family outside the park

HOW DETERMINED
Direct witness
Cries for help or other signal
Overdue from trip to park

 LOCATION KNOWN

REPORTED TO
Park staff on trail
Park dispatch via 911
Park dispatch via radio

INFORMATION NEEDED
Location: victim & reporting party
Incident type: trauma, ill, stranded, missing
Victim condition: alert, ambulatory, unresponsive, deceased, age
Terrain: trail, cliff, water, snow
Weather
Available daylight, etc.

 DISPATCH TAKES BASIC INFO
Transfers caller or contact info to ranger for investigation & action

INITIAL ACTION

ICS BEGINS HERE
Positions filled as needed

 Establish command structure
Continue investigation
Determine urgency
Plan initial strategy/tactics
Alert SAR resources

EACH ACTION MUST:
Be safe
Be effective
Be efficient
Minimally impact the environment

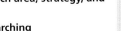

SEARCH

SEARCH RESOURCES

Investigators
Ground searchers (NPS, etc.)
Dog teams (YODOGS)
Helicopters (NPS, CHP, etc.)
Trackers
Divers
Mapping/IT specialists

Expand investigation
  (clues and witnesses)
Determine search area, strategy, and
  tactics
Continuous searching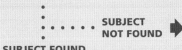

Field operations suspended.
Investigation continues.

 **SUBJECT
NOT FOUND** ▶

SUBJECT FOUND

RESCUE

RESCUE RESOURCES

Ground teams:
  Walk, crutch, horse, litter
Rope systems:
  Lower/raise rescuers & victim
  Reliable—most weather, 24/7
  Sometimes too slow
  More resources needed
Helicopter (NPS, CHP, etc.):
  Quick recon flight, land, rappel, short-haul, hoist
  Usually faster but constrained by
    weather, wind, darkness, altitude

**ACCESS THE SCENE AND
TRANSPORT TO SAFETY**
Choices depend on terrain, patient
  condition, weather, remaining
  daylight, etc.

MEDICAL RESOURCES

EMTs, parkmedics, paramedics
Medical control (Yosemite Clinic)
Regional air ambulances
Regional trauma centers

**MEDICAL CARE AT SCENE AND
DURING TRANSPORT**
May need only water, light, and a
  warm jacket or may need continuous critical care

DISPOSITION OF VICTIM
Release to self/family
Transfer to hospital
Transfer to morgue

DEMOBILIZATION
Prep gear for next incident
Investigate incident cause:
  Preventable?
Mission critique:
  What can we do better?
Documentation:
  All of the above & cost

THE BREAD AND BUTTER OF YOSEMITE SAR

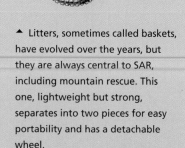

In part 2 of the book, you will read about SARs that are dramatic, heroic, bizarre, life-threatening, and all-too-often fatal. But first, a little about the more-routine accidents in Yosemite.

THE DAY-TO-DAY REALITY

Major SARs generally involve big walls, swift water, advanced medical care, and/or multiday searches, probably featuring helicopters, ropes, wetsuits, and volunteers. Rescuers might rappel, climb up, lower down, search, swim through rapids, or scuba dive in deep pools. Two or three of these major SARs might even be taking place at the same time.

But the truth is, most YOSAR responses are comparatively tame, and might even be boring to read about. You will almost never see them in the news. They are the bread-and-butter missions of YOSAR, and when things are busy and resources are limited, these incidents may be given lower priority. But if you or someone you care about is that sick or injured or stranded person in need of help, the situation might become critical to *you*.

▲ Litters, sometimes called baskets, have evolved over the years, but they are always central to SAR, including mountain rescue. This one, lightweight but strong, separates into two pieces for easy portability and has a detachable wheel.

▲ Many SARs are straightforward. A woman on crutches makes her way down a trail, assisted by a ranger. A "crutch-out": a simple solution to a common problem. NPS photo by Keith Lober.

▲ On June 8, 2008, while wading Tenaya Creek, a 25-year-old (at left) was swept off her feet. The Swift Water Rescue Team, with Dov Bock (right) and Moose Mutlow, responded. NPS photo by Keith Lober.

▲ Riding Bart, Fred Koegler leads Otis and a 14-year-old with an ankle injury from the Glen Aulin High Sierra Camp in 2008. A "horse-out." NPS photo by Patrick Dougherty.

A LITTLE HELP, PLEASE Emergency calls often come into the park's 911 center about visitors who are suffering from headaches, altitude sickness, chest pains, or vomiting. They are exhausted cross-country skiers, confused hikers, drug users, tipsy visitors falling among the boulders, and out-of-shape hikers who need help getting back down a trail that they should not have started up in the first place. These routine missions may involve broken ankles, knees and hips that give out, and collapses from heat and fatigue. Regardless, all are certainly serious to the person with the problem, and YOSAR will respond in a timely, compassionate, and professional manner. These photos and the illustration show how some of these missions are handled.

▶ A 12-year-old on a hike with her school group in 1974 was scrambling among the boulders. She pulled one loose, breaking a leg 100 yards from the Yosemite Medical Clinic, the corner of which is seen here in this photo of a "carry-out." NPS photo.

Since 1965, Fred Koegler has spent every summer as a seasonal ranger, almost always in Tuolumne Meadows. Few have worked for the NPS as long or have been involved with as many SAR missions.

As a Los Angeles County sheriff's reserve deputy and a member of the county's Montrose SAR Team since 1972, Fred has been on 1,050 SAR callouts. This is not to mention the several hundred missions for Yosemite over his five decades. One that Fred recalls with great pride was atop the nearly 11,000-foot-high Cathedral Peak late on August 23, 1989.

A mountaineer had fallen and was possibly dead. Battling 45-mph winds for hours, the rangers' climb up was desperate and dangerous, but when they got there they found life, not death. A navy helicopter tried four times and could only attempt one final, tricky Hail Mary hookup. Fred still glows recalling the moment the ship hung over him for just seconds and he snapped the litter onto the hoist cable.

THE MISSING GIRL

Stacy Anne Arras disappeared on July 17, 1981. That Friday, the bright 14-year-old from near San Francisco began a four-day horseback ride, a loop trip of the High Sierra camps with her father. Their first overnight stop was Sunrise High Sierra Camp. After a fast shower, Stacy took off for a brief hike. She was never seen again.

Despite an intense nine-day search that included 8,004 personnel-hours and 57 hours of helicopter time by four different agencies, costing over $100,000, not one clue as to what happened to Stacy was found. Theories included her running off with a boyfriend, falling into a crack, or being abducted.

Four months after Stacy disappeared, Yosemite's Kim Tucker, the National Park Service's first female criminal investigator, was brought in. She chased new and old leads in the hope of bringing some closure for the family and the park. To this day Kim has no idea what happened to Stacy Arras.

We use the terms "search" and "rescue" throughout this book. There are four phases to SAR, known by the acronym "LAST": Locate—the search part, which may take ten minutes or ten days. Access—actually reach the subject. Stabilize—look after the subject medically and physically. Transport—remove the subject from the area of predicament. As a search is generally an unknown, it is treated as an emergency, requiring some type of timely and deliberate response. Often, when the victim is found, a search will become a rescue.

YOU BE THE RANGER

Here's an example of how this might go. Let's imagine that a report comes in that a hiker is overdue from a day trip. A minute later, there's an unrelated report of an off-trail scrambler with a possible broken leg spotted up in the rocks. The first is a search, the second a rescue, but after the second report, the search may appear to be less of an emergency. This is not usually the case, however. Because the physical status and condition of the overdue hiker is unknown to us, it should be treated as an emergency.

But wait just a second . . . aren't they both emergencies? Yes. So now you are going to earn your pay! You need to weigh a lot of other things before a real decision can be made about the priority of either scenario, despite what I just said about the search. You'll want to know when the hiker was last seen and how bad the scrambler's injuries are. The only way to gather information about the scrambler may be to immediately send a small "blitz" team, e.g., two people with medical and rough terrain skills, to the scene. Meanwhile, you will assign one or more search investigators to gather all the information possible about the missing hiker, e.g., age, experience, physical condition, general health, equipment, and the weather now and in the near future. Assess what resources and personnel you'll need and what is available now. The questions are numerous, and the answers require careful thought. All things being equal, I put the priority with the search—but I will not ignore the rescue. However, there is no real definitive answer—I mostly wanted you to think about how complex and edgy this work can become.

▲ Ranger Jason Ramsdell briefs searchers on the Ottorina Bonaventura mission. On July 30, 2007, the 80-year-old began day-hiking from Vogelsang High Sierra Camp, elevation 10,000 feet. She soon left companions to return to camp for food. Known to suffer from memory loss, she took a wrong turn. Her remains were found 2 weeks later, several miles away. At the search's height, 4 dog teams, 2 helicopters and 150 searchers were involved. NPS photo by David Pope.

OUT ALL NIGHT

Rangers, campers and other volunteers turned out in force to find little Carrie Lou Lentz. From the June 30, 1932, *Mariposa Gazette*:

4-Year-Old Child Lost in Yosemite Found by Ranger

Everyone in Yosemite heaved a sigh of relief when . . . four-year-old daughter . . . was safely returned to camp after having been lost wandering along the banks of the Merced River from two o'clock in the afternoon until ten in the morning of the next day. Her father was busy setting up their tent in Camp 14 [Upper Pines Campground] when she started out sightseeing barefooted and dressed in a bathing suit. Every available ranger was detailed to aid in the search for the child but had no success until next morning when Mr. [Ranger] Scott found her sitting on a rock east of Happy Isles crying . . . Aside from a few scratches on her legs from the brush, she was in perfect condition, sleepy and hungry.

It was an emergency then (especially since it was a four-year-old girl), just as it would be today. A ranger took charge, quickly assessed the history of previous missing kids, evaluated the available resources, and made assignments. Teams went forth and looked in likely spots. The nearby Merced River and neighboring campsites became the obvious top priorities. Probably a bloodhound was brought in, or at least put on standby. There would have been a legitimate concern

▲ Ranger Billy Nelson and his horse Sheik are seen here with Carrie Lou Lentz.

HOW TO GET FOUND

+ Tell someone where you are going.

+ Be out in the open.

+ Use bright, contrasting colors.

+ Have and know how to use a signal mirror.

+ Use a loud whistle.

+ Consider using fire and smoke, but be very careful.

+ Try a cell phone, but do not count on it.

For take-along tips for getting found, copy or photograph page 204 in the back of this book.

about a child abduction. Carrie Lou Lentz disappeared one month after Charles Lindbergh Jr., the 20-month-old victim in one of the most famous kidnappings in U.S. history, was found dead. In fact, much of what the staff did then in looking for Carrie would be done today.

MODERN IMPROVEMENTS Fortunately for us, a search today, eight decades later, for Carrie's great-granddaughter, would benefit from innovations not available to rangers in 1932. First, of course, technology is light-years ahead of what it was then. In 1932, it would still be another year before Yosemite even got a two-way radio, let alone computers and cell phones. An evacuation by helicopter in Yosemite did not take place until 1949. Second, the body of knowledge and expertise on how to conduct a search is similarly much greater. And finally, we know a lot more about how people tend to behave when lost under various conditions.

▲ In 2006, Greg Raye was overdue from his trip into the wilderness of Kings Canyon National Park. It was believed he was scaling Mount Brewer, elevation 13,576 feet—a tricky climb in treacherous terrain. To aid in the difficult search, park officials needed specialists that could function safely in rock, snow, and ice at altitude. YOSAR was requested, and six members responded, including a YODOG and handler. The 52-year-old climber was found deceased on August 30. Far up the side of the peak, the team is seen here getting ready for the litter containing his body to be lifted off the mountain. NPS photo by Dov Bock.

A GAME-CHANGING COURSE In the early 1970s, a few forward-thinking SAR experts (Bill Syrotuck, Dennis Kelley, Jon Wartes) began assembling and analyzing data from search missions—what people do when lost, how far they go, what condition they are in after a certain time, and so forth. It was this great body of vital information, coupled with the glaring need for a national program on how and where to search, that would be the impetus for the Park Service's Bill Wade to facilitate a group of respected authorities to design a week-long, practical, hands-on course specifically for administering and directing searches.

▲ Steve Frazier, 49, left on a 5-day, 40-mile roundtrip hike from Happy Isles on October 28, 2008. Three days later a massive storm hit, trapping him at 9,700 feet with four feet of snow. On November 10, someone finally reported him overdue. No one knew his itinerary and his wilderness permit was vague, resulting initially in a 200-square-mile search area. He was found on November 12. He had kept a positive attitude and clear head, and had constructed a large SOS that could be seen from the air. NPS photo by Keith Lober.

Search managers have reliable data indicating that for hikers over 12 years of age who got lost, 25% were found within a radius of 0.87 miles, 50% within a 1.66-mile radius, and 75% within a 3.56-mile radius. Similar information exists, albeit with smaller sample sizes, on those with Alzheimer's, the elderly, hunters, and 30 other categories of people. These same incident management professionals know that for overdue hikers, only about 40% were adequately equipped, 92% did not travel after the first 24 hours, and between 30% and 40% traveled at night. There are a variety of other studies and analyses indicating that, of those subjects who died, 45% were dead within one day, 74% were dead within two days, 83% were dead within three days, and 92% were dead within four days.

—*Arizona Basic Search and Rescue*, 2nd Edition, Arizona Search and Rescue Coordinators Association, Ltd., Hereford, Arizona, February 5, 2013, saraz.org/saraznew/documents.html.

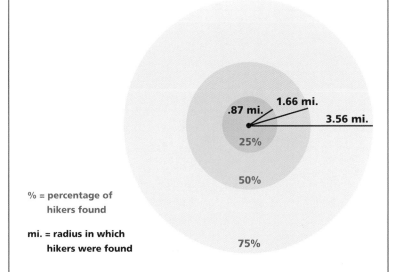

.87 mi.   1.66 mi.   3.56 mi.

25%

50%

75%

% = percentage of hikers found

mi. = radius in which hikers were found

That class, called "Managing the Search Function" (MSF) became an absolute game changer when looking for missing people. In the spring of 1974, this 40-hour classroom course was first taught to rangers and other key SAR people. At last, those in charge of finding someone lost had this ever-increasing database on behavior and related observations at their fingertips, as well as the collective operational wisdom of numerous persons directly involved with searches over the years. An MSF manual followed, to capture all of this material. In the 40 years since MSF came on the scene, it has been taught to tens of thousands of rangers, sheriffs' deputies, police officers, government officials, military personnel, SAR volunteers, and others involved with search tactics and management, both nationally and internationally. The course name has changed and content evolved and expanded. Quite a few additional courses, programs, and books and manuals have now come into everyday SAR usage. Where once there was a dearth of information, there is now a great wealth, such as the statistics in the box on the previous page.

NEED TO KNOW Before your eyes glaze over, you do not need to remember any of the statistics in the box. But it is essential you grasp how absolutely critical this kind of information is to search managers. This data helps them make key and time-sensitive decisions, set priorities, allocate resources, and design tactics and strategies to confine a moving individual or locate a person already down. It is impossible to say whether little Carrie Lou Lentz would have been found any faster with our great advances in search, but it is safe to say thousands are alive today because of how we search for lost people now.

THE SEARCH FOR LITTLE JOHNNY IRELAND

Who: Johnny Ireland • When: July 1964

The Story: A family fishing trip goes wrong.

Even before the Ireland family's car stopped that July day in 1964, 10-year-old Johnny was hopping out, eager to explore the little brook that slowly coursed nearby. Since leaving Los Angeles for a vacation with his parents and older sister, Johnny had been dreaming of going fishing. And in fact, White Wolf and nearby Harden Lake, nestled among the firs and lodgepole pines along the Tioga Road at 7,600 feet, should have been perfect for first-time campers and a young would-be fisherman. His parents and sister busied themselves unpacking the car and setting up camp. . . . No one missed Johnny until the shadows were already lengthening.

A MASSIVE EFFORT Led by District Ranger Doug Warnock, the search for Johnny grew to involve 100 searchers, specially trained bloodhounds, and a helicopter with a loudspeaker. For seven days they looked for the little boy in the striped maroon shirt—from dawn until dark and then again when the bright moon rose. The local newspapers quickly began to follow the story, one reporting, "An intensive rock by rock, gully by gully hunt for the youngster so far has turned up no trace of him. . . ."

Horsemen, hoping to catch a glimpse of a small footprint, briskly rode the rocky trails; men walked shoulder to shoulder through thick brush looking for tiny clues. They covered nearly 50 square miles of the park—classified as "friendly country," territory free of deep streams, steep cliffs, and dangerous animals—and then searched it again.

HOPE FADES As the week wore on, hopes of finding the boy alive grew slowly dimmer. As one ranger would later remember, "in the beginning there was much energy to the search and an almost continuous calling of Johnny's name but as each day passed the search become more dogged, his name was heard less and less." Unconsciously, subtly, many of them started looking for a little body rather than a little boy.

On the sixth day, the moment searchers dread the most arrived. Warnock and Chief Ranger Fladmark decided to suspend the mission the next evening. "We knew little things they had been saying all week were to prepare us for the worst," Mrs. Ireland said. "We should have been ready because, by all rights, John could have been dead. It was the most

desperate moment of our lives." But then, as searcher and veteran ranger Tom Thomas would recall 25 years later, a miracle occurred:

"One truck without radio contact was told by the driver of another that the search was called off and they should return to the base camp. As these men passed a meadow one asked to stop and he got out and simply called Johnny's name from the meadow edge. Johnny Ireland stood up in the middle of that meadow! As they had no radio, his arrival in camp was probably one of the most emotional experiences I have ever witnessed; for the parents were packing to leave and preparing to make arrangements for the memorial services."

Rangers James Riley and Gil Hall found Johnny less than 2 miles from the campground. Despite losing 14 of his 100 pounds, little Johnny Ireland was in remarkably good shape!

THERMAL IMAGING

These days, the science of thermographic imaging is often used on searches. This technology was initially developed by the military. Known as infrared or thermal-imaging cameras, these devices now can be held in the hand and are often used by structural and wildland firefighters to locate small burning spots—even through walls and under forest debris. A helicopter that is used for firefighting or for law enforcement will likely have such a tool on board as well. Also, they can pinpoint hot spots that might indicate an injured person. However, after more than 12 hours a dead body may not give off enough heat to be detected. Technicians also need to decipher whether they are seeing a body or sun-heated rocks. Trained users can distinguish between the heat of a person, bear, or deer; the most recent models of camera can even show the actual shape of the animal.

LITTLE BOY LOST

An eight-year-old boy with autism wandered away from his momentarily distracted parents as they started a short hike to Sentinel Dome on the afternoon of August 21, 2004. The report came in around 8:00 p.m. Due to the possibility of an abduction, the Glacier Point Road was closed and checkpoints set up at park exits—a standard procedure when children are involved. A hasty search was conducted on area trails, as was a grid search of the point last seen (PLS, a term in search management). Trackers and search dogs worked through the night. Just after sunrise, an infrared-equipped helicopter provided by the California Highway Patrol was in the air and ground teams were redeployed. Around noon, the youngster was located by the infrared equipment of the CHP helicopter—500 feet below the rim of Yosemite Valley on a small ledge above a cliff. The uninjured lad was raised back up to the top with the aid of ropes and rescue gear. Rescuers brought him to the trailhead and reunited him with his family. Like thousands of previous Yosemite searches, this one had a happy ending.

▲ Brandon Latham with the boy, who has a teddy-bear in his mouth. NPS photo by Greg Lawler.

▲ Searchers take pride in their efforts, such as after successfully finding the young boy in 2004. Notice the colorful shirts and uniforms representing the variety of units participating; not shown is the California Highway Patrol helicopter crew. NPS photo by Greg Lawler.

RACE AGAINST TIME AND TEMPERATURE

Who: Donnie Priest • When: January 3, 1982

The Story: An 11-year-old is the sole survivor of a plane crash, and time is running out.

At 3:40 p.m., Sunday, January 3, 1982, Robert J. Vaughn took off from Mammoth Airport, just east of Yosemite, in a four-place Grumman Tiger, identification number N-28912. Also on board were 11-year-old Donnie Priest and his mother, Lee. They were heading to Concord, near San Francisco. Their route was north to Reno, then west to Concord, thereby detouring around a storm moving into the Sierra. Within the hour, radar contact with the plane was lost; the last known point (LKP) was among the 12,000-foot peaks just east of the park boundary, near Tioga Pass. Vaughn soon radioed Oakland Air Traffic Control (ATC) that he was losing altitude in severe downdrafts and now below 12,000 feet.

A DEADLY CRASH A few minutes later the plane crashed on the east side of White Mountain, at an elevation of 11,100 feet. The two adults were killed on impact, but in the backseat Donnie survived uninjured. The storm struck, dumping 19 more inches of snow that first night, and by dawn the crumpled white and brown plane was covered with snow. The windows were broken and snow had blown in. "I was very cold and very, very hungry," Donnie recalled. "I tried to put my boots on, but my pants were frozen to my legs. I called but . . . I knew they had died."

TIME WAS RUNNING OUT
The blizzard raged on, depositing more than 4 feet of new snow. Nightly lows neared zero degrees.

"I tried to get a sleeping bag out, but all the luggage had frozen together. I curled up in some sleeping bag pads and tried to get warm," Donnie recalls. He was freezing to death. Many involved in the search expected no one to survive the frigid weather, even if they had lived through the crash.

INTO THE AIR Finally, on Wednesday, January 6, three days after the crash, the storm abated. The Naval Air Station Lemoore SAR Unit (see page 110) and the Civil Air Patrol (CAP; see the box) were finally able to take off. It was thought the plane would be within a few square miles of the LKP at about 12,000 feet. The terrain was rugged and the peaks, cliffs, and slopes were

---

FLIGHT INTO DANGER

According to the National Transportation Safety Board (NTSB), there were 207 reportable aviation accidents nationwide in January 1982, and on the day Vaughn crashed, there were nine accidents with a total of 11 fatalities. (Not all accidents required a SAR, however.) Within hours of the accident, a well-oiled search machine was in high gear, although no one was yet able to get into the field. In a downed-aircraft mission, even before a search plane gets into the air, a lot of planning and analysis must take place. Confusing matters in this case was the fact that Vaughn had amended his flight plan. In addition, the plane's critical electronic locating beacon didn't activate on impact.

The Civil Air Patrol is an integral part of most searches for downed aircraft in this country. Formally established in 1948, it is a Congressionally chartered auxiliary of the U.S. Air Force, principally consisting of civilian volunteers. As of 2017, more than 32,000 senior members as well as almost 24,000 cadets were part of the program. There are 4,300 volunteer-owned private aircraft as well as over 500 light aircraft belonging to the CAP itself.

covered in white. They came up empty-handed.

Since Sunday evening, the CAP, based on reports from ATC, believed Vaughn had been heading for Reno and must have become lost, west of his route. He could have flown in

▲ The rugged, snow-covered area where the plane went down.
▼ The nearly covered airplane (arrow) rests precariously on the avalanche-prone slope. Notice the way the snow has been windblown. NPS photos by Anne Macquarie.

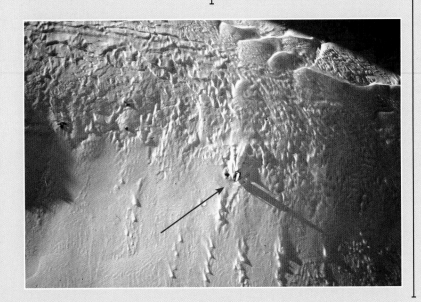

any direction from the LKP as he tried to escape the Sierra. For that reason, the search area was greatly expanded on Thursday. Again, nothing was found, and Friday's plan tentatively called for an even wider search.

A THURSDAY SURPRISE Ranger John Dill says, "I was the NPS liaison to the CAP. Thursday night Frank Burnham, the CAP investigator on the case, called me at our command post. He had just learned that, a short time into the flight, Vaughn had received permission from ATC to turn west on the direct route to Concord, across Yosemite, basically into the teeth of the storm. This information, vital to the search, had languished in a flight log for four days, but now we knew

that Vaughn had not been lost and may have deliberately continued west."

A NEW PLAN Dill continued, "So we decided to return to a small portion of Wednesday's area and re-search it intensely, in hopes that if the plane were there (not a sure thing), enough snow had settled or blown away since the storm to give us a glimpse of the wreck. This was a 'Hail Mary' plan, but based on better evidence." On Friday morning, five days after the crash, the crew of Angel 3, the Navy's Huey helicopter, briefed with John before lifting off. Onboard were Pilot Dan Ellison, Copilot Dave Urban, Crew Chief Reg Barnes, Second Crew Jerry Balderson, and Rangers Jim Sano and Anne Macquarie. All agreed with the plan. Flight Surgeon Dr. Bill Gooden waited in Yosemite Valley, unable to ride along due to weight constraints.

FOUND In 2016, Dan Ellison recalled, "We flew as close as possible to [Vaughn's] radar track. . . . Yet [after] an hour of searching [we] did not locate the wreckage [and] descended so I could look [for a] likely path . . . to cross the mountains." He went on, "500 feet above the terrain we flew for only a few minutes when Jerry reported, 'I've got something out at 10 o'clock.' I turned the helicopter until he called 'steady up,' and we flew right over the wreckage." North of Tioga Pass, it was just outside the park, on Vaughn's likely path. In her report, Macquarie said, "The vertical stabilizer and the back top part of the fuselage were the only parts of the plane we could see, the rest was buried." Angel 3 flew to Tuolumne Meadows, swapped Jim Sano for Chas Macquarie, and loaded his and Anne's ski and rescue gear. Returning to the snow-covered ridge, Dave Urban performed a one-skid landing on a rock outcrop to unload the rangers.

IN THE WHITE Chas and Anne warily plunged through the waist-deep snow, all the while evaluating the likelihood of an avalanche which could kill them and also carry the wreck down the mountain. Chas descended to the plane and was shoveling his way in when he heard a cry from inside. Anne joined her husband, and they soon got the boy out through the rear window. Donnie was hypothermic and his feet were bare and severely frostbitten.

A SUCCESSFUL MISSION Ellison continued, "We hovered over the wreckage and Barnes lowered Balderson on the hoist. He put Donnie into a harness and Reg hoisted them together up into the ship." Nearly out of fuel, they flew back to Yosemite Valley where Dr. Gooden stabilized Donnie in preparation for the flight to the hospital. Rangers Anne and Chas Macquarie, both highly experienced winter wilderness travelers, were left at

▲ Rangers Chas and Anne Macquarie broke out the rear window to remove Donnie from the frozen fuselage of the Vaughn aircraft; this is Chas. The boy has already been airlifted out by Lemoore. NPS photo by Anne Macquarie.

the wreck site, as the helicopter could not return for them, so they skied down from the crash site to Tuolumne Meadows. A week later, Donnie underwent surgery to amputate both of his frostbitten and gangrenous feet.

THE REST OF THE STORY The park saluted John Dill for his work. Jerry Balderson received the Navy and Marine Corps Medal, and Reg Barnes received the Air Medal, as did Dave Urban. Dan Ellison received the Distinguished Flying Cross and was honored as the Navy Helicopter Pilot of the Year for 1982 for that rescue. Donnie Priest was raised by his father and stepmother and went on to have a successful career in prosthetics.

Experts believe survival is mostly mental, a positive attitude and a will to live. Donnie discovered his mother

and stepfather were dead—even hardened adults would find this first test daunting. But he did not panic and soon tried to solve his crisis. What would you do as an 11-year-old, or as an adult? Would you survive?

EPILOGUE On October 29, 2008, at a gathering of some 300 former and current Yosemite employees, John Dill was presented with a Department of the Interior Superior Service Award for his lifelong contributions to search and rescue. Presenting this award was Associate NPS Director Karen Taylor-Goodrich mentored by John while she was a seasonal ranger in Yosemite. Standing alongside John as he received this honor was Donnie Priest.

HAL GROVERT REMEMBERS

Yosemite Search and Rescue Officer, March 1979 to April 1981

"Being the search and rescue officer in Yosemite was one of those transformative positions in the National Park Service. It was a unique position in and of itself. When I arrived at Yosemite in 1979, I went into the SAR officer job with what I thought was a pretty solid background in search and rescue. What was different from what I was used to were the sheer size of the rock walls and the volume of activity. I was the first SAR officer to come into the position from another park (Rocky Mountain National Park). It was a position that I definitely grew in, as an employee and supervisor. It taught me a variety of skills, and I can truthfully say it helped me in other positions in the NPS. It taught me critical thinking under pressure. It taught me about supervision, and dealing directly with upper management in the park and our regional office. And it taught me about developing and maintaining partnerships with volunteer groups, other agencies, and Lemoore Naval Air Station.

Two situations occurred around the time I became SAR officer that significantly changed how searches and rescues were managed. The first was a 40-hour course that had been developed called "Managing the Search Function" (see page 88). It was developed by NPS personnel and eventually taught by NASAR (National Association of Search and Rescue). This provided a significantly better organizational

◄ Rangers Tim Setnicka (left), Hal Grovert (center), and the author wheel out 15-year-old Victor Cox who drowned above Chilnualna Falls in Wawona on March 31, 1979. He went off-trail to view a cascade, lost his footing on the slick granite ledges, and fell 15 feet into a 10-foot-deep, eddying pool. He was able to remove one boot, but after 12 minutes in the frigid water, he became hypothermic and sank. NPS photo.

▲ Looking for a missing person has come a long way since the days before Managing the Search Function arrived on the scene. As visitation throttles up for the summer of 2015, members of YOSAR are seen here reviewing some lessons learned from a successful search in Yosemite. NPS photo by Alan Hageman.

structure and a much more scientific approach to searches. The second occurrence was that we became aware of the Incident Command System (ICS; see page 190). This system was being used in Southern California primarily with fire management. Until this time, we had a separate plan for every type of incident/emergency. We adopted ICS in the park and started training people in its strategy, tactics, and viability in the SAR function.

With this initial background in use and training, in 1990 I was asked to be one of the first two All-Risk Incident Commanders in the National Park Service, and became the first person to take an organized, trained All-Risk ICS Team on an NPS incident (mobilized in Philadelphia when the Persian Gulf War broke out).

My time as the SAR officer was one of the highlights of my career. I saw so many people at their absolute finest, people who gave so much, worked so hard, and risked their lives to save others. I still can vividly recall many of the searches and rescues during that time. It is a job that I will always remain extremely proud of, and to this day, I know that this position also taught me a lot about myself.

YODOGS: SCENT-POWERED SEARCH

Formed in 1999, YODOGS (originally a nickname for the Yosemite dog-rescue operation but now the official title) is a select group with some of the highest standards for both dogs and their handlers of any such unit in the United States.

COMMENDABLE CANINES OF THE PAST

Today, more than 20 dog-and-handler teams participate as YODOGS. Team members respond to the park's SAR coordinator and live and work throughout Central California. When on an actual SAR in Yosemite, they are paid as emergency hires.

The history of search and rescue dogs in Yosemite goes back to the early twentieth century. Bloodhounds had been used in Yosemite since at least the mid-1920s, and dogs like Switzerland's iconic St. Bernards have been on SARs even longer. The modern era of dog-assisted rescue in the park may have started in October of 1956, when the CALO Dog Food Company inaugurated a 24/7 statewide rescue unit of two bloodhounds, with search expert Russ Cone as the handler.

▲ Good dog! This photo was taken in 2005 during a search along Tioga Road for a "body dump"; the remains of a crime victim were thought to be someplace along the road. A few bones were found, later determined to be from a Jane Doe. NPS photo by David Pope.

BLOODHOUNDS TO THE RESCUE One of Cone's most famous cases, the search for six-year-old Terry Dunbar, took place in Yosemite on August 10, 1957. The youngster got separated from his family while hiking and somehow ended up 250 feet below the Yosemite Falls Trail, trapped overnight on a narrow ledge and out of yelling range. This was such a precarious spot that had the bloodhounds not been called in, he might never have been found alive. At the crucial moment, the dog's alert was so subtle that if Cone had not been so well versed, it might have gone unnoticed. Ranger Jack Morehead rappelled down and brought Terry up to his family (see page 10).

A DOG NAMED HOBO

In the summers of 1977 and 1978, the park hired Sandy Bryson as a seasonal ranger. She was a founding member of WOOF—Wilderness Finders—a highly respected search dog group out of the Lake Tahoe area, and a recognized expert and author of books on search dogs and their training. Most important for the park, however, she brought her German shepherd, Hobo, with her. He quickly became a key resource

for locating lost people as well as backing up law enforcement. When Sandy walked into a rowdy campsite with her German shepherd, things quieted surprisingly fast. And the night patrol felt far safer when Hobo was first to enter a park building after a silent burglar alarm went off.

A MISSING CHILD Sandy and Hobo were at their best when searching for a lost person, such as when young Orin Sample wandered away from Porcupine Flat Campground. The seven-year-old New Mexico boy had been playing with his younger sister in the popular, 8,000-foot-high campground along the Tioga Road. It was a warm and sunny mid-June day in 1977. Around 6:00 p.m., Orin started to go off on his own. His sister warned him not to, but the boy forcefully countered, "No, I'm going to look for pinecones." About an hour later the boy's father realized he was missing and called for park assistance, while also mobilizing many of the nearby campers to help him thrash through the surrounding woods.

THE RANGERS ARRIVE By 7:30 p.m., rangers were on scene gathering information, including shoe prints as well as several pieces of the boy's clothing to be used as scent articles for the dogs. With the fading light, the park's helicopter made a rushed sweep over logical spots and several hasty-team searchers began working their way

SPECIAL HOBO

Hobo was expertly cross-trained in both law enforcement and lost-person searches, which was the main reason Sandy brought Hobo up those summers. Today, however, search dogs are seldom cross-trained in law enforcement.

down along the small creek that ran nearby. Sandy and Hobo arrived long after dark.

BRING IN THE DOGS At 11:00 p.m., Search Boss Bob Johnson called everyone back to base, including the many campers who were now volunteering, to let the search zone cool down so as to enhance search scents for the dogs. In addition to mountain SAR teams being put on standby, two other dog teams from the Bay Area were en route and expected to be on site before dawn. A confinement strategy was being drafted, as was a standard grid search for first light, but in the meantime, Ranger Johnson wanted the dogs to go into the area without the further distraction of other searchers and their always-present scents. On missions such as this, the search area is almost totally, albeit unintentionally, contaminated by other people and their odors.

HOBO GOES TO WORK Dragging Ranger Bryson along, Hobo advanced upstream from the campground, which had now become the point last seen shortly before first light. Hobo was on the scent! The contract helicopter shuttled the two volunteer dog teams into a strategic spot, where they began working. The ship then began flying, looking for colors and movements not belonging there. At 7:35 a.m., Hobo and Sandy found Orin. In good condition, he was cheerful and talkative, and little the worse for wear. He did not have any pinecones with him. The seven-year-old had made his way nearly 2 miles, traveling uphill rather than downhill as most lost children normally do.

THE DOG PACK GROWS

Over the next 20 years, a number of the park staff purchased their own dogs and began to train them for searches. Ranger Gary Gissell may have been the first, followed by several others, including Rangers Maura Longden and her husband, Rich Baerwald; Ranger Julie Horne; and maintenance employee Jerry Van Hook.

DOG TEAMS PRE-YODOGS Before 1999, Yosemite SAR used dog teams, often successfully, as a mutual-aid resource requested from the State of California Office of Emergency Services (Cal OES). Cal OES called upon three state-recognized dog units, California Rescue Dog Association (CARDA), Monterey Bay Search Dogs, and Wilderness Finders (WOOF), to provide dog teams. The system worked well in urban and suburban settings, where searches were brief, the terrain more forgiving, and team fitness not a major issue. But at higher altitude, in bad weather, in areas demanding excellent terrain and navigational skills . . . some teams, not so much. At the same time, a few handlers who knew the Yosemite high country well were frustrated because under the existing system they rarely got the chance to use their skills. YODOGS was begun by two attorneys, Mike Freeman and Mike Bigelow, and Yosemite SAR Officer Evan Jones, principally as a result of the following two incidents.

THE CASE OF RANDY MORGENSON On July 21, 1996, 54-year-old Seasonal Backcountry Ranger Randy Morgenson started on a routine four-day patrol from his station in Kings Canyon National Park. An expert mountaineer, Randy was a veteran of 28 summers in the rugged Sierra and tended to range over tricky mountain passes and skirt remote, snow-covered creeks on his patrols. When he did not check in, a massive hunt was launched. At one time, over 100 searchers, five helicopters, and at least eight dog teams were involved. Despite an intensive effort for one of their own, searchers did not find him. It took five years before someone stumbled upon Randy's remains, on July 14, 2001.

In 1997, a year after Randy went missing, Evan Jones went to ranger headquarters in Sequoia National Park and assisted in a technical review of the search for his fellow ranger. During the week-long inquiry, Jones repeatedly became bothered by the way the dog teams handled themselves, particularly by how many handlers were often not prepared for the altitude and ruggedness of the Sierra.

THE SEARCH FOR DAVID PAUL MORRISON The second mission and the one that proved definitive for Evan was the search for David Paul Morrison, who was last seen in Yosemite on Monday, May 25, 1998. The 28-year-old chef from San Francisco intended to hike by himself to the 8,842-foot summit of Half Dome and back. This is a long and arduous 16-mile round trip with an elevation gain of nearly 5,000 feet. For the average person it takes a good 10 to 12 hours to complete. Morrison was a determined and experienced hiker, but was clad only in a sweatshirt, pants, and running shoes. During the five-day search, no one could be found who claimed to have seen Morrison on top, although there were unconfirmed reports of him having been seen in nearby Little Yosemite Valley. In addition, a major El Cap rescue overlapped with the first day of the hunt for Morrison, as well as a possible suicide in the area.

Even though it was already late May, nighttime temperatures in the search zone were dipping below freezing, and there were intermittent rainstorms and snowfall of up to 4 inches deep. A search anywhere is hard enough, but then throw in crummy weather, the skirting of tricky cliffs, marshy spots to be waded, impenetrable mazes of downed and dead trees, and poor communications, and you have Little Yosemite Valley. Before it was over, nearly 250 people,

▼ In September of 1974, when the search in Tuolumne Meadows detailed in the sidebar on the opposite page took place, search-dog teams were relatively uncommon and not as well organized as they are today. Several dog teams were flown in by the military from the Seattle area, including Bill Syrotuck (second from left) and his dog. Sandy Bryson (far left) also responded from the Lake Tahoe area with her dog, Hobo. NPS photo.

For more than 25 years, Commissioned Law Enforcement Ranger Maura Longden has been involved with climbing and wilderness management at the national level, as well as teaching SAR and high-angle rescue. On July 22, 1999, she was involved in the search for a 26-year-old woman who lived and taught in Yosemite. In emails with the author in July 2015, Longden related, "My husband and I were deployed with our two dogs, investigating her disappearance. It was obviously foul play, an abduction from her home in Foresta. The dogs were able to help put together the scene as well as locating an incredible amount of evidence. It highlighted the brilliance of search dogs and the occasional correct inference of their handlers." Earlier that February, a 37-year-old motel handyman had also abducted and murdered three women visiting the El Portal area. His subsequent arrest on July 24 for all four homicides was the result of an intense, collaborative effort of many people, including those from the NPS, Mariposa County Sheriff's Office, and FBI.

15 dog teams, and 4 helicopters had been committed to this search effort. Like some 30 others down through Yosemite's history, David Paul Morrison has never been found.

THE LAST STRAW In both of these cases, Morgenson and Morrison, SAR Officer Evan Jones was frustrated by the way the dog teams, and particularly the handlers, worked. Ranger Jones would be first to describe all involved as well intentioned and dedicated, worthy of thanks and admiration for their efforts. Many of them, however, were just not equipped mentally and physically to be in this area. Yosemite and the Sierra present challenges the average search-dog team is often ill-prepared to handle.

For example, one handler from Los Angeles showed up wearing a 65-pound pack. Once inserted by helicopter, he quickly wrenched his back and requested an evacuation, slowing down the search for several hours. Another handler spotted likely footprints but failed to mark the location. He then got lost descending from the area and was unable to relocate the potential clues. Despite being advised about the weather, others weren't prepared for the cold or the rain and snow. Some didn't even want to hike at all!

Evan Jones knew there had to be a better way. The answer was YODOGS.

THE MAKING OF A YODOG

To join YODOGS, dog teams have to belong to a certifying group in California, such as CARDA, for two years before applying. Once selected, they can still belong to both units at the same time and be available for callouts by the state. Members of YODOGS must be self-sufficient and properly equipped, and must understand that they may remain out for up to 72 hours, if necessary. All handlers are FEMA Type 1 certified, the highest federal level. YODOG handler Mike Freeman recalls going on a search mission with his golden retriever Susie and carrying enough food for both himself and Susie for three days, including more Power Bars than a normal human can tolerate. This was in addition to everything else necessary to survive and operate in the back country for three days. Search managers generally do not like to send teams out for this long because it's best to debrief the teams in camp every night in order to better plan for the next day. Still, it can be necessary.

ANY BREED CAN APPLY Any breed of dog is good for search, but for YODOGS, due to the terrain, bigger breeds—within limits—are preferred. Add in a sturdy coat for warmth in the Sierra high country. Handlers must pass the U.S. Forest Service Pack Test, which is to hike

3 miles with a 45-pound pack in 45 minutes, just like wildland fire-fighters must do. All the YODOGS are fit and will self-transport to their assigned search areas. Additionally, they receive the same training as other YOSAR personnel. The number of teams in YODOGS is maintained at between 20 and 25 to be able to deploy at least eight on a major search as well as two to four teams for a lesser incident.

SPECIALIZED SKILLS Each team is certified in at least two specialties: tracking, wilderness area search, human remains detection, water search, avalanche search, urban collapsed structure search, or forensic evidence search. All of these dogs, however, fall into two broad categories: air scent dogs and trailing dogs.

An air scent dog detects the smell in the air, called a scent cone, coming directly from anyone in the area, not just the missing person, and will follow the scent cone upwind toward the source, like a bird dog. A trailing dog is first shown the scent of the missing person, if possible, via a personal article like clothing or a blanket. Once it locates that specific scent trail, i.e., the odors and thousands of skin cells that person leaves on the ground and on bushes, it will follow the twists and turns of the person's path, ignoring other scents it may come across.

YODOGS and their motivated handlers are a crucial arm of YOSAR. Like search dog teams everywhere, they are dedicated to finding that missing person.

The average human has about 5 million olfactory receptors. Dogs are far more highly developed, having 150 to 220 million such odor detectors. That is why some dogs can even detect cancer cells in humans, not to mention exposing people and drugs hidden away in cars.

◀ On June 20, 2005, a 25-year-old man from Korea started on a multiday hike, despite being warned about deep snow hazards on his route. On August 6, his body was found 1 mile below Pywiack Cascade in Tenaya Canyon. Exactly how he died is not fully understood. Tenaya Canyon is extremely dangerous for those not fully prepared. NPS photo by Keith Lober.

HELITACK OPERATIONS

The term "helitack" comes from the words "helicopter" and "attack," and refers to the system of using helicopters and specially trained crews to battle wildfires. These helitack crews are used generally for quick attack of a wildfire to gain early control of it, particularly in places where conditions would make it difficult or impossible for ground crews to get access.

FIREFIGHTING IN THE PARKS

Responsibility for putting out wildfires in our nation's parks can be traced back to at least 1886 when Congress instructed the U.S. Army, then just arriving in Yellowstone, to "protect the forest from axe and fire." In 1916, when the more than 30 national parks and monuments then in existence were put under the newly created National Park Service, Congress mandated them to "conserve the scenery and the natural and historic objects and wildlife therein." Among other things this meant aggressively fighting wildfires, which all land management agencies have done for years. Generations of us grew up with Smokey Bear's admonition: "Remember . . . Only YOU Can Prevent Forest Fires!" Although this is still our mantra, it turns out that not all fire is bad.

SCIENCE WEIGHS IN Beginning in the 1950s, a scattering of scientific studies and local experiments suggested fire was actually beneficial to the ecosystem as long as it was managed and controlled. In the years since, the science of prescribed fire has become universally accepted as a key tool for maintaining a healthy ecosystem. The guidelines and variables for this discipline are complicated and advanced, but put simply: some fires are immediately suppressed, others are partially put out and then monitored, and some are deliberately set and safely managed. There are even undergraduate and graduate degree programs in this facet of fire and forestry management.

MODERN RESOURCES There are fire stations located in Yosemite Valley, Wawona, El Portal, and Hodgdon Meadows. Additionally, initial response to wildfires as well as key support in search and rescue is made by the park's helicopter crew from the Crane Flat Helibase.

WILDFIRE

In 2015 there were over 68,000 wildfires in the United States, involving 10,125,000 acres, or more than 13 Yosemites. Southern California (which includes Yosemite for these purposes) experienced 138% more activity than the 10-year annual average according to the government's National Interagency Fire Center. In 2015, there were 126 wildland fires reported in all of the national parks and monuments of California, including 69 in Yosemite (46 lightning ignitions, 21 human starts, and 2 prescribed fires). The largest fire in Yosemite history took place in 2013, and came to be known as the Rim Fire.

▲ The Yosemite helibase at Crane Flat, c. 2010. NPS photo.

▲ Bev Johnson jumping gingerly out of the park ship onto the top of Sentinel Rock before safety policies became more stringent. Not shown: the 2,000-foot drop under the helicopter's right skid! NPS photo.

YOSEMITE'S BIGGEST FIRE

When an illegal campfire spread from a remote canyon one sweltering August afternoon in 2013, California was in the midst of a record-breaking drought, the mountains parched and tinder-dry. The fast-moving fire was 40 acres in size when it was spotted topping Jawbone Ridge, nearly a dozen miles west of the park.

OUT OF CONTROL By day four, August 21, 2013, the Rim Fire, named for an overlook on Highway 120, had grown to 16,000 acres and was out of control. Over 850 people were prepared to battle it, with numerous aircraft on order for what was quickly shaping up to be an epic fight. Evacuation notices were issued to homes and businesses, including the park's little Hodgdon Meadows community. By day five, the fire was at 53,000 acres, 11,000 now in the park, and by the next day, it had doubled again. Historic buildings and two groves of giant sequoia trees were at risk.

The Rim Fire burned actively for more than two months, becoming the largest single fire in the histories of both the Sierra Nevada and Yosemite National Park, and the third largest ever in California. It would eventually consume 405 square miles, or 258,000 acres, including 79,000 in Yosemite. For much of that year, the Rim Fire was the largest fire in the United States. It cost $127 million to fight, and at its height 5,200 firefighters from 10 different agencies in the U.S. and elsewhere were working on it. Yosemite firefighters,

Currently, H-551, the radio call sign for the park's fire and rescue helicopter, is a Bell 205A++. This is a far cry from the park's first contracted helicopter in 1961, a three-person Hiller 12-E—with a high-visibility, Plexiglass bubble cockpit—that cost approximately $150 per hour to fly. In 2016, the cost for H-551 was about $2,000 per hour. While H-551 was referred to as the "park ship," in fact the park does not own any helicopter, nor has it ever. And H-551 is only stationed in the park during fire season, roughly May through October. It is considered a regional resource and may be used on emergencies outside the park, when available.

helitack crewmembers, and other fire management staff should take great pride in their skills and the dedication and leadership they bring to their craft.

EPILOGUE It wasn't until a year after this fire started that the hunter who set the original illegal campfire was identified publicly and charged with two felonies and two misdemeanors. The case against him was ultimately dropped after two key witnesses died.

AIR SUPPORT

The Yosemite fire and rescue helicopter provides a high performance, medium-sized ship that supports fire, search and rescue, law enforcement, resource management, and administrative projects. It can be engaged in firefighting and then, within a dozen minutes, be transitioned to a rescue and medical evacuation mode. In addition to an experienced pilot and mechanic, these missions will have a seasoned one- or two-person helitack crew providing safe and efficient aviation support to all those in the ship and on the ground, including safety at landing zones, load calculations and cargo management, and many other functions.

HELI-RAPPEL AND SHORT-HAUL Heli-rappel and short-haul are tools that deliver timely fire and SAR assistance in any terrain. Many of the park's highly skilled helitack firefighters are proficient in both. There are also an additional dozen or so Helicopter Rescue Technicians; these are rangers who provide advanced medical care via a quick helicopter response. Some of them are rock climbers trained in these specialized helicopter procedures.

The rappel operation lets a rescuer or firefighter descend by rope to the ground where the ship cannot safely land. The short-haul allows for a person to be inserted and extracted by being attached to the bottom of a rope fixed to the helicopter. None of this is done casually, and alternatives will be weighed to keep the mission as safe as possible. Similar programs exist elsewhere, but Yosemite's is deservedly recognized for its expertise.

LISA HENDY REMEMBERS

Emergency Services Manager, February 2012 to July 2016

" Most valued in my time as the emergency services manager at Yosemite was the camaraderie of working with Yosemite Helitack. When I arrived in 2012, the relationship between Helitack and the SAR Office needed attention to keep that partnership running smoothly and safely. We counted on each other for life-threatening missions, and joint funding of equipment and training. We were performing insertions on vertical walls while hovering out of plumb. No one else in the world did that. We were being looked to as a standard in high-angle helicopter rescue.

My office was in the Valley SAR cache, and as the traffic and the heat of summer bore down, it was always a joy to retreat to the helibase. During the Rim Fire in 2013, there was a need for wildland fire–certified ALS (Advanced Life Support) providers with helicopter rescue qualification (short-haul, heli-rappel). I spent much of the two weeks of the fire in Yosemite assisting with coverage on the aircraft. I learned so very much from the crew about their operation and priorities, and in return, I tried to listen for where the SAR program could support them better while we worked to get our rescues completed.

▲ Lisa Hendy heli-rappelling in 2014. NPS photo by Barry Smith.

From that point on, Jeff Pirog, the park aviation manager, Eric Small, the helitack foreman, Andrew "Boots" Davenport, the assistant foreman, Heather Wonenburg, the supervisor, and I started working to bring our programs back together at the core. Over the course of the next three seasons, we meshed the two operations into one of the safest, closest-knit, most versatile, and most solid helicopter rescue teams simply by starting with mutual respect.

When people ask me if I miss anything about Yosemite, I always say the helitack crew and the contracted pilots and support staff from Kachina Aviation. Notice I didn't say flying in the helicopter. Anyone can work where they get to do that, and I did it regularly for over 15 years. What I will always remember is how it felt to go on even the most hair-on-fire urgent mission with people around me who I knew were rock solid skill-wise, and who would look out for each other as a team. That is the greatest feeling of confidence any rescuer can ever have. I miss that. "

▲ Lisa Hendy during the park's 2016 three-day Short-Haul Refresher. NPS photo by Eric Bissell.

MIKE MURRAY REMEMBERS

Yosemite Search and Rescue Officer, July 1984 to December 1984 and
September 1985 to March 1987

When I first became the SAR officer in 1984, I was surprised that such a sophisticated program operated on a shoestring budget. Not much for equipment, nothing for training. Despite this, the SAR office was a hotbed of creativity and innovation.

The early- to mid-1980s was a period of advancement in helicopter rescue techniques at Yosemite. The use of the military, primarily from Lemoore, was well established. In 1982, the park began its heli-rappel program using the contract ship. However, many of the Big Wall rescues were where the helicopter could only hover beside, but not directly above, the victim(s) on a vertical cliff face. As a result, most Big Wall rescues involved lengthy litter raising or lowering operations, requiring substantial support.

SAR technician John Dill came up with using a sand-filled bag with an attached stuff sack containing a thin cord similar to the throw bags used in whitewater rescues. The helicopter could hover adjacent to and slightly above a victim on a cliff, and a rescuer could establish a light-line connection between the ship and the victim, which could then be used to pull a rescue rope from the helo to the victim. The rescue line could be used to deliver equipment or rescuers directly to the victim, or to extricate the victim from the cliff on a long-line beneath the helicopter.

After much thought about the geometry of rappelling diagonally from the helicopter to a vertical cliff face, ground testing, refining equipment, and determining the limitations, the time came to test the technique. John arranged for the park ship and, as a low-budget operation, I would be the victim on the cliff. We chose the Rostrum, a 700-foot cliff in the Lower Merced Canyon. I positioned myself on a large ledge down from the top, and set up a solid anchor system.

John arrived in the helicopter and threw the bag from the hovering craft at me. A perfect toss—on the first throw! I pulled in the cord, then the rescue rope attached to it, and anchored it to the cliff. The other end remained with John as he rappelled out of the hovering machine on a separate line. As he descended he was able to eventually transfer his weight from the heli-rappel line to the anchored rescue rope, then ascended the line to the ledge. He had just completed YOSAR's first controlled "pendulum rappel" from a helicopter to a vertical cliff face.

On actual rescues, the throw bag technique was most useful for delivering supplies to hypothermic or stranded climbers, thus avoiding a lengthy rescue. It would be some time before this technique was employed to deliver a rescuer to the cliff during a rescue.

◀ YOSAR's intentions are noted at the end of the thin line coupled to the throw bag. NPS photo by John Dill.

125 ft.

Read This Now!
* Do not anchor this rope.
* Pull the cargo to you GENTLY, as we lower it.
(There is a weak link in the line.)
* When you get the cargo, clip it to your anchor.
* We are not in a hurry. Take your time.
See other side now!

This is what we will do.

See Other Side Now!

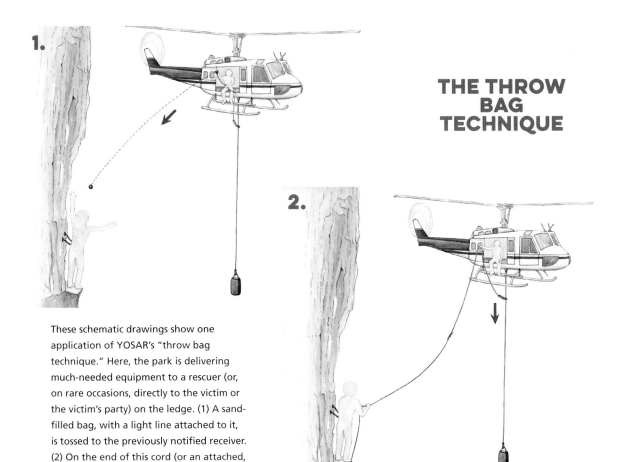

THE THROW BAG TECHNIQUE

These schematic drawings show one application of YOSAR's "throw bag technique." Here, the park is delivering much-needed equipment to a rescuer (or, on rare occasions, directly to the victim or the victim's party) on the ledge. (1) A sand-filled bag, with a light line attached to it, is tossed to the previously notified receiver. (2) On the end of this cord (or an attached, stronger second line) is a carabiner which

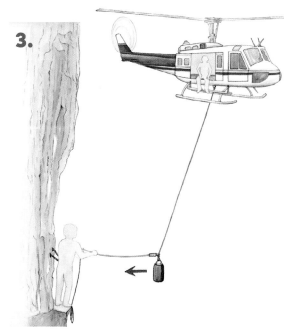

will slide down a rope with the vital gear hanging at its end. At the carabiner is a weak link designed to break if the helicopter needs to suddenly leave. If this happens, the equipment will remain with the helicopter. (3) The rescuer can then pull the rope, with this bag attached to it, over to the ledge. Despite the necessarily simplified text here, this technique is tricky and only used after all alternatives have been evaluated.

In any given year there are great examples of the bond between fire and SAR. Few if any, however, illustrate this trust and partnership more than the following Big Wall rescue on El Capitan on September 26, 2011.

THE SAGA BEGINS That afternoon, an Austrian who was leading the climb fell near the top of The Nose route, amputating the end of his thumb in the process. Amazingly, the severed digit tumbled 80 feet through the air only to land securely on a 1- by 2-foot ledge at the feet of the injured man's climbing partner—2,000 feet above the

ground! At 3:50 p.m., the park's emergency dispatch received the call, relayed by cell phone from a friend hiking to Half Dome several miles away.

TIME CRITICAL Valley District Ranger Eric Gabriel was the Incident Commander for this operation. He was an expert climber who had done El Cap five times as well as being a Park Medic. Gabriel requested H-551, the park ship, for a possible short-haul direct to the accident scene and for shuttling the rope rescue team and their gear to the summit. Gabriel knew the best outcome for the climber would include a surgical reattachment of the thumb, though that seemed like a long shot. Still, he asked that this issue be researched, and was told they had six hours if the thumb was unrefrigerated, 12 if refrigerated. To add to the pressure, Gabriel was also advised that once the victim was safely on the ground, he should go to microsurgery specialists in the Bay Area,

---

◀ Those certified in Yosemite Fire and SAR heli-rappelling must remain current, demonstrating their proficiency throughout their season. This July 28, 2007, photo shows this training. NPS photo by David Pope, himself a proud participant.

requiring an air ambulance. Speed was critical: the thumb was cut off at 3:00 p.m. and by safety policy, H-551 could not fly later than 30 minutes after the sunset at 7:20 p.m. Gabriel recalled:

My plan was two-pronged—Plan A would attempt to short-haul-insert rescuers and then short-haul-extract the injured climber, and Plan B would deliver about 15 people and . . . gear to the top . . . for a high-angle rope rescue. Plan A offered a reasonable chance of delivering the injured climber and thumb to the surgeons within the six-hour time frame. Plan B would get the injured climber off the wall . . . but not within the 12-hour window.

TOSS THE THROW BAG
A 12-person rope rescue team was positioned on top of El Cap by Pilot Richard Shatto. After sizing up the situation, he again launched with Helitack Foreman Eric Small and Assistant Foreman Jeff Pirog. Suspended below H-551 on a short-haul rope were Rescue Technicians David Pope and Jeff Webb. A thin nylon line was to be established between the granite wall and the helicopter, using an experimental

procedure that had been practiced, but never used in a real-life SAR. This "throw bag technique" required Shatto to hover for an extended time while Pope and Webb dangled 150 feet below.

IN A TIGHT SPACE Jeff Pirog rigged the throw bag with a thin nylon line attached onboard the helicopter and pitched the bag and line to the climbers' outstretched arms. It took seven tries before it was snagged. Then along with Eric Small, Pirog monitored tail- and main-rotor clearances while the machine hovered dangerously near the wall. Once the link was established with the climbers, the two rangers pulled themselves over to the narrow ledge, and Jeff Webb unclipped and tied safely to the wall while David Pope remained secured to the ship. Speed was paramount. The two pros swiftly readied the victim for an airy liftoff, tightly securing him into a nylon climbing and rescue harness.

LOWERED TO SAFETY Meanwhile, to maintain the physical line between Pope and the helicopter, Pilot Shatto had to hover nearby. When all was ready, David Pope and the injured climber gently lowered themselves back off the wall. Slowly

▲ Park helicopter H-551 is midway up the face of El Capitan. On August 24, 2010, the hottest day of the year, a 47-year-old Korean national who could not speak English pulled a rock onto himself, possibly becoming partially paralyzed. The plan was to lower rescuers to the victim from the summit and then lower him to the bottom. The plan changed. Rangers Keith Lober and Jack Hoeflich were lowered from the summit by ropes, then Lober and the victim were extracted by way of the throw bag technique and H-551. The remaining three Korean climbers then needed to be lowered to the bottom, as they were unable to self-rescue. The original victim lived. NPS photo by Clay Usinger.

swinging out, they placed their full weights onto the short-haul line. The two, now totally free of the cliff, were hanging directly underneath H-551. The helicopter landed in El Cap Meadow almost directly below, where an air ambulance was standing by. Later that night the thumb was successfully reattached. Although Jeff Webb and the victim's partner spent an uncomfortable night on the wall, they safely rappelled off the next morning.

The four men—Pirog, Pope, Small, and Webb—received Department of the Interior Valor Awards on May 8, 2014. Kachina Aviation contract helicopter pilot Richard Shatto deservedly received the Citizen's Award for Bravery.

LEMOORE NAVY SAR HELICOPTERS

From 1972 to 2002, and on through to its official 2004 decommissioning, the Naval Air Station Lemoore Search and Rescue Helicopter Unit was a true friend to Yosemite National Park. Once in the air, it was a 45-minute flight to the park from its base south of Fresno, California. It is impossible to adequately describe the superb rescue talent and high degree of competence always selflessly and eagerly displayed by this unit.

NAVAL SAR TRAINING

As conflict in Southeast Asia loomed in 1963, the United States Navy increased the training given to its pilots. One result was the formation of the Lemoore SAR Unit in Central California's San Joaquin Valley, which quickly became one of the premier SAR teams in this country. The unit originally flew the UH-34 Seahorse, which was underpowered for the altitudes of the Sierra Nevada. In 1970, the Seahorse gave way to the UH-1N Huey. With a service ceiling of 15,000 feet, the Huey was far better suited for the mountains; it even pushed this limit several times by landing and taking off on Mount Whitney, at 14,496 feet.

LEMOORE IN THE PARK Records are fuzzy, but the earliest account we can find for a Lemoore operation in Yosemite is for May 29, 1972, involving Blair Glenn, a climber hurt on El Capitan. In this case, the chopper was there solely to fly personnel to the summit. Less than a month later, they were back. On June 21, Lieutenant Commander John "Mercury" Morris, with two flight medics onboard, evacuated William Hendry, whose skull had been fractured by a rock dislodged by his partner's rope during an ascent of El Capitan. Hendry was lifted off and pronounced dead. Since the team was already in the park, Morris then agreed to evacuate a 19-year-old woman who had injured her ankle and could not walk.

CAMARADERIE AND KINSHIP The many dozens of rangers and other park staff who routinely worked SAR with the navy during these three decades would surely extol the high degree of competence and expertise of the many different air crews they worked with. There is a camaraderie and kinship, built upon mutual respect and admiration

▲ The crew of a Lemoore "Angel" on duty in Yosemite in 2000. NPS photo.

and trust, that quickly develops when individuals in public service risk their lives together. Below is a small example of this relationship, written by Dan Ellison, now a city commissioner in Helena, Montana. In it, he recalls a mission he was involved in while at Lemoore as a USN lieutenant commander. He was the Navy Helicopter Pilot of the Year for both 1982 and 1983, and earned a Distinguished Flying Cross for another SAR (see pages 91–93).

> It was May 1981 and we were called to assist with an unconscious climber on the Cathedral Rocks . . . severely injured by a boulder dislodged by another climber, and . . . now suspended by her safety line . . . on a vertical cliff face several hundred feet below the crest. Recognizing mountaineering skills would be needed I requested John [Dill] join the crew and serve as initial responder and he agreed without hesitation. . . . John rappelled down about 150 feet below the helicopter. . . . I hovered with roughly 5 feet of blade clearance off the cliff face. He caught the victim's safety rope, detached from his rappel line, and we returned to land in the meadow to conserve fuel and to let John work with the victim. . . .

> After coordinating with John by radio, I decided to use a Kendrick splint (Kendrick Extrication Device) and Stokes litter. While the Stokes was more secure for the victim, the

vertical cliff and elevation . . . ruled out using a tending line to prevent the litter from spinning during hoisting. We flew back up and lowered the Kendrick to John and returned to the meadow to refuel. John somehow put the victim in the [splint] while balancing on a ledge about 4 inches wide and several hundred feet above the Valley floor. I returned a third time, lowered the hoist cable and lifted both John and the victim off the ledge and into the helicopter. Back in the meadow, the rangers had found a visiting doctor who looked at [the victim] and said she needed to go directly to a hospital, so we flew her to Valley Medical Center in Fresno. In this brief account it's hard to portray the flying difficulty, although I'll never forget those three long hovers off the Cathedral Rocks. But the most impressive part of the mission was the remarkable skills of John Dill, without whose expertise my crew would likely not have been able to complete this rescue.

30 YEARS OF COOPERATION There are several practical reasons that Lemoore participated so closely in Yosemite SAR. The unit had been established to perform SAR and, fortunately, not many military jets actually crash. Crews were eager to maintain both rescue capability and mountain flying skills, and Yosemite was a natural fit. Lemoore often brought a flight medic, which was usually far more medical expertise than Yosemite could generally send out in the days before the Parkmedic program (see page 49). (Occasionally, however, one of the park's doctors or nurses might go.) Unlike with a for-profit civilian helicopter, the park did not have to pay anything for the navy craft and crew. (The hours flown on an actual rescue supplanted their required daily training and flying times.) Lastly and most important, Lemoore's flair and enthusiasm for each and every mission was unparalleled.

HUEY TO THE RESCUE Lemoore missions were flown in the UH-1N Iroquois, more often called the "Huey" or "Twin Huey." The ship was equipped with a 250-foot cable hoist, capable of lifting litters and personnel in and out of tricky, otherwise unreachable spots, invaluable in so many Yosemite SAR scenarios. In addition to its standard five-person crew, the Huey could carry an additional three to five passengers.

HOW MANY MISSIONS?

The exact number of missions flown by Lemoore in its 30 years of Yosemite SAR is difficult to fix. But of the more than 950 operations cited in the SAR unit's 2004 decommissioning ceremony, many were

▲ On April 7, 1973, a young woman fell off the Nevada Fall Trail, hitting the rocks below. Injuries to her head were so life-threatening, she might have died had Lemoore not been available. Incidentally, this spot is very close to where Robin, too, fell from the trail (see photo on page 76). NPS photo by Butch Farabee.

for Yosemite. The author is hesitant to use the word routine when describing the flying of *any* helicopter—civilian or military—in the Sierra. But by most standards, many flights were relatively easy, such as shuttling rescuers and equipment to the top of El Cap or taking dog teams into a search area.

NOT SO SIMPLE These flights (as well as for the park's ships) were relatively easy . . . until you throw in low clouds, thunderstorms, lightning, rain, blizzards, winds, darkness, high elevations, uneven landing surfaces, vertical cliffs, tall pine trees, remote locations, and the ever-present Murphy's Law. Any one of these could easily turn ordinary into something truly scary and unique. In the 1970s, most of the pilots and crews stationed at Lemoore had seen recent service over the jungles of Vietnam and were almost addicted to the excitement. There they often flew "Dust Off," a military call sign for a rescue or extraction, generally under less-than-ideal conditions. That same bravery saved many people in Yosemite as well.

RULES EXIST FOR A REASON

Per their own policy, Lemoore SAR would not assist the park if the subject of the mission was known to be deceased. They didn't wish to jeopardize crew and machine for these recovery missions, and Yosemite SAR managers respected that. On rare occasions, however, pilots and crew did violate this code. In one case, this came back to haunt them, illustrating why the policy existed.

A FATAL FALL Scrambling off a short climb on June 16, 1975, 19-year-old Peter Barton slipped, tumbling 150 feet down the broken cliffs at the base of El Capitan. When his partner, Dale Bard, started down for help, he believed there were still faint signs of life in his friend. Once notified, the park helicopter launched, knowing there probably was no place to set down. From inside, Ranger Dan Sholly, looking at hundreds of feet of treacherous cliffs over which a stretcher would need to be lowered, quickly asked for a Lemoore 'Angel,' since the park did not short-haul until a number of years later. Sholly, a Vietnam marine vet, was set down and worked his way up through an 800-yard maze of boulders and oaks to reach Barton. The climber was dead. Dan was soon joined by the 12-person ground team and shortly, Angel 6 was overhead. Lieutenants Tom Stout and John Sullivan were at the controls.

DANGEROUS DECISION Stout easily understood the danger of carrying the body back down over the often-vertical terrain. Barton's body, zipped into a black body bag and strapped to a litter, was moved to

▲ A c. 1970 Naval Air Station Lemoore Search and Rescue Helicopter Unit logo. These helicopter crews proudly displayed this cloth patch on their flight suits. NPS photo.

▲ When time and circumstances permit, helicopter crews love to show off their machines, such as in this 1980 photo with local park children. NPS photo by Butch Farabee.

a cliff edge for what should have been an easy hoist. Stout had been on numerous other Yosemite SARs, and rangers and helicopter crew both thought this would be, as they said, "a piece of cake."

EVERYTHING GOES SIDEWAYS On the second slow pass over the scene, Stout and Sullivan pulled a "hover check," rising 300 feet to guarantee sufficient power for the operation. Then they slowly lowered to within 30 feet of the victim. Rangers Dan Sholly and Tim Setnicka quickly hooked the thin cable to the stretcher. Within moments, just as the litter was about to pass into the ship, the familiar sound of the 1,100-horsepower engines changed, and the ship suddenly veered off. Dan and Tim dove for the ground as the rotor blades whished just over their heads. Auguring down, Stout tried to gain altitude in the little time he had. But the ship still rolled left, and made two spiraling, 360-degree turns before slamming into the stunted trees 600 feet below. Onboard were Stout, Sullivan, two crewmembers, a flight medic, and Ranger Paul Henry. With a crashing of metal and trees, the helicopter settled into the forest. As those onboard safely scrambled out, the $1.2 million Angel 6 burst into flame—with the body still strapped onto the litter—and burned to the ground. The cause of the power loss was never clearly understood.

A SINGULAR AWARD

Nearly three years later, the Lemoore SAR Unit earned a Department of the Interior Valor Award, granted by Secretary of the Interior Cecil Andrus. This was the first and only time this honor has been bestowed on any entity outside of the Department of the Interior. Here's the story behind the award.

RESCUE ON QUARTER DOME On May 28, 1978, two climbers were climbing Quarter Dome, just east of Half Dome. Suddenly, Gary Gissendaner lost his footing. He fell 70 feet and landed close to his partner, who was able to gently lower him to a sloping, dinner-table-sized ledge. It was 5:00 p.m. when rangers were first alerted, and darkness was beginning to close in. "Lemoore arrived at 6:25. After a quick reconnaissance, they planned their rescue." In the interim, three rangers had been put into place, 300 feet above Gary, ready to lower to him with a litter and medical gear.

AN INCREDIBLE OPERATION Aircraft Commander Lieutenant John Sullivan edged to "within 5 feet of the cliff face and hovered for 22 minutes—a harsh test for both man and machine." Copilot Don Swain watched the battery of cockpit gauges and Crewman John Deciccio lay on the floor, looking down past the skid, advising the pilot on

▲ The last photo taken of Angel 6, about 30 seconds before it crashed and burned. Peter Barton (deceased) is in the litter and about to be lifted into the cabin. NPS photo by Mark Forbes.

how close he was to the granite wall. Crew Chief Benny Revels then rappelled down a 300-foot rope to the victim. After reaching Gissendaner, he connected the unconscious climber to his own lines and disconnected him from the cliff. Pilot Sullivan then eased the helicopter away from the cliff face, gingerly compensating for the weight of the two men as he lifted them from the ledge and up and over the deep canyon. Within five minutes, Sullivan laid his human cargo to earth in a nearby meadow. All the while, as Revels dangled below the ship, he was unable to communicate with the pilot due to a dead radio battery. Gissendaner later died of his head injuries.

NO ONE IS SHOOTING AT YOU HERE

For decades, Lemoore SAR's main duty was to provide support to military aviation training, principally for jet pilots. In reality, however, most of its SAR operations were not for injured pilots but for the hurt and lost in and around the region and more often than not, for those in Yosemite National Park. As senior Lemoore pilot "Stormin' Norman" Hicks, himself a veteran of "Dust Off" flying in Southeast Asia, once told the author: "Yosemite flying is mostly harder than what I saw in Vietnam . . . but at least no one is shooting at you here!"

▲ A great three-decade-long partnership between Yosemite SAR and Naval Air Station Lemoore SAR formally ended in 2004. This photo was taken at Crane Flat Helibase on July 22, during a courtesy farewell visit. NPS photo by Keith Lober.

BIG WALL RESCUES

Without question, an iconic Yosemite rescue would involve an injured climber midway up the sheer Big Wall face of El Capitan or Half Dome, perhaps with a snowstorm thrown in to make it even more exciting.

"Big Wall" is not a technical term or a precise measurement, though all climbers know what it means to them. To this author, a Big Wall is determined by how high the wall is, how hard it is to climb, how long it takes, and how formidable the obstacles. They are demanding, even intimidating. We use the term Big Wall, capitalized, here to underscore that these climbs have an all-around high degree of difficulty. Such climbs are a breed apart. They include El Capitan, Washington Column, Lost Arrow Direct, Mount Watkins, Half Dome, and Leaning Tower.

AN INHERENT RISK

Climbing Ranger Brandon Latham estimates that the park sees some 80,000 to 100,000 climber-days annually, with roughly 100 climbing accidents per year, of which about 20 require an NPS rescue (10% of all SARs). The rest are self-rescues. These mishaps stem largely from judgment failure, climbers falling, rock falls, and weather. *Off the Wall: Death in Yosemite* (2017 edition) lists 113 people who have died climbing. Not all were on a Big Wall, although 27 did involve El Cap.

BIG WALL RESCUES OVER THE YEARS In many ways, Big Wall rescues are much alike from year to year. Victims change, injuries and circumstances differ slightly, the exact spots where accidents occur vary by a few feet, and of course individual rescuers age and move on. Changing over the decades are the equipment available to rescuers, the natural evolution of skills, and the increased trust and confidence that come from SAR teams having faced and conquered similar rescue challenges.

▶ On October 3, 1992, Yosemite SAR Officer Kelly McCloskey attends to a 28-year-old climber who fell while leading the 26th pitch of The Nose route on El Capitan. He sustained a compression fracture to a vertebra and suffered several breaks in his hand. During rescues, ropes often become twisted for a variety of reasons. NPS photo.

▲ El Capitan as viewed from Middle Cathedral Rock with 10 of the earliest, classic routes shown: 1) West Buttress 2) Dihedral Wall 3) Salathé Wall 4) Magic Mushroom 5) Muir Wall 6) The Nose 7) Wall of Early Morning Light (Dawn Wall) 8) North America Wall 9) Tangerine Trip 10) Zodiac. NPS photo.

HOW CLIMBS ARE RATED

In 1937 a climb-rating system was adopted by the Sierra Club, with Class 1 (walking) to Class 6. Class 5 (free climbing) required rope protection for safety but not for ascending. In the 1950s it evolved into the Yosemite Decimal System, with climbs rated from 5.0 (easiest) through at least 5.15 (hardest). Class 6, now called Aid ("A"), uses protection for both safety and ascending, with difficulty rated A0 to A5. There is also a Clean ("C") rating, C0 to C5, for aid without a hammer. A mixed free/aid or clean aid climb might be rated 5.8 A2 or 5.8 C3. (See glossary and sidebar for more.) Climb lengths are Grades I to VII. Grade I is short, maybe an hour, and Grade VI, several days. There are no Grade VIIs in Yosemite.

To illustrate the nuances of ratings, we have referred to The Nose route on El Capitan throughout this book. The earliest real guidebook to use these ratings, Steve Roper's 1964 *A Climber's Guide to Yosemite Valley*, had The Nose rated as VI, 5.8 A3. Chris McNamara and Erik Sloan's 2005 *Yosemite Big Walls* classifies it as a VI, 5.13+ or 5.9 C1 or 5.8 C2. Techniques, skills, and equipment have advanced the state of the art in the intervening 50 years.

A RESCUE WITH MULTIPLE CHALLENGES

Who: Neal Olsen • When: September 23–24, 1972

The Story: An unprecedented tragedy complicates an unrelated SAR.

▲ Neal Olsen and Jim Bridwell being lowered. NPS photo by Gary Hathaway.

This tale begins at sunrise on Saturday, September 23, 1972. Climber Neal Olsen was leading a difficult section on the 24th pitch of The Nose route on El Capitan, just above Camp V— a set of ledges about 900 feet below the top of the cliff. In an unlucky accident he pulled a 125-pound boulder down on himself. He tried to dodge it, but it still glanced off his head and back before striking his right leg and smashing it badly.

PLANNING THE RESCUE

By 7:30 that morning, Yosemite SAR Officer Pete Thompson was organizing one of the most demanding rescues in the history of North American mountaineering. Pete had an A-Team of six local climbers in his office:

Jim Bridwell, Bev Johnson, Tom Gerughty, Jim Breedlove, John Dill, and Loyd Price. Their mission: to develop an initial rescue plan, estimate equipment needs, and identify other technical climbers they wished with them. The idea was to lower a rescuer from the summit 900 feet down to the stricken climber. Then Olsen and his rescuer would be lowered to medical staff on the Valley floor, 1,800 feet below. At the time, only one other long-lowering rescue even remotely similar to this one had ever been performed, in Grand Teton National Park in August of 1967. In total 18 men and one woman—Bev Johnson—would be flown to the top of El Cap that day.

AN ADDITIONAL CHALLENGE

The team's task was made even harder as a result of a disastrous incident earlier that summer. Seven weeks before, just past midnight on August 1, 1972, a 17-year-old boy had torched the many tons of stacked hay in the government's horse barn (see page 40). The barn and stables were lost as were another seven older wooden structures.

One of these terribly flammable CCC-era buildings held the Valley SAR cache. Ropes, webbing, pitons, bolts, carabiners, sleeping bags, rain gear, and

related, vital equipment all went up in smoke. Thompson knew they were short on the right sorts of equipment to pull off a rescue of this size and complexity. He put Loyd Price, chief guide and an instructor with the Yosemite Mountaineering School, in charge of identifying what was needed.

OBTAINED FROM ALL OVER

To this day, a now-long-retired Pete Thompson is not exactly sure how the park ended up with some of what it got that day. The most interesting were the large rolls of one-half-inch rope. Tubbs Cordage, a yachting and sailing-line manufacturing company in the San Diego area, sent two 4,400-foot-long rolls and three 1,200-foot-long rolls of Goldlon, each tightly wound around a wooden spindle. Although plenty strong, the rope was not intended to take the kind of abuse it would be subjected to. Luckily, it worked out fine despite Thompson's trepidation at using a terribly wrong tool for lowering rescuers nearly 3,000 feet. Neither of the 4,400-foot-long rolls were ever used by the park.

The ropes were driven by local police departments to nearby El Toro Marine Air Station. They were then flown to El Cap Meadow in two large,

twin-rotor CH-46 helicopters. Other retail outdoor companies in the Bay Area, such as The Ski Hut and The North Face, sent real climbing rope as well as a seemingly endless supply of colored nylon webbing, hundreds of carabiners, 150 bolts, dozens of pitons, piton hammers, water bottles, dried food, and other long accessory lines and cords. These purchases were all picked up by the Bay Area Mountain Rescue Unit and transported by the California Highway Patrol.

Before they returned to their home base at El Toro that evening, the Marine Corps flew more equipment and manpower to the staging scene on top of El Capitan. There was a pile of equipment on the peak that night that had to be sorted and then placed in the right spot for the next morning. During the height of the stretcher lowering later in the day, several hundred people stood along the road and in the meadow, at the base of El Cap, most with their binoculars pointed toward the light-brown cliff.

A TRIUMPHANT RESCUE Six of the Camp 4 SAR-site climbers, including Bev Johnson, rappelled down to Camp V that first afternoon. Up top, the operation was mostly engineered by Loyd Price, although all of the climbers knew what to do and pitched in. They knotted together enough ropes to create two 3000-foot lengths. One rope made a directional change at the victim's tiny ledge far below; the other ran straight from the final lip of El Capitan to Olsen's litter, attended by Camp 4 superstar Jim Bridwell. Although it took more than 36 hours to fully orchestrate, once underway it took only 90 minutes for the two to be lowered down the remaining 1,800 feet of sheer cliff. It went off without a hitch. The five still on the ledge, as well as Olsen's partner, elected to come down that night, after dark. Al Garza, the park's chief electrician, built a huge light bank and illuminated almost the entire face of the great cliff. Neal's leg healed, and he continued to climb for the next four decades.

This mission earned a Department of the Interior Unit Citation for the El Capitan Rescue Team from Secretary of the Interior Rogers C. B. Morton. It was granted in recognition of the high degree of professionalism and valor exhibited.

▲▲ (top) Some of the ropes used. ▲ (above) Two days after his injury, a relieved Neal Olsen reaches the bottom of El Capitan. Climber Jim Bridwell, attending the litter, is glad to be down as well. Today, everyone in the picture would be required to wear a helmet. NPS photos by Gary Hathaway.

FROM THE TOP OF EL CAPITAN

Ranger Donna Lea Symns went on her fair share of SARs during the two years she worked in the park. After all, 55 people died while she was there. One death was particularly memorable to her, as it was only the second climber, after Jim Madsen (see page 64), to fall from nearly the top of El Capitan. On June 7, 1973, 19-year-old Michael M. Blake, a skilled climber from Santa Monica, was on the last few hundred feet of his several-al-day climb of The Nose route. The record is unclear as to what exactly happened next. The speculation is that his rope, while under tension, passed over a sharp object, possibly a piton, and was severed. He fell over 2,400 feet. Like many of the climbing deaths in Yosemite, it was a needless loss born of a simple mistake or a combination of them. Ranger Symns investigated the accident and then, along with others, recovered Michael Blake's remains.

▲ Monday, August 20, 2007, David, age 31, was leading the Regular Northwest Face of Half Dome, a strenuous Grade VI route. Both he and his partner believed they could do the climb in one day, although neither had done other Big Walls. At 6:30 p.m., now on the 17th pitch (of 23), David accidentally got off-route and fell 80 feet. Slamming into the granite, he hit his head as well as back and spine. Word reached the park's 911 dispatch at 4:30 a.m. Four hours later, Helicopter 551 began shuttling rescuers to the top. A litter attended by James Thompson was lowered roughly 600 feet to the victim (arrow). About a dozen hikers on the summit helped YOSAR raise David and his partner. In the photo, team member Werner Braun monitors the rigging at the edge of the cliff. The rescue scene was clear by 4:00 p.m. David suffered fractures to six of his vertebrae. NPS photo by David Pope.

AN EPIC RESCUE ON HALF DOME

On November 3, 1968, fewer than three weeks after Jim Madsen fell 3,000 feet trying to help his friends (see page 64), Yosemite Search and Rescue was once again faced with the need to save someone trapped in the middle of a Big Wall. The arching, 2,000-foot South Face of Half Dome was still unclimbed as of late October that year when master climber Warren Harding, 44, and his 28-year-old partner, Galen Rowell (yes, the famous photographer), decided to gamble with the late-season Sierra weather. Now rated as a Grade VI, 5.8 A4, the wall was expected, at the time, to be one of the most difficult climbs in the world.

For six days the pair inched up the endless granite face, spending long nights sleeping uncomfortably in homemade hammocks. The veterans expected to summit in a few days. Instead, with Harding leading, they were forced onto a dauntingly featureless 1,000-foot section. Galen would later describe it as "the most spectacular sixth-class lead I have ever seen," while Harding would call it his "most strenuous lead." Quite a declaration considering that these were two of the sport's celebrated heavyweights. While Rowell marveled at the sunset with a photographer's appreciation, he also warily inspected the wispy strands of white cirrus moving in ominously. He later recalled:

> Waking at midnight, I heard a new sound . . . running of water and dripping of raindrops. . . . [I] went back to sleep, not worried because the weather forecast carried no prediction of a storm and therefore this must be a local disturbance. But several hours later, I realized my down footsack and jacket were soaking . . . [the] tightly woven fabric let water soak in, but would not let it out. Pools formed at the bottom of the hammocks. . . . By dawn we were both soaked to the skin. Snow covered . . . the high country. The rain became sleet . . . then . . . snow.

DEADLY WEATHER Nearly 2 inches of rain fell in the Valley over the next 24 hours, and it was snowing at the 7,000-foot level—1,000 feet *below* where the two were now beginning to realize how dire their situation had become. Half-dollar-sized flakes of wet snow fell thicker and thicker, sticking to the granite around them. Both men shook all day with cold and, as Rowell remembered, "looked for a blue spot. . . . It never came. We passed a second night . . . [a] sleepless, cold, wet ordeal. Fourteen hours of November darkness."

THROWING IN THE TOWEL As day eight dawned, the climbers knew they were in true trouble, and might not survive. Rowell was completely soaked, his toes and fingers totally numb, but he still hoped

WATCH THE WEATHER

Even expert climbers can run into trouble.

There have been way too many Big Wall rescues as the result of both late-season heat and early, winter-like storms. Records tell us October (and sometimes even November) are often beautifully sunny and warm—ideal for scaling El Cap and Half Dome. These same archives also show a lot of seriously bad weather for these same months. Playing a form of Russian roulette, **climbers still go unprepared and/or will disregard warnings about the predicted storms. Also they often assume the prediction of fair weather is always correct.**

A helicopter may not be able to fly in stormy weather. If Half Dome is fogged in, for example, a ship might not make it to the top and rescuers might need to hike in by trail. Would an overnight delay prove fatal? **As every rescuer will tell you, don't count on a helicopter to save the day!** Even after a storm abates, flying may not be safe, due to melting ice and snow.

THE SHIRT OFF HER BACK

When Ranger Virginia "Ginny" Rousseau arrived in Yosemite in October of 1973, she had some doubts about her abilities. In email correspondence with the author in the fall of 2015, Ginny conjectured, "Could I carry the end of the litter? Lift someone? Defend myself in a fight? Go the distance? I arrived green, with few skills. I was not prepared in the least bit for what I was about to get into." Ginny taught herself to climb and became scuba qualified to join the park's Dive Team. "On my days off I would go fly with the Lemoore helicopter crews and rappel out of the ships. Great fun!"

She also learned some things her training might not have specified. "My first rescue was a young climber who had fallen. When we began assessing his injuries," she reminded the author, "you asked if I could take my shirt off and cover him up to treat for shock. I remember my reply. 'It would be a bigger shock to him if I took my shirt off than if I didn't.' The next day I headed to Fresno to buy T-shirts for under my uniform."

to make it down the 1,400 feet of snow-covered cliff to the base of Half Dome. In fact, he rappelled only 80 feet before realizing that his only chance might actually be to climb back up and hunker down, shivering and shaking with Harding. Rowell was freezing and so was his rope. Ice jammed his ascenders so that they no longer gripped the nylon link to his partner, 80 feet above. Struggling upward, he heard Harding on the CB radio with their support team below. He was throwing in the towel. Harding said, "We cannot last another night. Get us help today. A helicopter if possible. We are very, very cold."

CALLING IN AIR SUPPORT Rangers Pete Pederson and Pete Thompson were alerted to the nightmare far above and swung immediately into action. First, a fire helicopter from Sequoia National Park 150 miles to the south was requested. Then Royal Robbins in nearby Modesto received a call. Robbins was a friend of the park and probably the world's most experienced Big Wall climber. Robbins hurried to the Valley, as did Al Steck, another climbing great. The weather improved and they arrived shortly before the small chopper from Sequoia did. Late that afternoon, Pederson and Camp 4 climber Joe McKeown were flown to the top of the frigid peak. Thompson and Robbins quickly followed. The sun sank in the west and the nearly full moon rose in the east as Royal Robbins began rappelling down, eager to help his two friends below. Rowell remembers:

> About an hour after dark I heard a strange noise, so I unzipped the hammock and saw a man . . . not a hundred feet above us. . . . "Are you one of the guys from that chopper?" He was wearing a full down parka . . . carrying a walkie-talkie, a large pack, and had a headlamp strapped to his forehead. From now on if I ever envision a guardian, it will be in this form.

Over the next three decades, Galen Rowell became an internationally recognized photographer and photojournalist, and Warren Harding continued as one of the foremost climbers in the world. Both men died in 2002. Royal Robbins passed away in 2017.

▲▶ These photos were taken during the filming of a simulated rescue on Lost Arrow for *Sierra*. Portraying rangers on top are Wayne Merry, Bev Johnson, TM Herbert, and Loyd Price. Notice the ropes between the cliffs. Photos by Butch Farabee.

A TECHNICAL CHALLENGE ON LOST ARROW

On April 6 of 1970, YOSAR was faced with its most technically demanding rescue yet. It required a nearly professional-level feat of mechanical engineering to rig a rope and pulley system on top of the Lost Arrow Spire and then down around its totally vertical cliffs—and then back up again to the rim. The route, known as The Arrow Direct, is 1,400 feet and rated Grade V, 5.8 A3. We'll be focused on the top 300 feet. Andy Embick, 20, and his teenage partner Roy Naasz were on day three of the climb, and that noon they were only a rope-length below their goal, the sloping, 7-foot-square granite tip of Lost Arrow.

Often called The Arrow, this peak aims skyward, its 300-foot tip splitting off to stand 75 feet out from the main cliff at the top before it tapers 250 feet downward to a V-shaped notch that's 12 feet wide. The two climbers were on its vertical outside South Face, with the brush-covered base more than 1,200 feet below. Devoid of cracks and useful ledges, this wall is one of the more challenging in the park. With no small effort, Roy hammered in his third piton, a 2-inch-wide metal "bong," and slowly shifted his 180 pounds onto the nylon loop dangling off of it.

A LONG DROP INTO TERROR The bong pulled out. In the long blink of an eye, Roy suddenly dropped as though a trapdoor had been opened beneath him, falling into 1,200 feet of nothing. Climbers call

For photos of Lost Arrow Spire, see pages 163–4.

this "getting air," and if not for his belay rope, he would have died. Skidding down the rough, crystal-laced cliff face he smashed into a tiny ledge 25 feet below, aptly called "Second Terror." The young man had lost consciousness and hung limply at the end of his thin lifeline, his femur shattered (he would later learn that his ankle and wrist had broken as well). He quickly came to and was now alert. Andy climbed down to him and, after ensuring he was stable, safely tied Roy onto the tiny ledge. Because there was already a fixed line to the nearby rim, he quickly climbed out to get help. Amazingly, within two hours of the accident it was reported to Acting SAR Officer Tom Wylie. The Rodgers Flying Service helicopter out of Fresno was called and projected an arrival at 4:30 p.m., in about 90 minutes.

FINDING ROY Wayne Merry, a former ranger and now the Yosemite Mountaineering School director, agreed to be the operations leader. He and Loyd Price, his chief climbing guide, flew to the rim above Lost Arrow when the ship arrived. As he recalls:

> Loyd and I roped into the notch real fast and climbed to Salathé Ledge with sleeping bags and medication, getting there pretty close to dark. It was cold as hell—seems like it was about 17 degrees or so. Roy was straight down, 90 feet below Salathé. It was so steep you couldn't see him from the ledge.
>
> We tossed a rope into the gloom and I went down to Roy, who looked very tiny and very exposed on the wall, with a real white face and big eyes . . . sitting tied in on a little ledge just about the size of his hips and legs. The ledge was so small . . . no way I could stand on it, so I just stood in the slings with my shoulders level with him. I got out the Demerol. There was a little wind and so darn cold I was afraid the drug might freeze in the needle, but it didn't. I gave it in the shoulder. It hit him fast, and almost immediately he leaned over and barfed on my boots.

Roy would have to be re-medicated two more times before they could begin raising him out the next morning.

A COLD NIGHT UP TOP By midnight Loyd Price was so cold that he went up to the rim to warm up—he actually tied his hands to the metal ascenders to do so. Herb Swedlund joined Wayne Merry on the face to give Loyd a break—and became "desperately entangled" in the nine ropes running off the rim. Herb would describe the chaos of lines as looking like a "direct hit on a spaghetti factory." At sunrise the wall hummed with action as six other climbers joined Merry and Swedlund. Anchors were placed, pulleys were rigged, and ropes played out. They all knew what to do, and they did it well.

▲ On April 25, 1976, a 24-year-old woman fell 30 feet and hit her head while climbing an intermediate-level route on Middle Cathedral. She was knocked unconscious and (she was not wearing a helmet) and we believed she had broken her ankle. She and her partner, mistakenly on the wrong climb, had the proper gear but failed to use it. While being slowly lowered at night, Rangers Joe Abrell (left) and Tim Setnicka attend to the injured woman. Her injuries ended up not being life threatening, although she had, in fact, broken her ankle. NPS photo by Jon Kaunupace.

More than 3,500 feet of nylon rope were eventually used in the operation to rescue Roy Naasz.

FIVE HOURS OF RIGGING SAR Officer Pete Thompson, having returned to the park, directed placement of more anchors and ropes while Loyd Price designed an elaborate hoisting system. Few rescue techniques in mountaineering history have required greater skill, coordination, effort, and old-fashioned luck than this one did. Wayne Merry later told the author that getting Roy Naasz into the Stokes litter "was quite a feat, as the bad leg was on the side against the cliff. . . . [I had to] dangle on the ropes loading him in." Over the next five hours, through an intuitive but ingenious use of rescue gear, the litter with Roy in it would be pulled up to the rim.

A FALSE ALARM At midmorning, with more than 25 people now involved somewhere on or around the cliff, the delicate operation began. Kim Schmitz was leading with Jim Bridwell guiding the stretcher. Jim was on the radio to the top, dictating directions for how the litter should be moved, 6 inches to 6 feet at a time. At one point, Merry recalled, "A terrible scream rang up out of the void, and Bridwell's shocked voice thundered . . . 'We dropped him!'" Everyone froze. Jim hastily clarified—Roy had only toppled a foot onto a ledge. Everyone relaxed a little. Thirty hours after he should have died, Roy was in Lewis Memorial Hospital in the Valley. He would climb again.

▲ On October 5, 1976, 22-year-old Robert Locke fell and died while leading a difficult climb on Mount Watkins, across from Half Dome. Rescuers were flown in after dark and his body was raised 1,500 feet in a litter the next day. Here, attached to a nearby tree, is one of several systems being used to help raise the victim. Each piece of webbing, rope, line, and carabiner serves a specific function, all helping to anchor the ropes. NPS photo by Tim Setnicka.

CLIMBING AND RESCUE ROPES

In 1922, static (i.e., unable to stretch) hemp ropes were "fixed" up Half Dome to assist visitors, but even before then ropes were central to climbing and rescue in Yosemite. In 1939, DuPont Chemical Company began production of nylon, just as hemp from the Philippines (the primary source) became unavailable due to World War II. Nylon is stronger than hemp and has more intrinsic stretch. Today, climbing ropes are nylon and are dynamic, i.e., capable of stretching up to 40%, thereby acting like a bungee cord when stopping a falling climber. They are typically 50 to 70 meters in length and 8 to 11 millimeters in diameter. Rescue ropes are nylon or polyester, and are static, i.e., they have little stretch and so will not safely catch climbing falls; they are also much more efficient than stretchy ropes in rescue rigging. Static ropes may be purchased in longer lengths, typically in diameters from 9 to 12.5 millimeters, and can hold several thousand pounds of force before breaking. Both types of ropes have an outer sheath that protects the inner core against abrasion, critical for safety and rope-life.

TROUBLE ON THE LEANING TOWER

Of all of the Big Walls in Yosemite to rescue someone from, the 1,100-foot-high Leaning Tower is one of the most intimidating— maybe even more so than the much-taller El Capitan or Half Dome. Aptly named, Leaning Tower does exactly that, tilting several degrees from vertical. If you cautiously drop a stone off the top, the spot it crashes into at the bottom might be 60 or even 80 feet out from the granite wall's base.

LOOK OUT BELOW On the Fourth of July in 1992, Doug and Brad were on the third-to-last pitch of the climb, maybe 450 feet from the top. Brad was leading a moderately difficult A3 section when he pulled a

BIG WALL RESCUES: THEN AND NOW

In September of 1972, Neal Olsen smashed his right leg 2,000 feet up El Cap (see page 118). It took 36 hours to organize a plan, reach him, and then lower the injured climber to medical aid. Climber Jim Bridwell (center) prepares his gear to attend Olsen to the bottom of the cliff. John Long and Bev Johnson (left) look on with other rescuers. NPS photo.

An Italian climber was speed climbing The Nose on El Capitan on September 18, 2010. Swinging by rope to a handhold, he hit the wall hard, seriously injuring his right leg. By cell phone, he called 911 and at 10:30 a.m. YOSAR was en route. Ranger Chris Bellino was short-hauled in first to set anchors in the blank wall, followed by Keith Lober (left). In just under three hours, Alegre was short-hauled off and transferred to a medical air transport helicopter. NPS photo by Jorge Lantero.

large granite flake loose; it fell, striking Doug 15 feet below. Doug's helmet was smashed and, while it provided some protection, he sustained a serious head injury, with a scalp wound bleeding copiously. Looking down on this scene, Brad thought his partner was dead. He climbed down, yelling in the hopes that he was wrong. After several minutes he heard a moan. His friend was unconscious, having suffered a potentially life-threatening injury—one that needed attention that night or he might not make it. Brad removed Doug's helmet, bandaged the wound to the best of his ability, and replaced the head protection. He then ensured his friend was secure and placed him into a jacket and sleeping bag. Checking his pupils, he ascertained that Doug's condition was improving. As Brad talked to Doug, he also yelled for help, and was soon able to report their dire situation to some startled visitors below.

HANGING IN THERE As the rescue team flew close to the cliff to size up the problem, they saw both climbers on a portaledge (a hanging tent and sleeping platform often used by climbers on multiday climbs). Doug was lying flat, motionless, with Brad straddling him. The problem was, the broken and uneven cliff top offered no real place for the Yosemite contract ship to set down. It had to make risky, one-skid landings on each of its round-trip flights. And, if that wasn't bad enough, precious daylight was fading fast. Luckily, Ranger and Parkmedic Dan Horner was able to be placed on top to assist with the emergency medical situation playing out far below the summit.

A TWISTING DESCENT With his safety harness connected to the ends of two 1200-foot-long rescue ropes, Dan gently eased over the edge. The portaledge was 450 feet down, and nothing stood between him and the bottom below. He had to wrangle a medical kit, rope, other climbing gear, and a litter while being slowly lowered down the face. Since the cliff overhangs the top, Dan quickly found himself unable to touch the rock with his feet. The ropes slowly twisted. Although not unexpected, it was still disconcerting, and made looking up disorienting as well. In sum, he was being lowered a great distance, on the end of two long, twisting ropes, in the dark. His destination: a spot partway down the sheer cliff to where a man's life hung in the balance. As Dan neared the victim, he radioed the top, asking to be slowed, and then stopped. He was now just above Brad and Doug, which left him hanging some 40 feet out and away from them because it was . . . the Leaning Tower.

SHINE A LIGHT Dan had on a headlamp, but it was still dangerously dark with only a sliver of moon that night. Help came in the form of technology: on the road below at Tunnel View, close to a mile away,

Carabiners ('biners) are indispensable to climbing and rescues. Made of steel or aluminum, they come in several shapes, including oval and "D." Roughly the size of a human palm, they have spring-loaded gates and are either locking or nonlocking (both shown here). Both types are used for recreational climbing as well as rescue work. The sturdier ones, however, are designed more for rescue work and are capable of holding up to several tons.

oval locking carabiner

oval nonlocking carabiner

▲ Spotting scope and loudspeaker in action. NPS photo.

▼ For more than four decades, one of YOSAR's most useful tools has been a Questar, a powerful spotting scope. Its high-quality optics range from 40- to 80-power, and it is great for gaining valuable information about a Big Wall incident—such as who, what, and how serious—which will then help determine if a SAR response is needed. Additionally, a powerful, portable loudspeaker, as well as those mounted in ranger patrol cars, are used to communicate with people on a cliff. SAR responders use these tools to communicate about hand signals, such as "Raise one arm to answer Yes, two arms to answer No. First question: Do you understand?" Once this process is established, questions like "Is someone injured?" can follow.

Ranger John Dill had installed an intense bank of lights to illuminate much of the great cliff's face. Tunnel View also became a grand spot for those who stopped that Fourth of July evening to observe this extraordinary rescue as it unfolded.

THE THROW BAG TECHNIQUE Dan Horner was to connect with the climbers 40 feet away thanks to the throw bag technique (see page 106). To reach them, he lofted a baseball-sized bag with a thin cord attached to it through the outstretched arms of Brad, now standing upright, if badly lit, on the portaledge. Field goal! Once Brad had the small line secured, Dan gently pulled himself to where a now-conscious Doug lay gravely hurt. Dan tied off the rescue litter just inches above the portaledge so that he could kneel on it to treat the injured man. He assessed Doug's condition, administered pain-killers, and got him medically stabilized while continually relaying his vitals to the park's medical advisers. The big challenge was to get the victim into a temporary full-body brace to immobilize his neck and back—while still hanging off the wall. Dan and Brad then had to awkwardly wrestle Doug onto the litter, and tie him down securely. It was now close to five in the morning.

ALL THE WAY DOWN All that remained was to descend the next 650 feet, straight down. With the team at the top set to lower the litter, Brad, using a separate accessory line, gently paid out the main rope until it was vertical—and once again 40 feet away from the wall. The stretcher, with Dan tied to it, was now hanging free and slowly going down. Within minutes, they touched the bottom. It was now dawn, and Doug had survived his ordeal on the Leaning Tower.

TRIUMPH AND TRAGEDY ON EL CAPITAN

October is often a great month to hike and climb in Yosemite—but the weather can quickly turn deadly. Witness Sunday, October 17, 2004, when the first major storm of the season blew in. Freezing winds blasted El Cap at speeds upward of 50 miles per hour. Swirling snows repeatedly created whiteout conditions, ultimately dumping nearly 2 feet of new stuff on the peaks. During this four-day blizzard, SAR teams began a full-scale effort to rescue seven different climbers on four separate routes of the granite monolith. Before it was over and the last climbers pulled up on Friday, October 22, about 100 people were involved in this epic operation, including SAR groups from at least three outside agencies.

MAKING A BAD SITUATION WORSE To add to the complexity of operations, elsewhere in the Yosemite backcountry some 20 or so hikers, several of them ill-prepared, became marooned at elevations of up to

9,400 feet, hemmed in by 4-foot drifts. Some had altered their itineraries without notifying anyone. They created a potential major strain on the Park's SAR capability. Compounding the growing distress for SAR Officer Keith Lober, it was impossible to launch a helicopter for the first few days of the blizzard.

CLOUDED VISION YOSAR knew there were several climbing parties on the cliff when the storm first hit, and attempted to monitor their well-being and progress as a precaution. While the National Park Service does not, as a rule, monitor the progress of climbers, hikers, or anyone else, occasionally, such as during a serious storm, they may do so. Experience has shown that those tackling El Cap are generally very skilled climbers, but that doesn't seem to prevent frequent lack of preparedness, occasionally mixed with questionable common sense. SAR's attempts to track the climbers were hampered by clouds and blowing snow, which obscured the cliff face—it was difficult to know how the climbers were doing, or to plan for potential rescue operations.

CLIMBERS IN TROUBLE After the storm's first wave of wind and snow passed, those below saw that three pitches from the top of The Nose, two climbers from Japan, were not moving. They were 26-year-old leader Ryoichi Yamamoto, who had a reputation as an aggressive and talented climber, and his 27-year-old climbing partner, Moriko Ryugo. They were on a survivable—albeit marginal—perch with sufficient gear to weather the blizzard. We will never know exactly what

▲ In 2010, a 48-year-old fell 60 feet on El Capitan, suffering serious head injuries. Luckily, he wore a helmet. A 911 call was made at 8:23 p.m., but it was too close to dark to try flying a rescue team to the summit. For the next 12 to 14 hours, the patient's partner and two other climbers kept him warm, stopped arterial bleeding from a scalp wound, managed his airway as he vomited blood, and tried to keep his head and neck stabilized in case of a fracture. He made a full recovery, but had suffered a fractured skull, a brain bleed that required surgery, a broken neck, and broken ribs. He survived at least in part due to the basic medical care the other climbers were able to provide. At 6:30 a.m., using the CHP helicopter, Rangers Jack Hoeflich and Jeff Webb lowered onto the cliff. At 8:30 a.m., the victim was hoisted off and en route to the trauma center. Photo by John Fischer.

▲ October weather is unpredictable, evidenced by the blizzard obscuring El Capitan and the four parties up there in 2004. NPS photo.

▲ This is the helmet after the fall. It made the difference between life and death. NPS photo by John Dill.

A RESCUE ON EL CAPITAN

El Capitan missions are difficult because of limited access, often requiring 20 or more rescuers on top. Here YOSAR safely off-loads and prepares to go over the cliff edge.

The brake-bar rack serves for lowering a rescuer and/or gear, controlled with the friction of the rope going over and under the metal bars. For safety, there is always a similar, second system used.

A rescuer with a two-way radio for communication assists a victim while being raised or lowered.

went wrong, but we do know that on Wednesday, October 20, when rangers had a brief window of flyable weather, they were able to hover close enough to see that the pair was almost certainly deceased. They were the 23rd and 24th known deaths on El Cap.

A BRIEF RESPITE Lober had thought the two Japanese climbers were his principal concern. Upon learning of their deaths, it appeared that time was no longer so critical. This quickly changed, however, as word came in from other climbers. An experienced solo climber who had been up there for 17 days soon signaled a need for aid, and before long others began asking for help as well. Ultimately all three remaining groups on the great rock needed rescue. Lober knew better than to wait for the weather to improve enough to get a helicopter in the air. He couldn't gamble with more lives, which meant he'd have to get creative. He asked for help from well-trained SAR groups in nearby areas, including from Marin, Placer, and El Dorado Counties, and, as is always the case, their mutual aid was gladly given.

◀ On October 20, 2004, rescuers traveling the 11 miles to the top of El Capitan needed to break through up to 2 feet of fresh snow. Much of the time, they were in whiteout conditions. Initially, the SAR mission was for a Japanese couple climbing. Before it was over, 3 separate groups were rescued and 1 recovered by a team numbering more than 100. NPS photo by Mike St. John.

CARAVAN TO THE RESCUE At nightfall on the 20th, as the blizzard still raged, a caravan of four-wheel-drive SAR vehicles slowly made its way up the Tioga Road to where it intersects the trail to El Capitan. Some 20 rescuers began hiking, skiing, and snowshoeing to the top, about 11 miles away, through fresh knee-deep snow. Several snowmobiles were also pressed into service, although they only got a few miles. The rescue team was prepared to spend that night en route—in addition to their own camping and survival equipment, the SAR team also carried all of the ropes, carabiners, pulleys, edge rollers, webbing, tarps, tents, stoves, and medical gear needed to pull the remaining three groups off spots that varied in difficulty. One lucky break: all the parties were in the upper third of the cliff. They also brought reminders of the seriousness of their task: two body bags for the ill-fated climbers from Japan.

A BITTERSWEET RESOLUTION By midmorning on the 21st, the first of the SAR team had pushed through 2 feet of fresh snow to the very lip of El Cap. Murphy's Law being in full effect, the storm soon broke and patches of blue began to appear; they could have flown. Still, the sober, risky business of rescuing the remaining climbers lay ahead. The first to be removed that Wednesday morning was a solo climber who had almost reached the top. Next, a pair of young men from California on the obscure Never Never Land route were pulled to the summit on Thursday. While this was being done, Ranger Ed Visnovske was lowered to the dead couple. Their slight bodies fit onto the same litter, and they were raised to the top along with Ed. Lastly, a woman from Mexico and her partner from New York were taken off the Salathé Wall on Friday. All five of the rescued climbers were capable and extremely skilled—just victims of bad luck, bad weather, and maybe some bad planning. Despite the conditions they'd endured, all of those rescued were in good shape.

▲ Ranger Ed Visnovske is raised to the El Capitan summit with the bodies of the two Japanese climbers, Ryoichi Yamamoto and Moriko Ryugo. NPS photo.

▲ Greg Loniewski adjusts the raising system's safety backup while other team members lift up a storm victim. NPS photo by Lincoln Else.

▲ H-551 departs the summit as the El Capitan storm incident winds down. NPS photo.

ON AND OFF THE WALL

To highly trained YOSAR teams and elite helicopter crews, Big Wall rescues are demanding and scary, but maybe not more dangerous than some other operations—particularly those involving rushing white water. (Tell that, however, to the pilot and the rescuer dangling 150 feet below a helicopter while trying to get onto El Capitan to get to an unconscious person some 2,000 feet above the ground!)

A RARE OCCURRENCE Luckily for YOSAR and the park's climbers, mishaps that result in the need for such a rescue happen infrequently, maybe several times a year. Needless to say, despite all of the highly trained personnel and the ever-evolving equipment, Big Wall rescues are always tricky and dangerous. When you factor in adverse weather, a late time of the day, and/or maybe an awkward spot to reach, the gravity of the rescue mounts. Any injuries will certainly complicate the many decisions to be made, and speed may become even more paramount. What helicopter is available? Can it launch? Is this a short-haul operation? A heli-rappel? Do we need to lower SAR personnel down by rope from the top? Raise the victim? Lower the victim? These as well as other considerations, including a host of intangibles, factor into the decision-making process. And still, time after time, these decisions will be expertly made.

THE EVOLUTION OF BIG-WALL EXPERTISE

YOSAR has performed many of these demanding rescues since the 1960s, as Big Wall climbing became more popular. By 2016, it's estimated that between 100 to150 have been successfully completed, and with each, rescuers have learned something valuable. The vast majority of these have been high-angle rope missions (lowerings and raisings), but that's changing. Within recent years, the park has also performed a number of live insertions and extractions utilizing helicopter hoist, heli-rappel, and short-haul on Big Walls, including El Capitan.

KEITH LOBER REMEMBERS

Chief of Emergency Services, February 2003 to May 2011

July 15, 2009, was a busy day for YOSAR. The previous day the body of a person who had gone missing over a month ago had been located in the Merced River below Vernal Fall, and the young hotshots on the technical team were committed to a fairly complicated highline procedure to recover the body.

Valley District Ranger Eric Gabriel and I went out to where the team had begun setting up. It was a truly grand operation too, involving 30-plus swift-water rescue personnel all suited up in their neoprene with boogie boards standing by in case someone fell in the water, super advanced technical rigging stuff, and a line gun to fire a tether across the span of the river.

The operations boss found us muddling around. He was most unhappy with us on "his scene." He made it quite clear he did not need us there. And then told Eric not to touch anything and not to get in the way. Obviously he did not want any gray-haired old f—s mucking up his operation, and we were being summarily dismissed. At least as much as you can dismiss your boss. We were crestfallen, feeling dreadfully old and in the way. This younger generation of technical climber/rescuer was better, faster,

more physically fit, and more technically advanced than we had ever been. We had become obsolete and we had definitely been replaced.

About noon the park Communications Center received a 911 call from Daniel Scott (not his real name). He had become ledged out while scrambling un-roped on an unspecified dome near Merced Lake. Scott stated he would be needing assistance to get off the ledge. Dispatch also gave us the coordinates of our victim's perch triangulated from the cell-phone signal. The call was transferred to the SAR duty officer (SDO). Scott somewhat nonchalantly stated he did not feel in any immediate danger, only that he was unable to ascend or descend.

Eric and I listened in as Scott described the situation, telling the SDO that he had been hiking the Pacific Crest Trail when he decided to do some off-trail scrambling. Once off the phone, the SDO ignored us, looking over at the status board to see what resources he had left. To his chagrin the only personnel left were Eric and me. We were grudgingly assigned the mission. Eric tried to beg off, saying he needed to get back to his office. I talked him into accompanying me on

As if this photo were lifted from a copy of *Where's Waldo?* . . . can you find the stranded hiker on this vertical cliff face? ▶ The 21-year-old even took his boots off to continue to clamber higher. By some miracle he didn't fall to his death before H-551 with the SAR team showed up. NPS photos by Keith Lober.

the milk run. The SDO stated this would be a nonemergency, so on the way to the heli-base we stopped for a cup of coffee and a donut at the deli.

At the helicopter we discussed what gear to bring . . . a light technical rack . . . one 60-meter rope . . . oh yeah, my Bosch battery-powered rock drill. Off we went, content in that maybe the hotshots were getting all the glory, but we were at least getting a pleasant helicopter sight-seeing flight. The coordinates led us to a 1,000-foot exfoliated rock dome that on the map was identified as Marmot Dome. No subject after multiple passes. This was not really a big surprise, as cell-phone GPS coordinates are notoriously inaccurate.

On the third pass across the face Jeff Pirog, the Crew Chief, glanced left checking the rotor clearance from the rock face. Over the intercom I heard him exclaim, "Holy ___. . . . There he is!" Scott was 100 feet away,

directly left and level with the aircraft. He was standing on a 1-foot-square perch holding on with both hands and looking straight across at us. He was smiling, barefoot, and also 800 feet in the air. We hadn't found him because we were all looking down into the more reasonable terrain near the base of the wall. It never occurred to me to look this high up. It could not be possible for an un-roped hiker to get here. I had envisioned Scott comfortably sitting in a lawn chair sipping lemonade on a 100-foot-wide brush- and tree-covered ledge.

I was stunned at how seriously our guy had downplayed his predicament; he was standing on a minuscule ledge, clinging to the rock on a nearly vertical wall 800 feet above the valley floor! I felt nauseous. I had dangerously underestimated how dire an emergency this was and its complexity. We had brought only the most minimal equipment. It

◀ Ranger Keith Lober just descended to a tiny ledge above the victim and proceeds to put two bolts into the rock quickly to help secure Ranger Eric Gabriel, who is about to follow. NPS photo by Eric Gabriel.

▾ Gabriel, along with the victim, is a moment from being plucked from the cliff, 800 feet up.

▸▸ With pilot Richard Shatto steadying the controls, Crew Chief Jeff Pirog looks down, insuring all is synchronized with the load below. NPS photos by Keith Lober (below and right).

was immediately obvious that his position was too tenuous to retrieve him directly by short-haul. The pilot, Richard Shatto, was having a difficult time maintaining a steady hover. The aircraft was being pummeled in the hot afternoon winds gusting across the face, and Scott might be dislodged before he could be made secure in a harness. We had also clearly not brought anywhere near enough rope to accomplish a lowering from the top of the cliff down to Scott's stance almost 400 feet below.

We landed on top and Pirog rigged the craft to short-haul configuration. Eric and I discussed a plan, maybe sending the ship back to get the real technical team. We decided Scott's position was just too precarious. We would have to do it now! I was short-hauled to 50 feet above

Scott's perch, where I found a small ledge, just big enough to stand on with one foot.

There were no usable cracks in which to quickly place an anchor and free the ship. The only option was to power drill a two-bolt anchor. Fortunately for Scott, I had grabbed my beloved power drill at the last moment.

Richard hovered in the winds in close proximity to the wall while I drilled the anchor. I am without a doubt the fastest bolt driller on the face of the earth; this is especially true when I am scared, which I most definitely was. Not many people can say they have actually drilled rock bolt anchors while dangling from a hovering helicopter.

Eric was then short-hauled to my station where I had set up a lowering brake system using our one climbing rope. He clipped into the anchor and disconnected from the helicopter. I then lowered him down to Scott, who was then secured into a screamer suit. Scott and Eric were then short-hauled off the face.

Cell-phone coverage in Yosemite wilderness is effectively nonexistent. Scott was incredibly lucky: the location where he finally became stuck was just high enough for the cell signal to peek over the surrounding rock faces and hit the Sentinel Dome repeater site several miles away, the only repeater in that area of remote wilderness. Incidentally, Scott had sustained and recovered from two short falls just before deciding to call it quits and request help.

Later that day after we had returned, the technical team began filtering back in, reveling in their efforts, only to find the room plastered with two dozen 8x12 glossy pictures of our mission. Now, I know this shows a truly defective personality, but I could not contain my glee as the deflated youth gazed at the pictures and the realization came across their faces of what a truly critical lifesaving operation the two old guys had, and that this mission, without a doubt, would turn out to be one of the best that YOSAR would carry out that year.

While hiking in the park's Hetch Hetchy area on June 29, 2011, Mark Allee of the California Conservation Corps came across five hikers attempting to cross the Wapama Falls Bridge. A storm had dumped several inches of rain in 14 hours, causing water to flow at double the normal rate and plunge over the western end of the bridge. Initially, two hikers were knocked off their feet in the current, and Mark climbed onto the bridge to help. But while he was getting into position, the first hiker was swept to his death. Mark then noticed the second victim get pulled beneath the lower railing, trying to hold on. While exposed to the full fury of the water's flow, Mark was able to unhook the waist buckle on the hiker's backpack, which was swept away by the swift current. Despite all of Mark's efforts, the exhausted hiker was pulled off of the bridge and did not survive. Mark Allee was awarded the Department of the Interior's Citizen's Award for Bravery. Of 21 deaths in the Park in the year 2011, 6 were water-related.

Water-related death is one of the most common ways people die in Yosemite. Indeed, rural search and rescue teams anywhere will likely tell you that moving water is involved with the scariest rescue scenarios they routinely encounter. Water is deceiving and capricious. Currents and hydraulics (places where the river flows back on itself) are not always visible, and are predictably unpredictable.

UNSTOPPABLE POWER

Other variables include hidden obstacles, slippery surfaces, floating debris, numbing cold, and the sheer weight of all that water. However, the real killer that victims always underestimate and trained rescuers genuinely respect is water's unstoppable power. Think of waves, tides, and cascades. When this crushing force moves over, between, around, and under boulders and hidden logs, as it does in much of Yosemite, rescuers use extra caution. As of 2017, at least 174 people have drowned since records have been kept. Most of these people started out completely unaware, as in the case that follows.

SWEPT AWAY

On a lovely, warm Friday afternoon in July 1991, 13-year-old Steven was on a short family trip with his parents and younger brother. Wading into a shallow pond in a side creek of the Merced River above the Arch Rock Entrance Station with his father, Harold, the boy became curious when he felt the water speeding up a little, and began exploring. He followed the current downstream to where the water channeled through a small field of boulders and tumbled into the next pool. Startled, the boy lost his footing and slipped. The current, now stronger, instantly pushed him into the cleavage between two rocks and then slowly jammed him there, as tight as a cork in a bottle.

A FIGHT FOR HIS LIFE Struggling mightily, Steven was able to hold his head just above the surface. His father hurried downstream to help while he braced himself to keep the stream from forcing him deeper into the crack. While Harold tried with all of his strength to pull his son free, Steven's mother, Judy, raced to the nearby entrance station for help. Snowmelt sapped both father and son. Fatigue quickened as their body temperatures dropped. After 15 minutes, seemingly a near-lifetime of desperation, both father and son hit their limit. The boy sank ever deeper.

THE BOY VANISHES Then, to his father's horror, Steven suddenly disappeared beneath the rushing water. He had been sucked into some hidden void beneath two boulders, forced there by the river funneling between the rocks. Harold wildly groped underwater for his son. Propped against the deadly current, he now found nothing but water-polished granite. He was petrified with fear.

A MIRACULOUS RESULT Over the sound of the moving water surrounding him, a panicked Harold heard his younger son, James, shouting. Steven, the boy yelled, was out! By an amazing fluke, the creek had squirted the young man out the far end of the submerged tunnel and sent him tumbling into the shallow water below. Understandably stunned, Steven sat in the shallows shaking his head in disbelief and relief. Harold lugged his dazed, incredulous son to shore just as a dozen rescuers were arriving. Amazingly, Steven suffered only minor injuries.

A TRAGIC SACRIFICE

Around noon on a pleasant day in October 1997, 29-year-old Arjuna Babapulle and his 22-year-old wife, Juanita, were walking along the shoreline above Vernal Fall, near Emerald Pool, looking

▲ On May 5, 2004, while on patrol, Ranger Leslie Reynolds saw "a dripping man in his early 20s running down the road toward me, waving his hands. His 26-year-old friend had fallen into Tenaya Creek just below Mirror Lake and was trapped under the water, held in place by his foot." He had been climbing on a boulder near the bike path when he slipped and became pinned 125 feet downstream. It took YOSAR several hours over two days to free him. Ranger Ed Visnovske is on the ladder in the photo; notice the hand in the water. NPS photo by Keith Lober.

Steven's story highlights a number of dangers inherent in any encounter with moving water. Even if it appears shallow or peaceful, don't be lulled into a false sense of security. Know the following facts, and **never underestimate the power of moving water, especially as it flows around obstacles.**

+ As **moving water** funnels between rocks, it will dramatically pick up speed and force.

+ **Cold water** will rapidly—and insidiously—sap energy, body heat, and strength.

+ **White, foaming water** is largely bubbles—this means that it is air, and it will not support you.

+ **Submerged rocks and logs** form all manner of shapes and sizes of voids and holes. All are very capable of trapping a leg, an arm, or a body.

+ Be alert for trees, logs, and similar obstacles, known as **"strainers,"** lying in fast water (see the box on page 142). They can kill you.

PREVENT DROWNINGS

Most drowning victims are wading, soaking their feet, or just standing on shore, taking a picture—not swimming. That should be a strong lesson to **be extra cautious around water, as it is totally unforgiving**. Here are some key things to keep in mind.

+ **You are responsible for your safety!**

+ **Learn to swim!** There is no excuse for not knowing how.

+ **Water-polished rocks** along the shore's edge are treacherously slick, even when dry.

+ **Wet rocks** are dramatically more slippery because they are covered in algae that's invisible to the naked eye.

+ **Cold water** will shock and distract you and momentarily take your breath away.

Emerald Pool is closed to all swimming.

for the ideal spot for a picnic. Somehow, Juanita slipped into the water and started screaming, in surprise at falling, and from the sudden shock of how cold the water was. In reality her situation was not yet critical, as she was managing to stand still, despite being in water over her knees. However, she was afraid that she wouldn't be able to make it the few feet to shore without risking a second, more serious slip into deeper water—a situation made even more perilous by the fact that she did not know how to swim.

A FATEFUL DECISION Arjuna quickly stepped in to help his wife, despite the fact that he, too, was unable to swim. He soon stumbled on the slippery submerged rocks. Regaining his footing, he gingerly eased out closer to Juanita and, moving to slightly deeper water, was able to shove her toward the shoreline. By this time four bystanders had gathered, one of them with a rope. He threw it to her, and she was able to grab it and easily work her way back to safety.

THE FATAL RESULT When Arjuna pushed his wife toward safety, that equal and opposite reaction we all learned about in high school physics proved to be his downfall, nudging him into deeper water. A rope was tossed to him, but it was too late. Arjuna did not even know how to tread water, and he sank beneath the surface. Those on shore now faced a dilemma. Someone could risk wading or swimming out to where he was last seen, dive down, try to retrieve the fully clothed man, and then get them both back to safety—all of this before they themselves floated into the fast-moving white water not far downstream. No one risked it at first. Finally, 10 minutes later, a witness brought him up from the bottom and Arjuna was given CPR. Although he had not been underwater for long, it was too late.

AFTER THE FACT Arjuna D. N. Babapulle was awarded a Carnegie Hero Award for his selfless act. After analyzing the incidents in Yosemite in which rescuers drowned trying to save someone, the author believes this may be one instance of perhaps a couple that resulted in the rescue of the drowning person and the death of the rescuer.

DON'T BE A CASUALTY

Drowning people are notorious for killing their rescuers. If you are entering water you need to understand your risk and how to minimize and survive it. All courses in lifesaving stress using every conceivable on-shore technique first before entering the water, with the mnemonic Reach—Throw—Row—Go.

+ **STEP 1: REACH.** Reach out to the drowning person with a branch, fishing pole, towel, etc., and attempt to pull him or her to safety. If nothing is available, and you can be assured of your own stability, lie flat and try to grab the victim's hand or wrist.

+ **STEP 2: THROW.** If the victim is too far away to reach and a boat isn't handy, throw the victim a line, a life preserver, or another item that will float.

+ **STEP 3: ROW.** If a rowboat is available (which will probably never be the case in the scenarios we're discussing), row to the victim and then use an oar or paddle to pull the victim to the stern. Let the victim hold onto the stern as you paddle to shore. If the victim is too weak, hold onto him or her until help arrives.

+ **STEP 4: GO.** Swimmers without lifesaving training should not attempt a rescue. Even if you are trained, be sure to *keep out of reach of the person in trouble*. Toss the victim something rope-like and tow him or her to safety.

WHERE IS THE EDGE?

The word "edge" may seem precise, but when moving water is involved, the definition is fuzzier—and potentially crucial. If you are 100 feet from the edge of a river or the edge of a cliff, but you could slide all the way if you slip, you are already at the edge. Keep in mind that when you hike the Mist Trail steps below Vernal Fall, you may be only 12 inches from the edge.

◀ On July 3, 1980, a novice boater wrapped his raft around a notorious tree in the Merced River near the Valley campgrounds. Rangers Peter Fitzmaurice (rowing his own craft) and Hal Grovert made the tricky rescue. This tree, which had snagged other rafters, was cut down as a rare exception to NPS policy. NPS photos.

WHITE-WATER TRAGEDY

Who: A married couple • When: August 12, 1983

The Story: A peaceful rafting trip goes terribly wrong.

Life seemed good for Donna and her husband as they quietly drifted along the Merced River that afternoon. A few minutes before 5:00 p.m. on August 12, 1983, the 40-something couple was several hundred yards downstream of the Happy Isles Bridge. They were in a small, cheap vinyl raft and were both wearing horse collar–shaped life vests of the sort meant for a wading pool, not a serious float trip. Nor did they have any training for this kind of adventure.

A SUDDEN MISHAP Probably before either of them could say "Watch out!" the couple went over a barely submerged pour-over boulder and flipped upside down in the now much-swifter water. Immediately they became separated. The husband was pulled many yards downstream, through several small strainers (see the box below), before he

was able to drag himself onto the bank. Luckily, he was able to raise the alarm quickly by way of a passing shuttle bus driver. Within four minutes, Ranger Pete Dalton arrived on scene, and not long afterward others were responding and mobilizing for a swift-water rescue . . . or recovery.

ON-SCENE REPORT Ranger Dalton recalls seeing a life jacket float by as he searched the area. He checked every strainer, and soon found "Donna wrapped around a submerged log . . . under 1½ feet of swift moving water, in one of the river's main channels. . . . [Her] arms and head were the only portion of her body visible." A deep channel separated Donna from Dalton, who was some 40 feet away. He was lucky he saw her, as she'd been underwater for 10 minutes already. He recalls, "I attempted

to swim across the channel to an eddy . . . directly above where the victim was trapped. . . . Halfway across . . . I realized that even with the appropriate gear: wet suit, fins, and life jacket, the exposure to the strainers . . . downstream . . . would be high risk."

CRITICAL LACK OF KNOWLEDGE Not a white-water rafter, Donna did not know how to protect herself in these conditions. Had she taken a survival course, or an introduction to rafting or kayaking, instructors would have stressed the importance of assuming a shallow, on-your-back-with-feet-downstream position for passing over rocks in a boulder- and strainer-filled fast current. Nor did she know that with her feet pointed down-current, she could kick and maybe slowly move herself at a 45-degree angle to some kind of safety. Even if stuck on a rock midstream, she would have been far safer than she was in the rapids.

A DANGEROUS RESCUE Rangers Dan Dellinges and Gary Colliver had now joined Pete Dalton in the attempt to rescue Donna, who was jack-knifed at her waist over a log, both her head and feet pushed downstream by the

---

Even in low water, any swift-water river can be deadly. Powerful water moving over submerged obstacles results in deceptive currents and dangerous hydraulics. Particularly deadly is what's known as a "strainer." A tree may fall across a stream, or water-worn logs will jam up against rocks and sharp bends in the river and become lodged like straw in a haystack. These are strainers. You can be sucked into the branches and other underwater obstructions and be "strained" through them. You may not come out the other side.

▲ First responders work on a victim of a near-drowning in the Merced River, August 1, 2004. If not for EMS, he would not have survived. NPS photo by David Pope.

force of the river. The responders knew of instances—albeit very few—where someone had been submerged for up to 45 minutes in cold water and still survived. They battled to release Donna from the river's grip. The three knew if they lost their position, they could possibly become similarly trapped. In an interview with the author in 2015, a retired Gary Colliver recalled:

> I remember thinking Dan and I might get sucked under the same submerged log where Donna was caught. Dan and I . . . seemed unable to dislodge her. Finally, Dan said "One last try and we're out of here" . . . I was getting pretty tired. Dan let loose with a huge, growling, extended surge. . . . Dan's enormous effort was what broke her free. We handed her off to a team on the bank who quickly began CPR. What a thrill to overhear on the radio they got a heartbeat.

Sadly, that thrill was short-lived. The 25 minutes Donna had spent underwater induced hypoxia that plunged her into an irreversible coma. She never regained consciousness, dying eight months later. Gary Colliver, Peter Dalton, and Dan Dellinges earned Department of the Interior Valor Awards.

THE TAKEAWAY

Moving water is dangerous; if you're engaging in any sort of recreation on or around water, be sure you're properly prepared and know what you're doing.

+ **Get instruction** before starting out, even for a simple float down a river.

+ **Do not use cut-rate, inadequate equipment** on rivers and moving water.

+ Trees and limbs immersed in moving water always form **dangerous strainers.**

+ Water flowing over **submerged obstacles** forms powerful hydraulics that can affect your craft unexpectedly.

+ If you find yourself floating through rapids and strainers, **lie on your back**, raise your legs, and keep your feet pointed downstream.

+ On rare occasions, people have been submerged for up to 45 minutes in very cold water, yet successfully revived when rescued.

FATAL WATERFALLS

Some of the more dramatic deaths in Yosemite have occurred when visitors got too close to a waterfall. From 1913 with Snow Creek Falls (see page 34) to 2017, at least 54 people have died going over one of the park's named waterfalls, including 4 who committed suicide. Vernal Fall has claimed 18 lives, Nevada Fall 12, and Upper Yosemite Fall 11.

LESSER-KNOWN HAZARDS Other falls that have taken a life are Wapama in the Hetch Hetchy area, The Cascades near the Arch Rock Entrance Station, and Tenaya Canyon's Hidden Fall. The little-known, 25-foot-high Eagle Fall, not far from the Yosemite Valley Lodge, killed 22-year-old Gregory Brazil in 1975 while he was high on marijuana. The more than 340-foot-high Waterwheel Falls in the Tuolumne Wilderness killed Steven Brown, 9, in July 1971, when he got too close to the waterworn edge of the falls; he wasn't found until August 31. Amazingly, however, while taking a drink at the lip of the same cascades 20 years earlier, Eric Yeoman, 25, survived the plunge. Eric was able to walk away relatively unscathed. His wife, Norma, went over while going to his rescue. She also somehow lived, although she did suffer numerous serious injuries. Local campers carried her out to the road, taking nine hours to do so.

WHO DIED AND WHY As you might expect, all of the waterfall deaths, with the exception of the four suicides and Patrick Rose, 21, who went over Vernal Fall in October 1973, took place in the warmer months of May to September. People were wading, swimming, cooling their feet, taking photos, and a few were even trying to get a drink on a hot day. Not too surprisingly, 41 of these deaths were male, with 40 of them under the age of 40. The photo sequence on the next page shows a recent incident in which Vernal Fall claimed the life of one of these young men.

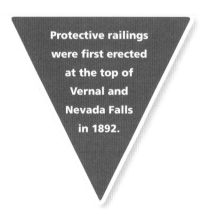

Protective railings were first erected at the top of Vernal and Nevada Falls in 1892.

▲ In 2005, a 25-year-old climbed over the railing 75 feet upstream of Vernal Fall (see circle). He slipped near the edge, slid into the current, and was swept over the fall. ▶ Two months later YOSAR tries to change the water's direction with sand bags to make finding the body easier. ▶ Ranger Ed Visnovske is lowered down the waterfall to check for the body. ▼ The Mariposa County volunteer dive team locates and recovers the body in the pool at the base of the fall. NPS photos.

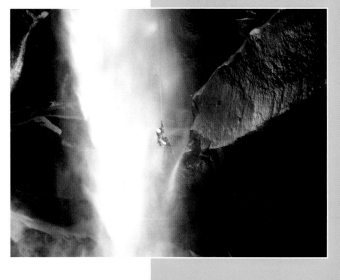

A BEAUTIFUL DEATH TRAP

Between Upper and Lower Yosemite Falls, Yosemite Creek plunges 675 feet over at least five smaller falls in a half mile. When the high-country snows melt, that creek is really a small, full-blown river with sloping, slippery, spray-splashed granite edges that make it a potential death trap for unwary visitors. Hikers often scramble down from the nearby trail to fill a canteen and take photographs of the incredible scenery.

ONE MISSTEP On June 16, 1990, Eric, 30, was snapping photos when he stumbled into the snow-fed cascades. He muscled himself out but again fell, bumping and sliding along the polished granite for 100 feet and then dropping over a minor cliff of about a dozen feet. He clung to a giant boulder, the river above his waist. Luckily, there were witnesses, and after YOSAR was alerted this became an "All hands on deck!" rescue.

SAR ON SCENE Quickly Kim Aufhauser and Joe Sumner were in their wet suits and in the air, the park ship putting them on a cliff a couple of hundred feet above Eric. Kim and Joe rappelled 180 feet down to the water's edge and would soon enter the moving water with safety ropes attached. Eric was unhurt but hypothermic, having been up to his chest in 40-degree snowmelt for several hours by then. Other

▲ Suspended from a highline, Ranger Ed Visnovske probes for a person who drowned in August 2005. NPS photo by David Pope.

▶ This is a schematic of a simple "Z-rig," named for the "Z" figure it forms when constructed. It is a rope and pulley system of mechanical advantage (MA), often employed in rescue work. Here the theoretical MA is 3:1: One pound of force in pulling will lift three pounds of victim or rescuer or gear.

A Z-rig may also tension a line, such as when a rope is used as a "highline" across a river. Note: this illustration does not show a second line or other necessary safety features that will also be built into the system.

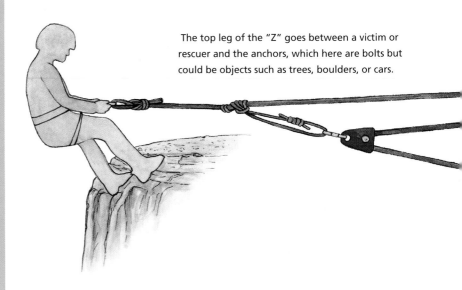

The top leg of the "Z" goes between a victim or rescuer and the anchors, which here are bolts but could be objects such as trees, boulders, or cars.

rescuers were now being flown in, including John Roth and Kerry Maxwell. While Kim Aufhauser and Joe Sumner concentrated on their man, a rope system employing simple mechanical advantage, called a "Z-rig," was being engineered to ultimately raise Eric and his rescuer up and, in due course, off the boulder. Joe Sumner recalls:

> When I reached [him] . . . Eric looked spent. I couldn't hear anything but the thundering of the water. I was wearing a wet suit and a life vest and carried a seat harness and a chest harness. I was to get him in both and then raise him out of the water but I couldn't even get him onto the rock. . . . He really couldn't help himself. All I could get on him was the chest harness. Kim and I couldn't see each other so I would hand signal to Kerry, who I knew was there but couldn't see either, and who would, in turn, activate the [haul] system. . . . I gestured for them to raise, hoping to get Eric onto the rock and then re-rig him into a more secure harness. Lifted, the rope slid several feet upstream, raising us both off the rock. We wound up face-to-face in a bear hug with his legs wrapped around me and his weight on me because of slack. . . .

> When we could finally hear each other I learned Kim had somehow stopped us from sliding into a powerful side cataract. If raised the entire distance in it, I am sure Eric would not have survived and I would have been in a lot worse shape.

REMEMBER!

+ **You are responsible for your safety!**

+ Most drowning victims were wading, soaking their feet, or standing near the edge and taking a picture.

+ Rocks at the water's edge, whether wet or dry, can be fatally slick due to sand and invisible algae.

For take-along reminders about water safety in Yosemite, see page 205.

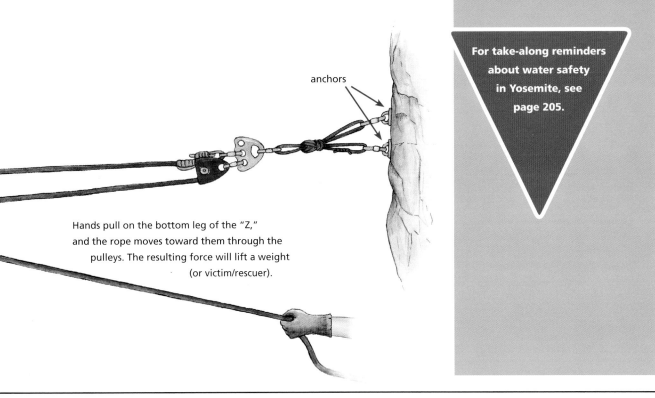

anchors

Hands pull on the bottom leg of the "Z," and the rope moves toward them through the pulleys. The resulting force will lift a weight (or victim/rescuer).

This is a throw bag, long used by rafters and kayakers for river rescues. About the size of a loaf of bread, the nylon sack has an approximately 70-foot long, 1/4- to 3/8-inch line stuffed inside of it. Held by a rescuer, its compact design permits it to be accurately thrown to someone in or near the water.

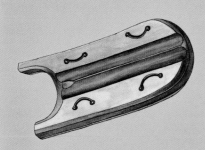

This is a rescue river board, a highly buoyant device made of nylon and Styrofoam used in Yosemite for swift-water rescues. It is a tool utilized by rescuers for initial attack to reach a victim or for backup in case a victim or fellow rescuer slips beyond initial help.

On the lip of the small ledge we realized we could not get him quite onto it. We needed to unclip, then slide into the waterfall and be hauled through the last 6 feet. We could not go up or move while a Z-rig was being set. Although it only took a minute or two, it seemed a lot longer.

When Kim let us go we swung into the far wall of the cascade and were under falling water. Eric went limp and was slipping from my grasp so I now had my arms tightly around his arms, now above his head. I was lucky my back was to the water and my nose and mouth under the top of my life vest with a little air pocket. My victim was getting the full water board treatment . . . lifeless and totally limp. I grabbed his hair and pulled his head out. Kim pulled us onto a ledge the size of a couch. Eric was not breathing, so we took turns doing mouth-to-mouth, but couldn't get air into him. I had . . . guilt . . . like you just killed the patient. Then there was one breath like inflating a balloon, I could feel his lungs fill . . . started breathing . . . still unconscious. Kim and I were exhausted but still had to drag Eric to the base of the last cliff.

During this entire SAR, windy and rainy conditions made helicopter operations difficult at best. Now out of the water, Eric was short-hauled to the Valley floor, luckily, just before it became too dark to fly. Darkness kept the ship from either removing the rescuers from the scene or leaving the Valley. Eric's core was 83 degrees. Stabilized at the park clinic, he was flown by Medi-Flight (which had no restriction due to darkness like the park did) to the trauma center in Modesto. Eric was released without permanent injury. Department of the Interior Valor Awards were presented to Rangers Kim Aufhauser and Joe Sumner on May 5, 1992. The citation that Joe received said, "In spite of Ranger Sumner's inability to swim . . . "

SWIFT-WATER RESCUES: THEN AND NOW

Like all SAR, swift-water rescues have evolved, with refinements to techniques and additions to equipment. Here, the author in a wet suit is on a rescue on the Merced River in El Portal, just outside the park, for the sheriff in 1974. Not seen are his swim fins, vital for navigating to the victim who is clinging to a rock in the rapids, downstream and out of sight. The author is not tied to the rope; rather he is holding onto a loop over his shoulder. Appropriate helmets and rescue river boards, as seen in the photo below, were not in use in Yosemite at that time. NPS photo.

Below, Moose Mutlow trains near North Pines Campground in 2006 with a rescue river board and helmet for swift-water rescue. Not all river rescues are done in the same way, but all require good planning. How they are safely performed—both then and now—depends on specifics, such as urgency, precariousness and location of victim, access to the other side of the river, hazards and obstacles, availability of trained individuals, and related circumstances. NPS photo by David Pope.

SCUBA IN THE PARK

With all of the high cliffs, rocks, and beautiful but jagged peaks in Yosemite, the use of scuba is not the first thing to come to mind as a search and rescue tool. But diving with air in a tank has been an indispensable asset to park SAR. As a rule, rescuers do not use scuba tanks to <u>rescue</u>, but only to <u>recover</u> someone who drowned, went over a waterfall, or was in a car that veered from the road and went into the Merced River.

A NEED FOR SPECIALISTS

The second documented instance of using artificial air in a SAR-type operation happened more than 20 years after the first instance, described at left. On July 8, 1965, 12-year-old Daniel R. Duda, a visitor from Brilliant, Ohio, crawled under the railing at the top of Vernal Fall, and in full sight of several witnesses, including his shriek-ing mother, slipped on the wet, water-polished granite and within seconds was swept helplessly over the lip of the 317-foot-high fall. His body became trapped amid the rocks and boiling hydraulics at the bottom, periodically bobbing to the surface, only then to disap-pear below. The park did not have anyone yet trained in the use of scuba and needed help. At that point in time, there were probably not more than two dozen rangers in all of the National Park Service certified to dive.

ASSISTANCE RENDERED The boy's family pressured the park to do something, and Yosemite Chief Ranger Bob Smith looked to out-side resources to see who might be able to help. Since at least 1964, Lake Mead National Recreation Area had hosted a well-trained dive team, and Smith finally asked for their assistance in early Septem-ber. Willow Beach Subdistrict Ranger Dick Newgren and Boulder Beach Ranger Al Denniston were flown to Mariposa in a trip that took them across Death Valley and then the Sierra in a four-seat Cessna-182 ranger patrol plane piloted by Park Pilot Warner James. All three rangers had graduated the year before from a local Las Vegas dive shop's class. More than 50 years later, Dick Newgren still remembered the day well:

> The day we flew over from Mead, the boy floated and then
> went back down. My boss, Chief Ranger Bernie Packard,
> insisted of Yosemite that we save our energy and we not hike

up to the dive site, but rather fly in. So we flew to the top of the waterfall by the park's three-person ship, from Sentinel Dome Helipad to above Vernal Fall. Yosemite rangers carried our weight belts, tanks, ropes, and rescue gear up by hand and Al and I took only our wet suits. Of course, it would have been easy and certainly safer just to walk the short 1 mile to the dive site, but it was both fun and exciting.

None of us really understood the dangers (or lack thereof) that existed in diving under the waterfall, and so we had rope safeties from both sides of the pool. There were foot-high whitecaps and blinding spray, scary until you went under and then it was crystal clear and pretty calm. The bottom has giant, VW-sized boulders with right angles and deep crevices. But it did not take us long, maybe 20 minutes of 'tank time,' to decide the boy was not there. We later learned he had floated out the night before and ultimately was located on October 16, wedged in the rocks halfway to Happy Isles.

THE YOSEMITE DIVE TEAM

Maybe the need to bring those three rangers over from Lake Mead was the impetus for Yosemite Ranger Tom Hartman to become the driving force behind the creation of the park's first dive team. Tom had recently transferred in from Channel Islands National Monument near San Diego and already possessed a great deal of dive training. Nearly 10 months later, on July 15, 1966, Hartman, along with Rangers Lew Alberts and Dick Marks, got official authorization from the Service's Western Regional Office to form a team. Even though Alberts and Marks were not officially sanctioned and were only minimally self-trained, they had already performed their first body recovery using their own personal equipment a month before.

▼ Ranger Tom Griffiths (front) and Chief Ranger Bill Wendt just recovered a drowned motorist. Late on May 27, 1978, an open convertible with four people inside hit a tree and bounced into the river in the Valley. Three escaped unharmed but a young man remained missing that night. He was found downstream the next day. NPS photo.

SEARCH AND RECOVERY On June 7, 1966, Gilbert Reid, while fishing below Pohono Bridge at the western end of the Valley, slipped on the spray- and algae-covered rocks and fell into the river. The 23-year-old was quickly swept into the nearby rapids, vicious with snowmelt from the high country. Not far below this stretch of white water is a long, calm, 10-foot-deep pool called Steamboat Bay. The young man's body was found there among the house-sized boulders the next day by Alberts and Marks. The need for a dive team was clear. Five months later, and after it had quieted down a little in the park, Lew Alberts and Dick Marks finally were able to attend an NPS-sanctioned dive class at the prestigious Scripps Institute of Oceanography, near San Diego.

THE GROWTH OF A TEAM All through the 1970s the Yosemite Dive Team was active, the size of it varying based on which rangers were in Yosemite and their skills. Near the end of the '70s the team had a maximum of six active divers, and the SAR cache had a full complement of scuba tanks, regulators, dive lights, and related dive gear. This equipment was not very sophisticated by today's standards, but was satisfactory for the era. Each diver was eventually supplied a wet suit, mask, fins, snorkel, and related personal equipment. Training dives were regularly made in the Yosemite Lodge swimming pool, the Merced River, including under the ice several times, as well as in

▲ On March 31, 1979, rangers work to recover a 15-year-old from above Chilnualna Falls in Wawona. Springing from rock to granite rock, he slipped and was swept over a cascade into a whirling pool of snowmelt, succumbed to hypothermia, and drowned. A small scuba tank was brought along in case the water was too deep to locate the boy's body, but it was not needed. Everyone is tethered by rope for safety. NPS photo by Tim Setnicka.

8,150-foot-elevation Tenaya Lake, perhaps the highest of any routine diving within the National Park System.

ROUSSEAU REMEMBERS In September of 1977, Virginia "Ginny" Rousseau attended the dive-training program at the Scripps Institute of Oceanography, the second of only three NPS women to go through this school. Over two decades, several hundred rangers would attend. The following is from a journal Ginny kept that summer.

> I was thrilled I was accepted but very nervous as I was a mediocre swimmer, but really more afraid I would fail and be sent home. I did not want to let those who supported me down. It would give ammunition to those who didn't believe women should be doing this job. I swam almost every day that summer in the Lodge Pool to get ready. . . . I focused on breast and side strokes and increased my endurance and strength. Technique over muscle. To also ensure success, I traveled to Fresno, on my own time, and completed a 40-hour NASDS (National Association of Scuba Diving Schools) course at Bob's Dive Shop. This gave me a good idea of what I would be getting into at Scripps. Like always there are the anxieties of the unknown. If I make it through the first week, I think I'll have a lot of fun.

> Well, if persistence counts for anything I won't quit, may drown but won't quit. And I won't do that—they have a reputation to uphold—they can't let me drown. Tomorrow should tell! At least swimming laps tonight made me more comfortable with the pool. . . . In the pool at 7 am, no problem with the test. Three guys didn't make the 150' the first time. Swam to end of [Scripps] Pier, dove down to get sand and it kept slipping out between my fingers. . . . This is really a fast pace! No time for stragglers or practice. . . .

THE END OF AN ERA During the three decades the Yosemite Dive Team was in existence, these scuba-trained men and women performed searches and body recoveries for victims of waterfalls, drownings, and vehicle crashes in the Merced River, both within the park and beyond its borders. In the mid-1990s, Chief Ranger Bob Andrew disbanded the Yosemite Dive Team, feeling that the time and money required for training and equipment was more than the park budget could justify. The slack for body recoveries in the park fell to the Mariposa County volunteer dive team.

NATIONAL WATERS

There are 88 ocean and great lake units within the National Park System, across 22 states and 4 territories, with 11,000 miles of coastline and 2.5 million acres of lands underwater. There are 14 national recreation areas with diving opportunities, such as Lake Mead and Glen Canyon. In 2017, there were approximately 215 National Park Service divers. They recover drowning victims, conduct biological and archaeological surveys, maintain docks and buoys, and monitor the condition of historic shipwrecks on submerged park lands.

DOPE LAKE

Who: Rangers vs. Entrepreneurs

When: December 9, 1976 to June 16, 1977

The Story: A legend is born.

We'll never know how much marijuana was on the plane when it crashed in a remote basin east of the Merced Pass Trail, 12 miles southeast of Yosemite Valley. Three tons is an educated estimate by a resolute researcher of the now near-legendary "Dope Lake Incident." The twin-engine, World War II–era converted Lockheed PV-1, with a wingspan of 72 feet, came to rest in the shallows of Lower Merced Pass Lake, elevation 8,800 feet.

At the controls of N80BD, falsely registered in Florida, was 31-year-old Jon Glisky, a former pilot in Vietnam. He was running drugs for the adventure as much as for the money. Also onboard was a friend and fellow vet; he too was a pilot. Having loaded the pot on the plane on a beach 150 miles south of Tijuana, this was the pair's second trip across the border that day. The plane crashed. Then, seven weeks passed.

THE BIG FIND On January 25, four employees on their days off from the Ahwahnee Hotel were hiking through the trees near Merced Pass and stumbled onto one white wing with an identifying number on it. Several days later they reported their find to rangers in the Valley and then SAR Officer Tim Setnicka. Soon, courtesy of a Lemoore helicopter, Rangers Joe Evans and Bruce McKeeman were searching at the remote crash site.

The doomed plane had left an obvious path of debris through broken pine branches, with the mangled fuselage and most of its illicit cargo ultimately ending

▲ On February 1, professional diver Bob Tostenson from Fresno prepares to enter foul water through a hole right above the fuselage of the plane. NPS photo by Joe Blackburn.

◀ Tools and clothing abandoned when NPS returned on April 13. Burlap bags that were once full of pot are in the background.
▼ U.S. Customs Service helicopter being loaded. NPS photos by Joe Blackburn.

up sealed beneath 12 inches of frozen lake ice. Scattered about the shoreline were numerous burlap sacks full of marijuana, all waterlogged. Also interested in the missing craft were four other federal agencies: Customs, DEA, NTSB, and the FAA. The NPS took the lead since the plane was in the park.

For two days, a professional diver from Fresno as well as several rangers slipped through a hole cut in the ice. Dodging jagged metal and with limited visibility, they retrieved bags of dope (maybe half of the load)

and sought the occupants in the wreckage. The Sierra weather then closed in with a vengeance and the five agencies chose to wait for spring to further unlock the mysteries of the ill-fated drug plane. This was a mistake.

HOW TO SUCCEED IN BUSINESS
A month later, unusual vehicle activity at a trailhead, along with quiet gossip among the local mountaineers, began filtering in to park officials. Enterprising entrepreneurs were mining the 6-acre, snow-covered lake and had been for days, maybe even

weeks! But as soon as the navy chopper popped over the rocky ridge like a Vietnam gunship, the climbers scattered like a covey of quail. Everything from chainsaws to sleeping bags was abandoned.

Despite wild rumors, no one will ever know how much "Yosemite Gold" was harvested before park rangers took back Dope Lake. Reputedly, however, a few near-penniless climbers soon bought new cars and took expensive vacations. On June 16, the pilots' bodies were found underneath the last of the twisted metal.

◀◀ A piece of the white, blue, and red tail from N80BD, as first seen by NPS on January 29, 1977.
◀ Sonny Lawhon chainsaws one of several holes in foot-thick ice for access to the wreckage below. An unidentified U.S. Customs Service helicopter pilot stands near the nose cone of the aircraft. NPS photos by Joe Blackburn.

SOMETIMES ANIMALS NEED RESCUING TOO

On April 4, 1975, during the
search for a missing skier (whose
body wouldn't be found for
seven more weeks), the author
had a surreal encounter. The
nighttime search was proceeding
in an orderly fashion, despite
the blowing snow; I was second
in line from the left, moving
slowly along and poking into
spots which might offer the
missing man some protection.
Near 11:00 p.m., I saw movement
out of the corner of my eye.
There was a fully grown duck,
a cinnamon teal, settled into
the snow at the tips of my skis.
Knocked out of the sky by the
blizzard, it was doing its best at
ground level. Gingerly, I placed
the surprisingly calm animal
into the large front pocket of
my waterproof outer garment.
I thought the duck would struggle. Not so. With its head and
beak poking out of the top of
the pocket, the duck seemed per-
fectly happy to go along for the
ride. We returned to Badger Pass
at 3:30 a.m. and another ranger
released my newfound friend
later that morning in better
weather in El Portal.

Animals occasionally get rescued as well as humans. These stories rarely make the news, but you can bet the rescuers will always remember them. Here are the stories of a few lucky animals.

A HORSE TO WATER

On the morning of June 21, 1995, Park SAR personnel were respond-ing to a request by neighboring Mariposa County to assist with a drowning victim outside the park. As they proceeded "red lights and siren" along the highway to Mariposa, paralleling the Merced River, they saw a saddled but riderless horse swimming frantically down-stream through some very dangerous Class 4 and 5 white water, with rocks and boulders everywhere. They slowed to a stop and watched as the confused animal was able to swim into a calm eddy along the stream bank but then became stranded, lying on its side on sub-merged rocks. Fortunately, it had ended up on the same side of the river as the road. One of the rescuers was able to crawl out and get the horse onto its feet, leading it upstream to a flat rock shelf. The animal struggled but finally was able to get out of the water. How-ever, it was still trapped by the steep bluff. The incident had been radioed in and coordinated with the Mariposa Sheriff's Department, and before long, the stranded horse was tranquilized by a veterinar-ian and lifted off the riverbank by a utility boom truck. It was later learned the pet had fallen in several miles upstream; its fortunate rider had managed to jump clear before it fell in. Although banged up, the horse survived and was later reported to be doing well.

MULE PLUNGE

On July 9, 2004, around noon, a concessionaire mule train loaded with supplies for the Merced Lake High Sierra Camp was traveling in the Merced River Canyon, traversing the Bunnel Switchbacks several miles above Nevada Fall. Something spooked the four mules, which were strung together by rope, and they tumbled off the trail and slid and somersaulted for approximately 200 feet across low-angle granite slabs, coming to rest upon a flattish rock bench. Amazingly, the animals sustained only slight injuries. A park trail crew working nearby helped to quiet and stabilize the mules.

◄ Rangers prepare for a backcountry patrol in 1926. On the left is Chief Ranger Forest Townsley.

Once park personnel had assessed the situation, it was decided more resources and equipment were needed to safely extricate the animals. The concession stables foreman, the park's trails supervisor, and two YOSAR members were flown to the accident scene in the park's helicopter. To help them gain purchase on the polished, slick granite, the mules' metal shoes were covered with tape to simulate sticky rubber climbing shoes. A rope system was set up to belay the mules as they made their way back across the slick rock and up to the trail. Three of four mules danced, high-stepped, and stumbled as they were led across the slabs back to safety. One animal, weighing about 1,000 pounds, slipped and rolled, but was caught by the rope safety team. She was able to right herself and safely continue. When all four mules were back on the trail, they were repacked and continued up the trail to the camp.

A DOGGONE RESCUE

On Thursday afternoon, June 9, 2011, a black lab named Sweety escaped its leash and chased a squirrel over the stone wall at Tunnel View, a popular lookout at the western end of Yosemite Valley. The 11-year-old lab disappeared down a steep embankment and into an area of many cliff faces. NPS Custodian Greg Warren happened to be there at the time. He radioed for help and then tried to find the pet, but was unsuccessful. Rangers who responded were also unable to locate Sweety; since it was a typically busy summer day, they were pulled off and assigned to other incidents.

The following Saturday, Ryan Leahy, a park employee, was in a wooded area below Tunnel View and heard a dog whimpering from farther down in the trees, out of sight. Leahy and Ranger Matt Stark rappelled down 100 feet to the dog. Uninjured, the pet was trapped on a small exposed ledge. Custodian Warren, along with some of the park bear management team and several additional rangers, rigged a harness and lifting system and brought the dog safely back to the rim.

HANG GLIDING AND BASE JUMPING

The **BASE** in BASE jumping stands for **B**uilding **A**ntennae **S**pan (bridge) **E**arth (cliff); the term was coined in 1978. The Park Service generally prohibits BASE jumping, with a few exceptions. The Park Superintendent's Annual Report for 1980 reports on the following: "Cliff Jumping program—120 illegal jumps, 324 legal jumps (began Aug. 1 and terminated Sep. 9, 1980), 10 serious injuries, 15 arrests & 35 citations. This activity will not be permitted again." But despite the official prohibition, there are still an estimated 100 or more illegal jumps annually from El Cap, Half Dome, and occasionally elsewhere—often at dawn or dusk to take advantage of the cover provided by poor light.

Parachute jumping from top of El Capitan by permit only. (August 1 - October 31) Violators may be prosecuted under Section 2.36 of CFR and the Endangered Species Act. -16 USC 1531 -

▲ Signs were prominently displayed around El Capitan in 1980 to help control BASE jumping from there. The trial period was terminated after only 40 days due to serious abuse of the regulations. Photo by Butch Farabee.

THE FIRST BASE JUMP

Before Mike Pelkey could turn around, Brian Schubert literally leaped from El Capitan into history on July 24, 1966, becoming the first person to dive off a cliff (or other fixed object) with a parachute. Three seconds later, Mike followed, making his 183rd successful jump, but the first from anything but an aircraft. Their jumps were successful in that they lived to tell the story, but neither walked away unscathed—in fact, they did not walk away at all. More like they hobbled and scooted. Brian, forced to land in the confusion of boulders at the bottom of the monolith, seriously injured several bones in his feet. When Mike hit the cliff while floating down, he fractured an ankle, and then hit the granite at the bottom.

ILLEGAL THRILLS Since Brian and Mike's jump in 1966, there have been several thousand BASE jumps in the park, most illegal. Criminal investigators in Yosemite estimate that there have been 150 to 200 arrests and citations for this act of "illegal airborne delivery." It is a cat-and-mouse game in which jumpers try to evade rangers while rangers try to catch jumpers. But there is also a far darker side to all of this. With trees, cliffs, boulders, rivers, roads, limited landing space, poor light, unseen air drafts, and the need for speed and stealth, this adrenaline sport in the park causes too many injuries. Broken arms, legs, backs, and heads are common, not to mention internal injuries. And far worse, there are deaths.

DEATH FROM ABOVE Since 35-year-old James Tyler, a professional stuntman with over 1,000 "regular" jumps, cartwheeled uncontrollably down the face of Half Dome in 1982, it's certain that six others have died in the park while BASE jumping. (Another, Frank Gambalie, made a successful leap in 1999 but then drowned in the Merced River when rangers began to pursue him and he refused to be caught.) Later that same year, Jan Davis, 58, an experienced BASE jumper, was engaging in a much-publicized and videotaped act of civil disobedience on El Capitan. In midair, she made a simple yet fatal mistake with her unfamiliar, recently borrowed equipment. Videos from several sources show her frantically grabbing behind her, seemingly for the pilot chute, which for this one special jump was in a different location—a pouch on her leg.

The last two to die, Dean Potter, 43, and Graham Hunt, 29, wore wingsuits and then, trying to avoid crashing into each other, crashed into the cliffs during a jump on May 16, 2015. They made the leap from Taft Point instead of the cliffs that have historically been the site of BASE jumping, such as Half Dome and El Capitan. Dean Potter was an acclaimed career climber, well liked and respected in international mountaineering circles.

HANG GLIDERS BECOME LEGIT

Hang gliding is much more disciplined, organized, and safe than BASE jumping, and has been enjoyed in the park since 1973, when the first flights were allowed on a restricted basis from Glacier Point.

▲ Taft Point is one of those off-the-beaten-path scenic spots that Yosemite is famous for. A mile from the Glacier Point Road, it is on the south rim of Yosemite Valley by way of an easy dirt trail. Overlooking the Valley, the view from Taft Point is breathtaking. It is also the spot where Dean Potter and Graham Hunt BASE jumped with their flying squirrel–like wingsuits one last time on May 16, 2015. Photo by Josh McNair, CaliforniaThroughMyLens.com.

That year, 170 flights were made, and hang gliders have returned to participate almost every year since. Unlike the parachutists, the hang gliding community proved very agreeable to self-regulating, helping to write guidelines for themselves and aiding the park in figuring out how to safely administer the sport.

DEFYING GRAVITY Only practitioners who demonstrate a very high level of competence, confirmed with official credentials, are permitted to glide. A dozen or so devotees are authorized to fly each morning, launching early due to wind patterns and so as not to distract other visitors. For many years, the park even had a ranger who was a qualified hang glider pilot at the launch site to interact with the group. Now volunteer site monitors oversee the activity each day, which has become a familiar routine.

HERE TO STAY? Hang gliding is not without its detractors. Some want it banned from the the park, claiming this isn't what Yosemite National Park is all about. And at the other end of the spectrum, BASE jumpers decry being unable to enjoy their sport while hang gliders can, claiming there is little real difference between the two. One can make a case for this and, had the BASE jumpers been less anarchic in 1980 when they were given a three-month trial by the park, they might be able to pursue their passion legally today. Regrettably for them, the 90-day trial ended after just 40 days after participants rode pogo sticks and bicycles off El Cap, allowed more than the agreed-upon 12 jumpers per day to participate, and otherwise made what some saw as a mockery of the rules.

SAFETY CONSIDERATIONS If hang gliding is done by highly skilled enthusiasts, it's been shown to be safe and relatively accident-free—the sport has resulted in no deaths in Yosemite, ever. The sport probably peaked around the time when 1,560 trips were recorded in 1976.

Are you ready to try it? If so, let's go. But be careful: You are near a sloping edge close to Glacier Point! More than once someone has stumbled while shuffling the last few downhill steps and ended up falling into the rocks and oaks and pines below, potentially needing help from the park to get free. More likely, you're now in the air but still near the cliffs. You'll be tested by updrafts and squirrely currents as the air heats up. This has thrown a few of your peers back into the cliffs on that side of the Valley, requiring a more serious rescue effort from YOSAR. Now the landing—be alert! Although it's not common, ankles and knees can collapse on impact, and several backs have reportedly been broken. Then there was that one rescue from the bi-g-g-g tree.

▲ Only moments before this photo was taken, the hang glider launched safely from near Glacier Point. Within the next minute, this enthusiast will probably turn to the left and take a tour out over the Valley. NPS photo.

HANG GLIDER MEETS TREE; TREE WINS

In Leidig Meadow rises a stately, often photographed 100-foot-tall ponderosa pine known as the John Muir Tree. It stands by itself, far from its neighbors. Hang gliders have used the meadow as a beautiful open landing zone for more than four decades, mostly successfully. But not on July 5, 2008. That day, a 66-year-old enthusiast from Alabama launched at 8:45 a.m. on a path that took him past Yosemite Falls. After a flight of 15 minutes, he prepared to land. Not only was his approach too high, his glider was also unresponsive as he attempted to turn . . . and he went into the tree straight on. On the one hand, this was his first flight in Yosemite. On the other, he had 30 years of experience, and still managed to crash. He was not injured, but did end up with his craft precariously trapped more than halfway up the tree. He justifiably feared that he and his $5,000 aircraft would fall free, hitting limbs on the way down and incurring who knows what sort of damage. When Dov Bock, David Pope, Werner Braun, and Keith Lober woke up that morning, they surely did not dream that their team would need to climb

up through the large branches of this living tribute to the celebrated environmentalist to rescue a hopefully embarrassed hang glider pilot.

▲◀ You have to be at least a little stirred while watching the colorful hang gliders float above; imagine looking down from up there. The sport has been surprisingly safe for more than four decades. There are exceptions, however, like with the gentleman in this tree, assisted by Rangers David Pope (left) and Dov Bock. NPS photos by Keith Lober.

BURIED WHERE THEY LAY

It's not often in this country and in this day and age that you hear of someone being buried where they fell, certainly not in Yosemite. But park management has had to make this delicate, sometimes controversial decision four times to date.

THE YOSEMITE POINT BUTTRESS

The first person interred where he fell was Franklin Johnson, a medical intern from San Francisco. On May 27 of 1956, the Sunday before Memorial Day, the 28-year-old doctor and a friend were fighting their way through the rugged brush of Indian Canyon. They decided to head uphill off-trail, which didn't seem like a big deal at the time. After all, they could always retrace their steps. But once the pair reached the rim of the Valley, Johnson chose to strike out on his own, looking for a different way back to Yosemite Valley. The news articles about this SAR do not tell us how much hiking experience Dr. Johnson had, which is relevant since his route would quickly drop down through the Castle Cliffs or maybe skirt the very deceiving Yosemite Point Couloir. While we know he was a smart man, he should neither have left his friend nor taken this unknown route, certainly not without proper preparations.

A HIDDEN DANGER This area is heavy with brush and trees, as well as ledges, cliffs, rock jump-offs and slide downs, and any number of other hazards, including rattlesnakes. It's a jungle of obstacles, convoluted and tortuous; ropes are probably necessary for descents. It is unlikely you'll know where you are at all times, and once you choose a route down, it's far easier to continue on jumping and sliding than to fight your way back up. Herein lies the hidden danger Johnson found himself in.

Scrambling and climbing downward with no descending equipment, the 28-year-old ended up falling 80 feet onto a narrow, sandy ledge high on the brush-covered terraces just to the east of Lost Arrow Spire. During the five-day search that ensued for him, a small helicopter out of Fresno was pressed into service, only the third time such a machine had been used in Yosemite. It was mostly used to try to spot Dr. Johnson, or rather, some colorful piece of clothing or equipment that would lead to him. It is always a great idea to wear bright, contrasting clothing when hiking for this reason. This most definitely is not the time for camouflage attire!

HIKE SMART

The cliffs and rugged scenery that make Yosemite so beautiful also make it downright dangerous. That means that for most of us, hiking off the trail is a terrible idea that is likely to lead to trouble. Remember, the more you prepare, even for a short hike, the more enjoyable and safer the adventure will be. Here are some basics to keep in mind:

+ **Tell someone your plan**, including when you expect to return, and then stick to it.

+ **Check the weather** forecast and be prepared for unexpected changes. Avoid ridgetops and other exposed places during a lightning storm.

+ **Wear substantial, appropriate footwear**.

+ **Bring a map, compass, whistle, and headlamp.**

+ **Consider a quart of water for each two hours** of strenuous hiking; needs may vary. Watch for dehydration, even when it's cold out.

+ **Frequently snack** on slightly salty foods to replace salts.

+ **Avoid shortcuts** and cutting switchbacks. Never cross a railing or a fence.

+ **Do not let young children run ahead** and out of sight.

LAS · YP · YPB · YPC · Indian Canyon

◀ The uppermost feature in this photo is Yosemite Point (YP); the large cliff face below it is the Yosemite Point Buttress (YPB). The slender finger separated from the cliff, just left of YPB, is the Lost Arrow Spire (LAS). Immediately to the right of the YPB is the Yosemite Point Couloir (or gully; YPC), and, finally, just off the photo to the right is Indian Canyon (IC), up which Dr. Franklin Johnson and his companion made their way. Once on the rim above the Valley, somewhere between IC and YP, Johnson chose to return to the Valley. His route down may have seemed obvious when he began, but it soon turned into a brushy labyrinth of craggy cliffs and broken ledges that would be difficult for *anyone* without proper equipment. The author has seen one grainy, black-and-white photo in the Mariposa County sheriff's files taken at the time Johnson was buried showing a long-forgotten pile of rocks in this area. NPS photo by John Dill.

A HOPELESS ENDEAVOR Even if Dr. Johnson had been spotted, there was no place the pilot could have landed in the area. And in 1956, the option to do a short-haul below the machine did not exist, even if the two-person ship could hover there. In the end, Dr. Johnson was not located from the air, but by rangers and members of the Sierra Club who were literally tracking his progress downward via scuff and slide marks, boot prints, and broken branches. The search area was fairly limited by today's standards. They had a good idea where he was last seen and could extrapolate his intended route back to the Valley. What they discovered was that he apparently died immediately. And where he came to rest was in a spot so incredibly difficult to access that bringing a body down by hand seemed impossible. Because of this, permission was asked of and granted by the family to bury him in place, which the rangers did.

NIGHT OPS This author believes that Dr. Johnson would have died under these circumstances, even today. Assuming the victim's friend would have returned to the campsite and waited a while before reporting him overdue, it would have been getting dark. In fact, it would not be unusual in a circumstance like this for a companion to wait until after sunset to see if he showed up. Reports don't mention anyone hearing any shouts from the area where he fell, which might indicate that he was already incapacitated or perhaps dead that first afternoon.

Today, a nighttime SAR operation in this treacherous area would be feasible, although still risky. Early on, a loudspeaker would be set up in the Valley while search managers capitalized on innovations in cell phone technology. Trailing scent dogs might be moved into the area, while avoiding destruction of any footprints. If available, a FLIR-equipped helicopter (Forward Looking Infra-Red) would be utilized as soon as possible, even before sunrise. A real concern would be whether Dr. Johnson changed his mind after his friend left, and walked out of the initial search area. This possibility is always considered by searchers.

Would Dr. Johnson be found more quickly today than 60 years ago? Very probably. We can only guess if FLIR, "pings" from a cell phone, expert climbers, or even a YODOG, would have gotten to him the next day. Would he have been alive? We will never know.

DEATH ON LOST ARROW SPIRE

On March 19, 1960, 17-year-old Irving Smith was a talented young climber who aspired to be the youngest person to reach the top of The Arrow, nearly 300 yards to the east of Upper Yosemite Fall. At that time, the youngest to successfully climb the prominent rock shaft had been 18.

INTO THE NOTCH Smith and his 24-year-old partner, Gerald Dixon, needed to rappel into the loose, rock-filled notch between The Arrow and the granite headwall. This requires two separate rappels of over 120 feet each. Once in the 12-foot-wide notch the plan was to move a few feet around to the South Face of The Arrow and begin climbing, with an intimidating 1,400 feet of air below them. Smith was first down the second rappel. Dixon never saw what happened; he only heard a faint cry from below and then the distant, unmistakable thump of a body hitting rock. Did Irving Smith rappel off the end of his rope? Or as climber-historian Steve Roper believes, perhaps he fell while walking about the "prehistorically dark and dank" bottom of the notch.

A DIFFICULT DECISION The teen's father conferred with Park Superintendent John C. Preston and eventually decided, with input from Chief Ranger Elmer Fladmark, to let the boy remain where he ended up. Several of the best technical rock climbers in the world volunteered to retrieve his body, including Warren Harding and Ranger Wayne Merry. Preston deemed a recovery attempt not worth the risk, even for well-qualified Big Wall climbers. He then issued a Superintendent's Order, closing the area around where the boy had come to rest to further climbing for a year. Smith is generally considered the first modern-era climber to die while actually climbing in the Valley.

◂ The prominent crack running vertically beneath and to the left of Lost Arrow Spire (notice the shadow of its tip) is called the Lost Arrow Chimney, a difficult climb first done in 1947 in five days. Somewhere near its top is the final resting place of 17-year-old Irving Smith. NPS photo.

A MYSTERIOUS DISAPPEARANCE

Quin Charles Frizzell, who disappeared on June 4, 1966, was a more unusual case. The 31-year-old was a nuclear scientist with Top Secret clearance at Lawrence Livermore National Laboratory. He vanished on a solo hike to Yosemite Valley from Tenaya Lake. Considered highly competent by those who knew him, he nevertheless failed to tell anyone his route and itinerary. Definitely a bad idea. A challenging 10-day search for Mr. Frizzell focused on Tenaya Canyon, a nearly six-mile-long catch-all, a Bermuda Triangle if you will, for Yosemite National Park. Other hikers had become stranded and delayed while traversing down Tenaya Canyon, but no one to this point (that we know of) had died there. And to add to the mystery, the Cold War tensions then existing between the United States and the Soviet Union inspired a nagging suspicion in some quarters that perhaps the young scientist had defected and fled the country.

CHALLENGING TERRAIN All searches are serious, but this may well have been the most complicated such operation in the park up to that time. Beginning with alpine Tenaya Lake at 8,150 feet, Tenaya Canyon drops down over 4,000 feet to Yosemite Valley. It is a 3,000- to 4,000-foot-deep glacially carved rift edged by some of the most imposing granite walls in the world, with tumbling waterfalls; dark pools; and long, brush-covered rocky terraces. In short, it is as rugged a piece of real estate for a ground search as Yosemite has to offer. For even the most seasoned hikers it is a tricky, grueling, all-day (if you are lucky) trip. There are a million-and-one places to fall, or become stranded or disabled . . . or worse.

HELP FROM ALL OVER The author has heard that 150 searchers were involved in this search. I've never seen an actual report, but that would be a reasonable number, given the terrain and the length of the effort. Mountain Rescue Association (MRA) teams from around the state, including units from San Diego, Sierra Madre, Riverside, and Montrose participated. In addition, unaffiliated volunteers drove in from the San Francisco Bay Area—and ultimately banded together to form the Bay Area Mountain Rescue Team. At least one helicopter had its engine fail in midair flying across the base of Half Dome and had to land in the Mirror Lake area, suffering minor damage. The park's fire chief, Lee Shackelton, was onboard the two-person ship and once told the author, "Kissing it goodbye flashed through my mind!"

A GRIM DISCOVERY On April 8, 1971, a human skull and a credit card belonging to Mr. Frizzell were discovered on a brushy 15-foot-wide ledge below Mount Watkins, not far above Tenaya Creek. Rangers

TRACKING PEOPLE

We know that tracking dogs search for missing people by following a trail; the same is true for human trackers. While dogs use scent, two-legged searchers looking for missing people use footprints, scuff marks, and related minor surface disturbances as their trail. Those who walk away from a campsite, get off a path, or become confused while cross-country hiking will leave traces that skilled trackers can follow. It is claimed that a person can be followed across solid rock. Some members of SAR teams specialize in this proficiency, becoming indispensable primary resources.

Two things that need to be done immediately as a search begins are to isolate a good shoe or footprint and identify the point last seen (PLS). This PLS may provide the direction searchers will begin with. This tracking skill was incorporated into modern SAR techniques in the late 1960s by legendary U.S. Border Patrol agents, such as Jack Kearney and Ab Taylor.

YOSEMITE CEMETERIES

The park has three cemeteries. The main and best-known cemetery is immediately west of the Valley Visitor Center and was opened around 1870. There are at least 45 marked graves and a number of unmarked ones, principally in which American Indians are interred. A good description of this historic site is *Guide to the Yosemite Cemetery* by Hank Johnston and Martha Lee. The second cemetery is in Wawona and is several hundred yards northeast of the Pioneer Yosemite History Center, on a small hill. At least 10 people were buried there from roughly 1878 to 1905. The third cemetery contains five men in marked sites who died between 1884 and 1918. Largely forgotten until rediscovered in 1957, it is on the road into Foresta, near Big Meadow.

▲ Partial remains of Quin Charles Frizzell as found by the author. Bones were inside the socks still inside the boots. About half of his skeleton was located and interred in place. He may have survived his fall of 100 feet. The yellow is a piece of deteriorating fabric. NPS photo by Butch Farabee.

could find nothing more of the missing man—no more bones, no pack, clothing, or other clues. Based on the skull and credit card, however, the sheriff-coroner of Mariposa County was able to sign a death certificate. The widow moved on with her life and wrote to the park that if anything more was ever discovered, "Please bury him in place." On a very hot Thursday, September 14, 1972, the author would end up doing just that.

OFF THE BEATEN PATH On the 13th of that month, I was called into the park's Law Enforcement Office to meet with Chief Ranger Jack Morehead and Lee Shackelton. Also present was a young man in his late teens who was . . . unkempt would be a kind word. I will call him "John Jones." Young Mr. Jones had been exploring Tenaya Canyon when he discovered human bones and the remnants of a small backpack. He had brought in a human knuckle to prove his find. Both Jack and Lee knew of Charles Frizzell; Mr. Jones and I knew nothing about him. We were told of the search and the widow's instructions. Per my superiors, I was to accompany John Jones back into Tenaya Canyon, maybe 2 miles upstream of Mirror Lake, and try to determine what had happened to Mr. Frizzell. I was then to bury what we could find of him there.

PUTTING THE PIECES TOGETHER We spent a fruitful morning on that obscure ledge. It appeared the skull and credit card had either rolled downhill or been carried by animals. Based on what we could see above us, it looked like our victim had slid and tumbled maybe 100 feet. A faded, nylon backpack rested in a small tree nearby, and a disintegrating piece of yellow fabric was present, both possible distress signals. If so, hopefully he didn't suffer long. One almost-disintegrated sock—still in a leather hiking boot—rattled with foot bones. Looking into rodent burrows under the nearby rocks and scouring the area within 25 or so yards, we collected about half a skeleton. I was unsure of what to do next. So, I followed my instincts, perhaps informed by watching too many movies, and dug a shallow, 2-foot-square hole. I put the remains into this small grave, outlined it with golf-ball-sized rocks, and placed a cross of similar-sized rocks over it.

WHAT WENT WRONG? Tenaya Canyon is a Grade III, Class 4 effort—a very demanding trip, requiring mountaineering skill and, for most hikers, some rappelling gear. Add to this that Frizzell was definitely off route. We know that he was in good condition, as this trip certainly requires, and he was an experienced hiker. But he was hiking alone—a terrible, terrible idea in this treacherous canyon. When his pack was found, there was no rope or descending equipment. Nor was there a whistle, mirror, extra water bottles, or equipment for bivouacking in case the trip took longer than he thought. Some of these items could have been lost in the fall or taken away by time and the elements, but not all.

The public will often put too much faith into a helicopter finding someone. Helicopters are great for many things, but definitely not as aerial observation posts in an overdue-person scenario. The odds are increased many-fold if there are contrasting colors, mirrors, signal panels, or something else to see from up there. Every seasoned search manager in mountainous terrain knows of cases in which someone was not seen, even while searchers in a slow-moving helicopter were looking directly at the person. If there is some kind of thermal imaging equipment onboard, then the metrics may improve considerably. In the end, if Charles Frizzell had recognized the very serious situation he was facing and had just stopped in place, rather than continuing over increasingly vertical terrain, even if that meant not getting back to his important job on Monday morning, he might have been found alive.

OVER THE FALLS

Last of the four deceased people to be intentionally left in place was 27-year-old Francois Serge Durand de Fontmagne, from near Lyon, France, who died on August 15, 1995. Just after 3:00 p.m., the NPS radio dispatcher received a 911 call from the Nevada Fall emergency phone—someone swimming above the fall with a friend had just

WHAT ELSE COULD I SAY?

On our way back down to Tenaya Creek, Mr. Jones and I stopped to eat and talk a bit in the shade. I thanked him for being a Good Samaritan, for not only leading me back up there and but also for sweating all morning and helping to inter Mr. Frizzell. He must have taken my thanks as a cue, as he then proceeded to pull out a softball-sized baggie of pot and asked nonchalantly if he could toke up! This was 1972 and in the middle of Yosemite's hippie era. Marijuana use in the park was blatant. That John wanted to light up after a morning of helping to bury a missing nuclear scientist did not really surprise me. "Okay, go ahead and light up, today is a freebie. But if I see you tomorrow, you could be going to jail." He had been gracious with his time and effort and had acted as a responsible citizen—what else could I say?

been swept over. With a nearly 600-foot drop, not to mention the rocks at the bottom, the victim was presumed deceased. The winter before, 1994 to '95, had been a big snow year, and the waterfall was still ripping, though it was late in the summer. Even 20 years later, veteran NPS Investigator Steve Yu, then a Camp 4 SAR-Siter, recalls: "The volume of water going over the edge was intimidatingly impressive. . . . I can feel the vibration of the falls in my chest, I can hear the deafening white noise, I feel that slight, almost-nausea flip of my guts . . . knowing what had happened to Durand."

IGNORING THE SIGNS French was Durand's first language, but he could speak and read English fluently, using it as his primary language

▲ In 1977, a 22-year-old crawled between railings at the top of Vernal Fall for a photo looking over the edge while standing *in the stream.* He slipped trying to jump to dry rock. In this photo, Tom Griffiths (left) and the author recover his body on the cliff. Both Vernal and Nevada Falls have posted warning signs that Durand and this young man disregarded. NPS photo by Tim Setnicka.

for business. He totally ignored the posted warning signs where he was swimming. Despite knowing the river disappeared over a lip not far away, he and his companion chose to go swimming anyway. In addition, the companion was shooting the obligatory tourist photos. In fact, he may have had Durand in the camera's viewfinder when Durand suddenly vanished out of sight and over the fall.

The section of the Merced River between the world-famous Nevada and Vernal Falls is a jumble of boulders and smaller rocks, forming hundreds of cracks, gaps, and other miscellaneous voids of all manner of shapes and sizes. The day after the accident, SAR-Siters Steve Yu and Vicky Travis were sent to photograph the warning signs at the top, then down to the bottom of the waterfall to begin to search for the dead man. Steve recalls that day:

> Before we hiked down, we peered over the railing at the top. And there, where the slab at the base of Nevada Fall hits the talus, we see a broken, human body. I hate to admit it now, but we were giddy with excitement. Searches are often long, tedious, and boring; to find a victim . . . was exhilarating. The IC [Incident Commander], Grady Bryant, told us get down there and confirm what we were seeing. Yes—crumpled, broken, obscene, lonely, and sad lay Durand.

Before Steve and Vicky could finalize plans to extract Durand, they were called back to the SAR cache: their skills were needed on El Cap for a rescue. A team would return for Durand's body the next day. But with the afternoon sun came the rising waters of the snow-melt. Durand de Fontmagne disappeared. To Steve Yu, a heavy blow.

THE BODY (PROBABLY) FOUND Periodically, searchers would scour the river. Finally, more than three months later, on December 2, Rangers Keith Lober and Steve Yu braved falling ice at the base of the fall to look again. Twelve feet down a 6-inch-wide crack in the bedrock, and only visible by powerful flashlight, were human remains. There was now no way to get to the body, driven through the narrow crack by the force of the water, wedged under a great many tons of granite. Technically, it was impossible to prove this was really the Frenchman—but nobody else had been reported missing.

There was, however, a confirmed instance of someone going over Nevada Fall. Two weeks after Durand needlessly went over the fall, and I repeat needlessly, 31-year-old Daniel Kahler from San Diego was wading and sunbathing in nearly the exact spot that Durand had been. After warming up and now needing to move on, Kahler began wading back to where his friend was waiting. Before he probably really knew what had happened, the current grabbed him off the slippery rock bottom, and on September 3, he too disappeared under the footbridge and went over Nevada Fall. Kahler's body was, however, quickly found that day.

LEFT TO THE RIVER High explosives could have broken the rock encasing Durand's body, but they would have also created unacceptable environmental damage—triggering nasty letters from the park's Congressional delegation—and likely would have disintegrated Durand's remains. In this case, park management really had no choice but to leave what was surely Francois Serge Durand de Fontmagne where he lay.

PROFESSIONAL TO THE CORE

Down through the years, more than 1,800 people have come to their end in Yosemite—some naturally and a great many, such as the four singled out here, in a traumatic fashion. Rangers, SAR-Siters, investigators, doctors, nurses, paramedics, and others have to deal with this reality more often than they would like. Each death is significant and is respectfully handled, and most of this effort goes unseen by visitors to the park. The next chapter looks at some of the ways these professionals go about the less public side of their work.

> "Twenty years later and now a father of three, it's not so cool. The thrill is gone. There is more scar tissue on my soul after too many death notifications, too many hard conversations with families, friends trying to sort out the wreckage of their lives. Mothers and fathers trying to make sense of why their child sent to Yosemite on vacation is now in a body bag. It is important to feel relevant and useful, but when the action involves innocents, it's a tragedy on a small scale in terms of the universe, but reality-rending for those immediately involved."
>
> —Steve Yu, ranger-investigator and former SAR-Siter

PART 3

BEHIND THE SCENES

◄ Ranger John Dill orients park staff to the California Highway Patrol's helicopter rescue program, seen here with one of its machines in June 2010. NPS photo by David Pope.

INTO THE DELUGE

In the pitch black night of February 6, 1999, in torrential rain, Rangers Mary Hinson and Keith Lober and a rescue team of four others climbed down 800 feet, including 400 feet of rappelling, to a 17-year-old boy. He had wandered from the trail into the Inner Gorge between Upper and Lower Yosemite Falls. He now had hypothermia, a dislocated ankle, and a broken wrist. The rain and sleet were so intense that the soil liquefied and flowed out from under the rescue team's boots as they climbed to him. The so-called watertight headlamps on their helmets were half-filled with water. Most terrifying, however, were the boulders crashing by them, loosened by the near-hurricane-force winds, including one rock that partially cut Mary's rope in three places.

The teenager survived only because of this Yosemite SAR team. Rangers Hinson and Lober received Department of the Interior Valor Awards. The other four rescuers received Department of the Interior Citizen Awards for Bravery, which are bestowed on non–Department of the Interior employees.

WHO PAYS FOR A RESCUE?

After reading about all of the bad luck, reckless decisions, and slaps upside the head from Mother Nature in this book, you might be wondering who picks up the tab when **YOSAR** gets called out on SAR. The answer may surprise you.

AN EXPENSIVE HIKE

On a Saturday morning in March of 2015, a man we'll call Mic left his friends to go for a short hike to the base of Lower Yosemite Fall. He left his cell phone locked in the car, and he and his friends had no specific plan for meeting up after his hike. They last saw him scrambling up a large boulder, having told them he was going to reach "the peak of Yosemite." This was Mic's first time in the park and, unfamiliar with the area, he may have been referring to Yosemite Point Buttress, just east of Upper Yosemite Fall. In the midafternoon his friends reported him overdue, mistakenly saying he'd been headed for the top of Yosemite Falls. This led to some early confusion in what would become a multiday search. The park soon received aid from the Madera, Tuolumne, Mariposa, and Marin County volunteer SAR teams, along with a California Highway Patrol helicopter.

FOUND IN THE FIELD Some 48 hours later, Mic was spotted by visitors who recognized him from a missing-person flyer. He was in a rocky, forested area some 50 feet from a popular, maintained trail not far from where he had last been seen. Looking at Mic's camera afterward, investigating rangers determined he had started up toward "the peak of Yosemite" (there is no such place) on a steep, obscure, and dangerous social trail. He fell far enough to suffer serious head trauma, among other injuries. Possibly suffering from a concussion, he was unable to communicate with the people passing by on the busy trail below. When found, he was thoroughly soaked from the series of rainstorms that passed over the park the night before. He was lucky to survive, given that both nights he was missing were wet and cold.

THE PRICE NOT PAID Mic did not pay for the 80 searchers (including park staff and volunteers), nor was he charged for the CHP helicopter. His rescue was free to him even though the final bill for this search and rescue was just over $16,000. He was, however, billed for both his medical treatment in the field as well as at the clinic.

▲ On June 13, 2008, YOSAR team members Jon Gleason (left) and Sam Piper assist in carrying out a 21-year-old climber from the base of Middle Cathedral Rock. The climber fell 8 feet and broke his ankle. NPS photo by David Pope.

GOVERNMENT POLICY

The federal government does not charge for search and rescue, though Yosemite does seek cost recovery for the emergency medical services it provides. A policy for many years, this applies to the National Park Service, Coast Guard, Army Corps of Engineers, Air Force, Border Patrol, Forest Service, Army, and all other federal agencies with life-saving responsibility. There is a cost to SAR, obviously, and your taxes and mine help pay the bill. Over the years, however, the NPS has made a couple of efforts to recoup some of its expenses from the rescued.

AN ATTEMPT TO RECOUP A May 4, 1967, memo from Western Region Associate Director Robert B. Moore indicated victims should pay for helicopter use, but if unable, the NPS would take care of the expense. This policy quickly became unmanageable and was soon abandoned. In July of 1974, Yosemite rangers began citing certain individuals into the U.S. Magistrate's Court within the park for violations of the Code of Federal Regulations, Title 36, § 2.34, which encompasses disorderly conduct. Subsection (a) (4) covers an individual who: "Creates or maintains a hazardous or physically offensive condition." In other words, some people do dumb things and there should be consequences.

A WILD RIDE

On September 17, 1992, a German visitor fell while climbing the Northwest Face of Half Dome. He plummeted 30 feet, sustaining multiple injuries. Mike LaLone, a ranger, parkmedic, and accomplished climber, was asked to heli-rappel to the accident scene. With a thunderstorm approaching and winds kicking up, the operation was becoming riskier.

"Our first flight was to place a ranger on the summit of Half Dome to keep hikers from throwing rocks [and frisbees] over the side, a common occurrence," LaLone recalls. "We used a whiteboard and told the victim's partner help was coming. I made a rappel of approximately 200 feet to where my victim was. It was mostly free, and I recall reflecting as my feet touched the cliff wall for the first time that I was 42 years old, too old for this nonsense. Actually not true, as I love SAR, but the things you think of dangling 1,000 feet up. Now on the ledge, the ship long-lined the EMS equipment into us. He had a depressed skull fracture, along with back and lower leg injuries. Stabilizing him, his partner and I immobilized him in a Stokes basket.

continued on facing page ➤

Every year climbers and scramblers, hikers, BASE jumpers, and others ignore posted warning signs, a widespread forecast for severe weather, or something comparable, and need to be rescued. The "hazardous or . . . offensive condition" part of Subsection (a) (4) identified above was applied when these violators put SAR responders in significant harm's way. For at least the next 20 years, the few violators whom were cited in this way would agree to donate up to $500 to the park's Mountain Safety Fund as part of a plea agreement. This money would restock ropes and other gear. This practice has become rarer over time for a variety of reasons.

THE BOTTOM LINE

As a rule of thumb, searches are more expensive than rescues. For the average search (though there really is no such thing) that goes on longer than two days, costs mount quickly. One major factor is that in a longer search, helicopter use generally increases, due to the need to transport and supply more personnel in the field, as well as to spend more hours air searching.

SOME STATES WILL CHARGE YOU Several states will, or at least can, hit outdoor enthusiasts with hefty bills for SAR services. In some areas, the laws are written so that just about anybody can be forced to pay. In others, you've got to do something reckless to get billed.

THE ANNUAL TALLY

In 2014 (more recent national figures are unavailable), search and rescue costs for the entire National Park Service were just over $4 million. There were 2,658 missions involving 3,483 subjects, and including 164 fatalities. In 2015, Yosemite had 216 SARs at a cost of just over $463,665, for 275 individuals with 15 deaths. As a comparison, in 1976 the NPS had 2,841 incidents at a cost of over $630,600, while in Yosemite there were 131 missions costing $103,400 (1976 dollars).

Figures can be misleading and always need elaboration. For example, the NPS national figure for 2014, $4,020,000, includes costs for such things as military aircraft. SAR units in the park do not pay for these resources, however; the sums are recorded based on a predetermined cost per type of helicopter or airplane along with the cost of its crew. And for both the NPS figures and those for the park, the final tally includes the expenses of people already working that day. Of Yosemite's 181 missions in 2014, 86 cost over $500, a limit used by the national office of the NPS for reimbursing the park.

People skiing out of bounds at a ski area or hikers who venture into closed areas, for example, might be penalized. Some states have implemented or are considering a communal fund (something like an insurance pool) for a person involved in certain outdoor sports, including hunting and fishing, to pay into. This in turn pays for their rescue if necessary. New Hampshire, Utah, and Colorado have systems like this.

WHO'S TO BLAME? Some readers are likely thinking that anyone who engages in a risky sport like climbing and then needs to be plucked from El Capitan, or who gets carried out of Little Yosemite Valley while trying to set a personal best in chancy trail running, should pay for their misadventure. And a case can be made for this sentiment. In fact, for truly negligent behavior, an offender can be cited into court and a fine may be levied. But the many gray areas are what inform the current policy. Appendicitis in a backpacking Boy Scout? A child wandering from a campground? A victim of lightning or a falling limb or rock? A driver of a car going over a cliff or the pilot of a small plane that crashes in the park? A child slipping and going over Nevada Fall? A sunbathing wader swept into the rapids? It's a hard line to draw; where would you place it?

ONE FINAL CONSIDERATION A second concern that most SAR managers will raise is that the fear of a large fine or bill for rescue may dissuade people from seeking help. Postponing that call to save money could easily result in further injury or even death, making the eventual SAR that much harder.

▲ Spending taxpayer money is never taken lightly, but neither is the safety and expertise of rescuers. Dov Bock, aided by Jeff Pirog, stands on the helicopter skid, ready to descend to the ground in this heli-rappel training in 2007. NPS photo by David Pope.

"Lemoore tried four times [to pick him up] but the winds were too squirrelly. In the end, the short-haul with the park's H-551 was our only real choice. A small window of opportunity opened despite the surrounding storm with the turbulence and lightning. I was able to safely connect the litter to a long rope below H-551, and without wasting much time, it was off. The window closed, forcing me to rappel roughly 900 feet down the route with [his climbing] partner.

"His partner asked about payment, due to his experience in the Alps. He was surprised there would be no charge. Also, well after dark, as we were in the trees on the Vernal Fall Trail [hiking back to the Valley], we both noticed flashes of light ahead of us. Two climbers from a day climb had lost their flashlight and were using the strobe on their camera to light short stretches of trail. They were fairly happy to see us. Two SARs for the price of one!"

For this rescue, a Department of the Interior Valor Award was presented to Yosemite National Park Ranger Mike LaLone on November 22, 1994.

JIM REILLY REMEMBERS

Yosemite SAR Officer, December 1984 to September 1985

" As a ranger, I remember responding to a major rockfall incident in the Upper Yosemite Fall valley, which resulted in multiple deaths and injuries (see the box below). I remember providing medical assistance to a young boy who had been hit by a Volkswagen-sized boulder and was holding hands with another boy who was buried beneath that boulder. We stabilized the first boy, placed him in a litter, and waited for the helicopters that arrived at dusk. Our helicopter hovered and lowered a cable to hoist the litter. On the way up, the litter got caught in the branches of a tree. I remember praying, and I'm not a religious guy, that they wouldn't cut the cable, as the protocol was to cut rather than lose the ship and crew. Fortunately, the experienced Lemoore pilot was able to disengage the litter [from the tree] and our boy lived, though he was in very bad shape.

In another incident, I remember getting multiple cries for help on El Cap. We had a lot of wet snow on top and rain falling on top of that. It had turned the wall into a waterfall. Three parties were stranded on the face and getting hypothermic. We pulled together [SAR-site] climbers and brought a helicopter into the Valley beneath the clouds. Every time we got a break in the clouds, we put a helicopter up with rescuers and equipment. I was on the last flight [to the top], but the clouds closed in on the landing zone and we had to scoot back down to [El Capitan] Meadow before they closed in there as well. That

▲ Here the trail crew is uncovering one of the deceased. NPS photo.

On November 16, 1980, three hikers died and at least seven were injured when the Yosemite Falls Trail beneath the Forbidden Wall suffered a catastrophic rockfall. A school bus-sized chunk of cliff fell from 200 feet up, exploding like shrapnel. Ranger Mike Durr recalls, "I heard what sounded like a jet airplane landing in the Valley. I understood the rumbling noise and, as both acting shift supervisor and SAR officer that day, I was in the hot seat. This was major. SAR-site climbers and rangers began to run up the trail; hikers streaming down reported death and destruction. We needed lots of help. Navy helicopters from Lemoore and Fallon responded, as did a civilian ship. Then two air ambulances came. When the news helicopters began appearing, the FAA closed the airspace. Within days, cliffs above Valley trails were being surveyed for other large, potentially hazardous rock. Those few found were dealt with by park crews using high explosives. It was not until the following June that the Falls Trail was finally reopened.

▲ While descending from Half Dome on February 23, 2009, a 37-year-old climber suffered major trauma from a snow avalanche. A California Highway Patrol ship from Fresno, H-40, lifts the victim out the next morning. He recovered from a broken femur and is believed to have returned to climbing. NPS photo by David Pope.

left just the climbers on top. They lowered ropes to the three teams, rappelled down in wetsuits, provided them with warm fluids, and helped them climb out. The [rescue] climbers saved the day on this one.

I remember a night (July 27, 1985) during a major lightning storm when a number of young people climbed the cables on Half Dome to the top, maybe while under the influence. I recall that two of them were sitting on the edge of the face when one was struck by lightning. The other tried to hold onto him, but his weight was too much and

he had to let go. The victim fell nearly 2,000 feet to the talus below. John Dill and I pulled together a ground force thinking we would have to do a major lowering of multiple victims from the top if the lightning stopped and the weather didn't clear. We also had the problem of getting a medical team to the top, given the lightning and the metal cable route they would take going up. We knew that because of the storm and because it was night that we had little chance of getting a helicopter up there. Medi-Flight had a prohibition against flying at night, as they

had previously lost at least one helicopter and three occupants. In spite of that, John kept calling them with updates. Around 1:00 a.m., the sky cleared, the moon came out (only temporarily) and Medi-Flight decided to go for it, and literally saved the day (or night in this case). Pilot Al Majors landed the Medi-Flight helicopter on top of Half Dome three times, bringing down the three patients. All survived. "

TECHNOLOGY TO THE RESCUE

A radio message was first sent
from a plane on January 21,
1911, by the U.S. Army Signal
Service. This was accomplished
with a Wright biplane trailing
a 100-foot-long antenna. The
nascent U.S. Forest Service was
looking for any and all innovations that might be put to use,
particularly since they had just
dealt with major fires in the
Northern Rockies the previous
year. By 1919, foresters were
experimenting with radio sets
borrowed from the army.

With the possible exceptions of modern emergency medicine and the Incident Command System, there is arguably no milestone in the evolution of SAR more significant than the advent of two-way radio.

RADIO COMES TO YOSEMITE

In late summer of 1931, the University of Washington, at the direction of the U.S. Department of Commerce, placed six stationary and four portable radios in nearby Mount Rainier National Park as a trial. And in 1933, Yosemite and six other national parks finally got two-way radio capability.

OFF TO A SLOW START The National Park Service's 1934 Annual Report expressed a lack of faith in the technology, with statements such as "experiments do not justify at this time any conclusion that radio can take the place of telephone communication in high mountain areas." However, minds had already begun to change after May 20 and 21, 1934, when two-way radios were first used on a SAR in Yosemite to help coordinate the rescue of two Bay Area youths who, according to the Yosemite superintendent's monthly report, "caused a great amount of excitement, and exposed rescue forces to unusually

▲ Communications are central to all SAR, exemplified here by this radio small enough to be secured in a rescuer's chest harness. Yosemite's earliest radios, call-sign KNKS, were first used on a SAR in May 1934 (see the main text). They were used again a month later in searching for Temporary Ranger William L. Corless, who was "lost for two and half-days in the treacherous Tenaya Canyon. He was hungry and exhausted when found."

THE MODERN ERA

Radio and related wireless technology have gone light-years beyond anything the rangers in 1934 could have envisioned. In 2016, Yosemite had over 1,440 radios for conducting both routine and emergency business. Augmented by the Yosemite Telecommunications Shop, the park's Emergency Communications Center (ECC) is second to none in the NPS. Nine full-time dispatchers field radio and telephone traffic for Yosemite, Lassen Volcanic National Park, and Devils Postpile National Monument simultaneously. Its state-of-the-art system includes connections with California and U.S. Department of Justice databases. The ECC handles both the 911 system and fire dispatching. In 2016, the ECC answered 3,388 cell and landline calls for 911 alone, and at least 60,000 regular telephone calls.

▲ In July of 2005, SAR Officer Keith Lober (right) confers with regional volunteers searching for the remains of a possible "body dump" (victim of a crime) along remote Tioga Road. Computer programs focusing on search probabilities and strategies continue to become more sophisticated and vital to SAR. NPS photo by David Pope.

CELL PHONES

Innovations in cell-phone technology and in civilian uses of satellites will be one of the most important advancements in search and rescue for years to come. Throughout the National Park Service in 2014, for example, cell phones were used 936 times (out of 2,587 incidents) to notify officials of a SAR. In Yosemite there were 95 such calls in 2014 and 105 in 2015.

Carry a cell phone, but do not rely only on your phone for emergencies. Most of the park's backcountry and portions of Yosemite Valley do not have cell service. Even where coverage exists, batteries die (always carry a spare power pack) and technical limitations may cause the location provided to dispatch to be off by miles. You should know how to find and relay the phone's coordinates manually (there's an app for that). Wilderness rangers in Yosemite are required to have two forms of communication, and a cell phone is not one of them; they are, typically, a park radio and a satellite device.

arduous and hazardous effort, by stranding themselves high up on the northwestern face of Half Dome." Today, radio technology is also used by civilians to call for help in several ways.

A BRAVE NEW WORLD OF TECH

In Yosemite, cell phone calls currently account for up to 50% of requests for help (see the sidebar), and a 911 voice call often automatically displays the caller's location to the dispatcher. (As of 2017 Yosemite does not have text-to-911.) Even when the phone is not used to call for help, SAR and law enforcement can sometimes use cell data: transaction records (voice, text, and internet data) may show the phone's approximate direction or distance from a cell tower at the time of the call, and triangulation among several towers may pinpoint the phone's position. (Not all towers or service providers have these capabilities.) Furthermore, cell forensics can suggest likely areas for the phone's location based on computer-generated maps of signal strength for the towers involved.

Satellite phones, though more expensive than cellular, are now standard for many remote-area parties, bypassing the need for towers. In 2014, 114 incidents were reported by satellite phones throughout the National Park System; in 2015, there were 12 in Yosemite.

▲ Wilderness navigation is key for everyone spending time in the outdoors, but this skill is rapidly disappearing. Overreliance on cell phones and GPS-related technologies is a concern for SAR. Here a YOSAR team member is participating in an advanced map and compass course in 2007. NPS photo by Keith Lober.

GLOBAL POSITIONING SYSTEMS We're all used to having GPS in our phones or cars. You can also purchase a separate, handheld GPS unit to help you find your way in the wilderness. GPS navigation systems provide location and time data in all weather conditions, anywhere there is an unobstructed line of sight to four or more GPS satellites. The United States government created the initial system, but at least two others now exist, all freely accessible to anyone with a compatible receiver.

A BEACON IN THE AIR In 1970, Congress mandated that emergency locator transmitters (ELTs) be installed in all U.S.-registered aircraft. Congress didn't get tough about privately owned aircraft until 1972, when a small plane went down in remote Alaska with two congressmen, one of whom was Louisiana's powerful Hale Boggs. (A 39-day search proved fruitless and no bodies have ever been found.) ELTs, activated either manually or automatically from the impact of a crash, signal their location via government-operated satellites (see the sidebar) and are now enhanced with GPS in many cases. Emergency position-indicating radio beacons (EPIRBs) and personal locator beacons (PLBs) are basically ELTs designed for marine and land use respectively, using the same satellite system. From the first save in 1982 to the end of 2016, they have assisted at least 41,000 people and saved millions of dollars in search costs. Many handheld PLBs available for hikers are relatively inexpensive and there is no charge for service.

ALL-IN-ONE DEVICES A recent innovation is the range of handheld personal messaging and emergency alerting units, similar to PLBs but operating through commercial satellites. Like the SARSAT-supported devices discussed above, they are popular with pilots, sailors, and backcountry travelers. As with phones, there is a subscription charge for the services, which include emergency alerts to a commercial dispatch center, messaging, and showing your tracks on social media (a potentially life-saving feature if you are later unable to send an emergency alert). SPOT and InReach are two common brands.

THERE IS NO BAT SIGNAL With over 700 firms making some form of emergency alerting product, getting started can seem overwhelming. To learn more about these many products and to better understand the subject, you can get started here: sarsat.noaa.gov and searchandrescue.gsfc.nasa.gov. Cell and satellite phones, satellite alert devices, and radios can be lifesavers, but they also breed complacency and a false sense of security, with a loss of skills such as map reading, staying oriented as you hike, and planning ahead. Technology will not keep you from falling off a cliff.

THE RISE OF THE DRONES

Unmanned Aerial Vehicles (UAV), often called drones, have been around for years, often referred to in the war on terror. Their smaller, far-less-expensive cousins now serve many civilian uses, including a burgeoning role in SAR.

Radio-controlled drones can be equipped with optics for real-time imagery and thermal sensing while providing an aerial platform for search. Missing children and dementia patients have been found. Drones can deliver life jackets to flood victims, string a rescue line across a river, and even deliver medical supplies at an accident. Their role in SAR is evolving, their value being discovered.

Drones are both fixed wing (plane) and multirotor (helicopter) and are cheap to fly. These miniatures require piloting, and have limitations on battery life and distance from the operator. Now regulated by the FAA, restrictions include altitude, available daylight, and licensing. Although Yosemite does not currently use drones, other organizations do. An international network known as SWARM (Search With Aerial Rc Multirotor) is made up of more than 1,100 volunteers dedicated to using drones for SAR. For further information see SARDrones.org.

OUTSIDE THE PARK

A relatively little-known part of Yosemite National Park is a crucial set of resources located in the small town of El Portal. In 1958, the National Park Service acquired the approximately 1,200 acres located adjacent to the park's western boundary so that over time, necessary utilities, maintenance shops, offices, and critical housing could be relocated out of the Valley. It is called the El Portal Administrative (Admin) Site.

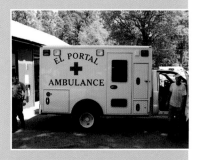

▲ Yosemite began ambulance service in El Portal in 1982, staffed by Ranger Jim Tucker and volunteers. This 2009 photo shows El Portal Ranger Brendan Bonner and SAR-Siter Werner Braun working on a more current emergency vehicle. NPS photo by Keith Lober.

DIVISION OF LABOR

In the Admin Site, there is a shared legal jurisdiction between the NPS, Mariposa County, and the State of California, which is significantly different from that of the park proper. Memorandums of understanding spell out which agencies have what responsibilities and authorities within this jurisdiction. Although there are some exceptions, the state and county authorities take the lead on most higher-level criminal matters within the Admin Site.

RANGERS ON SITE Historically, depending on the year's budget, Yosemite's Protection Division has staffed an El Portal Subdistrict Ranger Station on the site. The county does not have a substation there (over the years there has been a resident sheriff's deputy), and the California Highway Patrol maintains no resident post there. Thus, the state and county authorities are usually in El Portal only for emergencies and related incidents.

FIRST RESPONDERS The National Park Service plays a significant role both on the Admin Site and in the greater El Portal area, which stretches out downstream along both sides of the Merced River for several miles. Frequently, NPS search and rescue and emergency medical personnel are first on scene.

AN INCIDENT IN EL PORTAL

The following is an example of SAR and EMS mutual-aid response in El Portal. On December 29, 1996, a vehicle slid off Highway 140 and overturned in the Merced River at what is referred to as Patty's Hole. River flow was near flood level and extremely dangerous, even for persons wearing the proper flotation and personal protective gear. Two years earlier, a commercial rafting guide had drowned here under similar river conditions. Charles "Rick" Foulks, Greg

▲ Coordinated by park rangers, a day was devoted to training in El Portal for a mass casualty incident such as this simulated accident of a school bus full of children in 2009. Drills like this require the cooperation of many agencies. NPS photo by Keith Lober.

THE TOWN OF EL PORTAL

El Portal is about a dozen miles west of Yosemite Village on California State Route 140, also known in the area as El Portal Road. The highway runs through El Portal for approximately two miles. Summertime residents of El Portal plus motel guests in the surrounding area can number as many as 4,000 people. Ever since Highway 140 was completed through the Merced River Canyon and on into Yosemite in the 1920s, the park has provided assistance to residents and travelers.

Magruder, and Deron Mills were on the El Portal Swiftwater SAR Team at the time, and their skills were put to the test that day.

DIRE CONDITIONS One passenger was ejected from the vehicle and quickly drowned. A second passenger was clinging to the vehicle's side, while a third person was actually trapped inside the car in a small air pocket. The water temperature was below 40 degrees, placing both surviving victims in extreme danger of hypothermia as well as drowning.

RANGERS TO THE RESCUE Foulks, Magruder, and Mills used an extension ladder off a fire truck to cross from the shore to the upside-down vehicle where they pulled the second passenger onto the car, placed him into a life vest, and assisted him to safety. They then broke one of the car's windows and pulled out the trapped person. Since he was suffering from hypothermia, with a core temperature of only 88 degrees, once he was in a life vest they then secured him into a litter and moved him along the ladder to safety. Despite the frigid conditions the victims suffered, they both survived. The rangers on this emergency justifiably received a Department of the Interior Exemplary Act Award.

In this photo, the CHP is about to hoist a 39-year-old climber with an injured hip off the Royal Arches on April 17, 2010. NPS photo by David Pope.

A despondent 22-year-old went missing in mid-June 2008. He was found alive with the aid of the Fresno County Sheriff's SAR team. NPS photo by David Pope.

MUTUAL AID

Several times a year, YOSAR is called to support search and rescue missions outside the park's jurisdiction. In fact, federal laws as well as state and county agreements encourage this cooperation. Years ago, this mutual aid was most often requested for a SAR in the river near El Portal. As described earlier, a car would skid on the ice and go in, or a swimmer or rafter might be swept onto a rock, and Mariposa County would ask for help. In addition, the park has lent its mountaineering skills for injured "peak baggers," avalanche victims, and missing hikers. Sequoia National Park has asked for assistance on particularly difficult SARs, usually involving the Short-Haul Team. Now that the park has a helicopter powerful enough for higher altitudes and tougher conditions, H-551 is increasingly asked to assist with calls for trickier missions. When possible, the park gladly responds.

IT GOES BOTH WAYS In this mutually beneficial arrangement, the park sometimes asks for help from its neighbors, generally when there is a large search and a need for extra personnel or for a specialized resource, such as dog teams. When Yosemite eliminated its dive team in the mid-1990s, Mariposa County pitched in, providing trained scuba divers, several of whom were off-duty NPS employees. For years YOSAR has relied on the California Highway Patrol for its winch-equipped helicopter and highly skilled crews, mostly in the off-season when H-551 is not around. The park has coordinated training missions and routinely collaborates with the California Office of Emergency Services. Over the years, a mutual respect and SAR bond has been forged.

A RECORD-BREAKING INCIDENT

Billionaire Steve Fossett was a record-setting aviator, sailor, skier, mountaineer, and all-around adventurer. In 2002, he became the first person to circumnavigate the world by balloon. In 2005, he repeated the feat on a solo, nonstop, and unrefueled trip in a single-engine airplane. And then in 2007, he set an around-the-world sailing record. Ultimately, he set 91 aviation and 23 sailing world records. He also swam the English Channel, finished the Alaskan Iditarod Trail Sled Dog Race, ran the Leadville 100 Ultramarathon, and climbed the highest peaks on six continents. His records and accomplishments go on and on. But his remarkable career ended on September 3, 2007. That Labor Day he was taking what he referred to as a "morning ride" in a borrowed, little two-seat aerobatic airplane, not far from Yosemite National Park. He did not return. The search for Fossett—both publicly and privately funded—was one of the largest, most intense, most highly publicized such efforts in history, yet it failed.

THE END OF THE STORY On October 1, 2008, 13 months after Fossett disappeared, a hiker found his pilot's license and over $1,000 scattered at the 10,200-foot elevation north of Devils Postpile National Monument, east of Yosemite. This was in Madera County, but the Madera sheriff's SAR coordinator asked Yosemite for aid, mostly for the use of its helicopter. At 6:00 p.m., Ranger Matt Stark and the crew of H-551 finally located the burned wreckage of Fossett's plane, about one half mile from the initial evidence. There was no body inside; bears and other animals had almost certainly removed it. Over the next two days, H-551 and YOSAR personnel returned to help search for human remains as well as provide assistance in the investigation. Finally, on October 17, H-551, with two Yosemite rescue personnel and four Madera County sheriff's deputies, returned to the crash site. Ultimately, bone fragments with sufficient DNA were found, linking them with Steve Fossett.

▲ "The mosquitoes were getting almost as much blood as I," says Eric Gabriel, seen here starting an IV. Helitack crewmen John DeMay (middle) and Morgan Pierre assist. Five hours after falling, the victim was in an air ambulance (see sidebar). NPS photo by Jason Ramsdell.

"That rescue is the best save I have ever had," professed Ranger Eric Gabriel. "He [the victim] took a bouncing, 140-foot fall and was tightly wedged in that snow moat [trench] for over three hours." On August 12, 2006, a 38-year-old man was scrambling up 12,590-foot-high Mount Conness in Mono County, only feet outside the park when he fell. By some miracle, an off-duty Yosemite SAR-Siter heard the man's scream and quickly organized a rescue. Initially, the Mono SAR team was on the mission but soon asked the park to assist. Aided by Yosemite Helitack, H-551 short-hauled Rangers Gabriel and Jason Ramsdell onto a ledge just below the victim, at the 11,000-foot level. "He coded [heart stopped] a couple of times on the way [by air ambulance] to the Reno hospital and his core body temperature at the Emergency Room was 84 degrees. But he made a full recovery with no problems."

IF YOU DIE IN YOSEMITE

Only two parks in our National Park System—Yosemite and Yellowstone—have ranger/coroners. Why in Yosemite? It may have begun in July of 1905, when the State of California mandated that all counties begin officially recording deaths in their jurisdiction.

RANGER AS CORONERS

As of January 2017, 23 Yosemite rangers served as deputy sheriff-coroners for either Mariposa or Tuolumne counties. Some served both counties. Madera County is such a small part of the park that, at this time, there are no rangers serving in that capacity, although this has not always been the case. If a coroner were needed in that corner of the park today, a regular Madera County official would handle the incident.

SOME HISTORICAL PERSPECTIVE

Until the early 1900s, the function of certifying deaths in California counties fell to a coroner's jury, convened by an official such as the sheriff. Witnesses might testify, and the jury might even travel to the scene. They would reach a consensus, rule on the cause of death, and file the requisite legal papers.

THE PARK'S FIRST CORONER The transition to the current system for the park may have begun in August of 1919, when 49-year-old Emma French, from Los Angeles, drowned while swimming in the Valley. A week later, Assistant Superintendent Ernest P. Leavitt assembled an inquest, becoming the park's first deputy coroner.

THE SHERIFF STEPS IN

Today, the sheriff of a California county is elected and is the chief law enforcement officer and also the coroner. In cases in which a death is not attended by a physician, or is otherwise unusual, the sheriff is responsible for fixing a cause of that death as homicide, suicide, accidental, natural, or not determined. The sheriff relies on deputy coroners, investigators, medical experts, and a host of complicated laws and regulations.

WHAT ABOUT THE PARK? Yosemite spans three counties: Mariposa, including Yosemite Valley and Wawona; Tuolumne to the north, including Tuolumne Meadows; and a small section of Madera County, on the southern edge of the park. Because of the park's Partial Exclusive Jurisdiction status, many Yosemite rangers also serve as deputy sheriff-coroners (see sidebar).

WHAT WOULD HAPPEN TO YOU?

More than 1800 people are known to have died in Yosemite since 1851, and the park now averages 15 to 20 deaths each year. If you happen to be among them, this is how your death is likely to be handled. Many of the following functions are done simultaneously and in some cases may even be handled by the same ranger.

▲ The body of a hiker who slipped off the Mist Trail in May 2009 is recovered on July 15 by Ranger Aaron Smith, who is wearing a disposable hazmat suit and facemask. NPS photo by Dov Bock.

First, a ranger at the scene will assume responsibility for documenting the incident, whether on a SAR, in a hotel room, or maybe even at the clinic. The basics of who, what, when, where, how, and why are identified and recorded. Witnesses are interviewed and the scene is photographed and/or described in detail. The area will be secured, as will any relevant personal property. A death investigator is soon assigned to your case. This ranger will process your body, such as taking fingerprints, and will seek to determine if civil laws have been broken while ascertaining if legal liabilities face the government or its partners, such as a concessionaire.

Then, your remains are delivered to a pathologist for an autopsy, blood tests, and gathering of related data. Finally, a ranger serving as a deputy sheriff-coroner will process the observations and possible conclusions of all the investigations—in and out of the park—and suggest a cause of death to the sheriff, who will ultimately sign the death certificate.

TELLING YOUR FAMILY A ranger will notify the first next of kin, and if this is outside the park, a police officer will be present. Press releases about your death will be withheld until your family is contacted. A valuable aid to first responders and investigators is the family liaison, a person in the park trained to comfort and assist survivors and others affected. Death in Yosemite National Park is not taken lightly, and rangers charged with these duties handle them compassionately and professionally.

NO DUTY TO RESCUE

This 1991 case stemmed from an incident in Grand Teton National Park, but it has direct bearing on Yosemite SAR. Ben Johnson and three friends went climbing on June 28, 1987. Two got down, the third was rescued in the middle of the night, and the fourth, Johnson, went missing. At dawn the next day, rangers in a helicopter spotted Johnson in a pool of snowmelt—dead. Johnson's estate alleged he would not have died but for the Service's negligent failure to: (1) adequately regulate recreational climbing in the park, and (2) conduct a reasonable rescue effort after one of the companion's second report.

The United States Court of Appeals, Tenth Circuit, found no statute imposing a duty to rescue, nor a formal NPS policy to do so. The decision whether, when, or how to initiate a search or rescue is left to the discretion of the SAR team; in other words, the SAR team has discretionary authority over each situation. The Court said that if the plaintiff's argument had been accepted, it "would jeopardize the Park Rangers' autonomy to make difficult, individualized search and rescue decisions in the field."

A CASE OF JURISDICTION

Who: Donald Barnes and Charlotte Bacon • **When: February 8, 1975**

The Story: Rangers are forced to think fast after a plane crashes in bad weather.

Thirty-seven-year-old Donald Barnes, along with thirty-year-old Charlotte Bacon, were flying his single-engine Cessna 182 from Las Vegas to his home in Modesto, California, on February 8, 1975. Their route took them directly over the 11,000-foot snow-covered peaks on the park's southern boundary, as a serious snowstorm was moving into the area. Apparently, Barnes thought he could beat the storm, and perhaps he added pilot error to the dangerous weather. He crashed just as he was nearing the park.

CALL FOR HELP A commercial airliner passing far overhead first heard the faint signals from the plane's ELT (see page 180) and sounded the alarm. Aviation officials believed the ill-fated craft was inside the park; Yosemite was notified by the Air Force Rescue and Coordination Center (AFRCC) at Scott Air Force Base, Illinois, the overall coordinator of resources for these sorts of incidents. The author was the incident commander, or search boss (as it was known in those days), for the park's response. The AFRCC directed the military in Tacoma, Washington, to fly in special handheld emergency locating devices overnight. Satellite radio communications—possibly a first for a civilian search and rescue—were installed in the park's command post by noon on February 9.

▲ Ranger Joanne Cross prepares a tarp on which to position the deceased in order to drag them over to the waiting helicopter for hoisting inside. NPS photo.

INTO THE SNOW Despite heavy snows and more severe weather in the forecast, two four-person teams started into the area on skis late that afternoon from different directions, a distance of more than eight airline miles. Flying was not an option. Two additional four-person teams were poised to leave the next morning. All faced tremendous avalanche hazards. The dense, new-fallen snow is frequently—but not affectionately—termed "Sierra Cement" due to its high water content, and it is terribly difficult to ski through. Indeed, four decades later, Ranger Joe Abrell recalled, "We had a hell of a time because the snow was so deep." It became quickly apparent, given the new snow and the aircraft's uncertain location, as well as the distances to be covered, that the ground teams should stop and remain in place, at least for the time being, in the hope that the weather would improve enough to fly.

HELICOPTER SUPPORT Also on standby in Yosemite Valley the night before was a Naval Air Station Lemoore Angel, piloted by Lieutenant Commander "Stormin' Norman" Hicks. Norm had been on many Yosemite SAR missions, and park rangers respected him and his seasoned crew. The next day, February 10, a several-hour window of flyable but still marginal weather developed. At first chance, the navy aircraft took off with four rangers aboard in addition to the regular crew. Despite thick cloud cover, within seconds of rising above the Valley rim it picked up the plane's emergency signal.

A SUCCESSFUL SEARCH In less than 15 minutes, the small, mostly white plane was found. It was badly mangled, having augured into deep new snow at 11,000 feet on a ridge of Post Peak. No signs of life could be seen, although without physically looking into the crumpled craft, this could not be verified. And just to add even more complexity, the rangers realized that they were now slightly outside Yosemite's southern boundary. They were no longer within the park! Unable to set the helicopter down due to altitude and critical weight concerns, Hicks was forced to put the four rangers, including Randy Morgenson, Joanne Cross, and Ron Mackie, onto a bare rock outcropping a mile away while Hicks went for fuel at Castle Air Force Base. He returned, picked up the rangers, and they then jumped into the deep snow near the crash scene.

▲ The spinning rotors added a tremendous windchill factor to the scene. Notice the snowshoes. NPS photo.

WHO'S IN CHARGE? Now comes the interesting part. Technically, as trivial and inane as bureaucratic boundaries may seem in a case like this, none of the rangers had any legal right or jurisdiction to act. Indeed, they knew that they held no authority to serve as coroners or official investigators, despite being right there. However, because of the awful weather predicted to hit the area and surely bury the wreck and the victims in just hours, the four would be the only officials on this scene for days, perhaps weeks.

CREATIVE THINKING In need of a fast, practical solution to this dilemma, Captain Ovonual Berkley of the Madera County Sheriff's Department was contacted by phone and patched through to the rangers on Post

Peak by the park's radio communications center. Ron Mackie was quickly deputized from afar as he stood beside the twisted aircraft. Berkley urged the park team to remove the two frozen bodies and get off that mountain ASAP. Stormin' Norman and his crew were primed to leave, given the weather they could see coming.

The rangers on the snow moved swiftly. Within an hour of the recovery of the victims and the team being safely hoisted back into the hovering helicopter, snow would begin to fall, locking in the downed aircraft for the winter. I do not know, maybe it is still there.

INCIDENT COMMAND SYSTEM

▲ During President Barack Obama's 2016 family vacation to western national parks, he visited Yosemite on June 18 to 19. Six large military helicopters were stationed in the Valley full-time while the Obamas were there. Here, Marine One (the call sign for any U.S. Marine Corps helicopter that carries the president) arrives in the Ahwahnee Meadow. Not seen is the large-scale ICS supporting the visit. NPS photo by Alan Hageman.

Ever wonder how the Forest Service manages a 100,000-acre forest fire for weeks? How the Coast Guard handles large oil spills? How the Federal Emergency Management Agency (FEMA) responded to Hurricane Sandy? Let alone how large teams of people are coordinated for manhunts or large high-security events such as the presidential inauguration?

THE SYSTEM WORKS

Today, all federal fire, law enforcement, and other emergency response agencies as well as most comparable entities at both the state and local levels, and in a number of other countries, use the Incident Command System (ICS) to manage larger events. It is a uniform approach to the management and coordination of both emergency response and significant nonemergency events. Responsibility, methods, and procedures for well over 100 positions within the ICS are formally defined, and the necessary qualifications, standards to be maintained, and obligations of each of these job functions are spelled out in detail using common terminology.

FORGED IN FIRE While ICS is a quasimilitary paradigm, it actually began with a fire in the hills above Oakland, California, in 1970. California had received little or no rain for six months, setting it up for perhaps the worst wildfire period in decades. The fires burned from September 22 to October 4. According to one source, 773 wildfires burned a total of 576,000 acres throughout California, destroying 722 homes and killing 16 people.

COORDINATION ISSUES At the peak, some 500 local, regional, state, and federal firefighting departments and related medical and law-enforcement agencies were involved in these catastrophes. Each was working furiously to put out fires using its own management processes. Command structures, procedures, and protocols for decision making all differed. More often than not, a fire truck could literally not talk to another truck just up the street because of a lack of mutual radio frequencies. People working side by side were not using the same terminology, and might not be able to request further assistance due to dissimilar requisition processes.

▲ The Operations Section Chief is a key member of the Command Staff in an ICS organization. Here Keith Lober provides leadership for a simulated mass casualty school bus accident in El Portal on April 4, 2009. Dana Tafoya, Mariposa County Emergency Services Coordinator, is at left. NPS photo.

One fire department would send a truck to the next block, only to discover that it was not what was needed, or didn't have the staff or the necessary equipment for the job at hand.

CREATING A SOLUTION Almost immediately after the fires, the U.S. Forest Service, with special funds appropriated by Congress, joined with two of California's divisions, Forestry and the Office of Emergency Services, to begin creating a system in which each fire and law-enforcement department could work seamlessly with its counterparts. In 1972, Firefighting Resources of Southern California Organized for Potential Emergencies, or FIRESCOPE, was launched. Over time, a sophisticated process evolved from FIRESCOPE, known as ICS. In 1981, it was formerly adopted by the major fire agencies in Southern California.

That same year, Rick Gale, as the chief ranger of Santa Monica Mountains National Recreation Area (SMNRA), ratified it just for his park. Gale, however, was also one of the most senior fire managers in the Department of the Interior at that time. He quickly began spreading the word about the value of ICS. Two years later, from March 3 to 5, 1983, Great Britain's Queen Elizabeth II visited Yosemite. This event was managed by ICS, although ICS was not yet formally adopted by the NPS, with Valley District Ranger Dick Martin serving as the incident commander. This was the first time a national park area used ICS and likely the first time it was employed for managing a nonfire incident anywhere, albeit unofficially. Finally,

BIG HITS OF ICS

Basic ICS was first used by the NPS on large fires, such as the Yellowstone fires of 1988. Beginning earlier, in 1981, however, parts of the NPS (and eventually other agencies such as FEMA) began managing nonfire events with ICS. Major events included Queen Elizabeth II's visit to Yosemite (1983), the *Exxon Valdez* oil spill in Alaska (1989), the 50th anniversary of the attack on Pearl Harbor (1991), the aftermath of Hurricane Andrew (1992), catastrophic floods in Yosemite Valley (1997), and the visit of President Barack Obama and the First Family to Yosemite (2016). All SARs in Yosemite, no matter how small, are managed by ICS.

On the morning of September 11, 2001, SAR Technician Donna Sisson had climbed Higher Cathedral Spire. She returned to the Valley SAR cache around 11:00 a.m. and immediately sensed an eerie vibe in the room. Some of the park's team was gathered around a television watching news coverage of planes crashing into the World Trade Center's twin towers. "Something was wrong in a way we had not experienced before," she recalls. "We were at the ready but our SAR packs were inadequate and the mission unclear." O'Shaughnessy Dam at Hetch Hetchy Reservoir went on 24-hour security, law enforcement rangers were placed at all entrance stations, and field operations such as traffic control were short-staffed as rangers were detailed to critical security assignments in other parks. All SAR personnel were placed on standby, which meant they could not climb or attend to personal business. The heightened alert went on for several days and, while most took it as part of the job, some took issue with the requirement to report to duty and the mundane assignments.

in 1985, the NPS formally adopted ICS, the fifth agency within the federal government to do so.

ICS SPREADS LIKE WILDFIRE Given that ICS was originally the product of wildland firefighting, in its early years it was spearheaded by the National Interagency Fire Center, headquartered in Boise, Idaho, and used exclusively for managing large forest fires. Under Rick Gale, SMNRA first used ICS officially on a nonfire event in 1984 during the Summer Olympics, instituting what's known as the "all hazards" concept, which mandates that emergency responders use consistent procedures no matter what the incident.

On March 1, 2004, the Department of Homeland Security called for standardized incident management among all federal, state, and local agencies and developed the National Incident Management System (NIMS), which integrates ICS. Firefighters, law-enforcement officers, and most other first responders go through at least the 80-hour basic ICS training. At the most demanding and complicated end, incident commanders and key staff train for years, in both the classroom as well as in real-life shadow applications, to manage the largest nonmilitary events this country is routinely called upon to handle.

HOW THE SYSTEM WORKS TODAY

ICS allows agencies that may never have worked together to operate together under a familiar framework. (An analogy might be that drivers, for the safety of all, agree to drive on the same side of the road.) Using ICS command structure, the incident organization can grow in complexity depending on the needs of the operation and can then be reduced in size as the incident winds down. For example, an Air Operations Unit or a Medical Unit may be required for one problem; for the next, it may not be needed and may be disbanded or held in reserve.

The author was involved in an impressive example of such flexibility, when the Deepwater Horizon oil well blowout and catastrophic oil spill took place off the coast of Louisiana in 2010. The U.S. Coast Guard had ultimate authority over the situation, but combined all decision making with British Petroleum, the owners of the well. To help keep track of developments and inform all the players, a huge Incident Command organizational chart was written on large sheets of paper and posted on one wall in each of the two big-box-store-sized Incident Command Posts. At the height of the incident, there were upwards of 700 people in just the management structure, in addition to the thousands of workers actually on the beaches and elsewhere, cleaning up. At one time, the author oversaw two separate

▲ A key element of NIMS (see page 192) is standardizing training to the greatest degree possible. Yosemite SAR Officer Keith Lober and some of the YOSAR team review the basics of a raising system, suitable for rescue work. NPS photo.

groups with 1,200 people working under him, yet the space on the official organizational chart given to identifying these groups and their roles was but two or three lines out of many hundreds. Over several months, as the need for certain functions and workers was reduced, the large paper chart got smaller as well.

ICS IN THE PARK Here's an example of how the system works in the park: If a young child goes missing from a campground, a search will begin. One ranger will be identified as an incident commander (IC), and he or she will begin utilizing ICS. The size of the search and how quickly it grows will depend on the child's age and health, as well as the weather, external hazards, and other factors. The effort will be coordinated from an incident command post (ICP). Hundreds of searchers, helicopters, dog and horse teams, and dozens of other resources may ultimately be involved, each of them with a well-defined role and purpose as well as preestablished procedures. When the child is found, the organizational structure will melt away, only to reform the next time it's needed.

AN INTRICATE WEB ICS is simple in concept. However, with its many roles and functions, along with the complex training required of these positions, it is a highly sophisticated system. It could be as important to SAR as are two-way radios, helicopters, and emergency medicine. A sample ICS organizational chart follows.

INCIDENT MANAGEMENT TEAMS

Incident Management Teams (IMTs) have evolved from only fighting wildfires to now managing all-hazards incidents, e.g., dignitary visits, hurricanes, and floods, in addition to large fires. A Type I Interagency IMT handles large events at a national level with up to 58 people designated in each of the 16 teams existing in 2017. They are dispatched by the National Interagency Coordination Center (NICC) in Boise, Idaho. Type II IMTs perform at the regional level; the NPS has several teams as of 2017 which are generally dispatched by the NPS regional offices. States also have Type I (California) and Type II Teams. People in one position may serve in similar positions elsewhere. The NPS identified two Type-II All-Risk IMTs in 1990, a first for the federal government. Hal Grovert, former Yosemite SAR officer led one team. After the 1991 *Exxon Valdez* oil spill, the NPS organized the first national Type-I All-Risk IMT. Today, All-Risk IMT is more commonly known as All-Hazard IMT.

INCIDENT COMMAND STRUCTURE

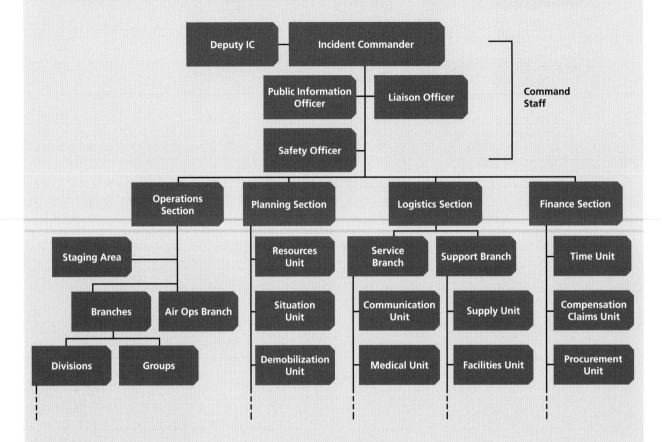

Note: Some of the positions identified in this basic ICS Organizational Chart are described here in limited detail. For a large incident, there could be hundreds of people included here.

+ Incident Commander (IC): ultimately responsible for incident activities including the development and implementation of strategic decisions and goals. This is always done in concert with the specialists and other professionals in the organization.

+ Liaison Officer: the point of contact for representatives of assisting and cooperating outside agencies, e.g., other police, fire, public works, military, and Red Cross, as well as victim families and other civilians affected by the event.

+ Operations Section Chief: oversees all field operations directly applicable to the primary mission and is responsible for executing the plan of action for the day. For a large-scale search, this could include the parallel use of helicopters, ground searchers, and YODOGS.

+ Planning Section Chief: responsible for the collection, evaluation, dissemination, and use of information needed for development of plans, including missing person data, status of resources, mapping, and weather. Also oversees event documentation and demobilization as the incident winds down.

+ Logistics Section Chief: responsible for providing facilities, services, and materials in support of the incident, e.g., food, sleep/rest areas, medical services, communications, and incident command post facilities.

+ Finance Section Chief: responsible for all finances and cost analysis of the incident, timekeeping for participants, tracking compensation claims, and paying for supplies.

RESCUING THE RESCUERS

Who: The author and his friend Mark • When: February 1973

The Story: A snowy adventure turns into a death march for two prepared outdoor enthusiasts.

IT WAS A NICE DAY With the forecast predicting a beautiful day, I convinced my fellow ranger and good friend Mark to go on a snowshoe hike. It was all downhill and about 4 miles by the map. From near Badger Pass (the park's downhill ski area), we'd drop into the Bridalveil Creek drainage and exit with a short rappel into the Valley over The Gunsight, a notch in the cliffs near the top of Bridalveil Fall. I used my 4-foot-long beavertail snowshoes and Mark was similarly equipped. We had ropes, bolts, drills, and a piton hammer as well as a two-way park radio and basic bivouac gear. With blue skies above and fresh snow below, off we went on our day trip.

We easily worked down into the drainage and along the creek. Then our luck turned. At noon and way past the point at which we should have turned around, our death march commenced. With each step, the webbing on our feet would catch the 6-foot-high, snow-buried manzanita bushes, and we started plunging down between their brittle branches. Climb out, snag, tumble in. For hours. Climb, snag, fall. Sweat rolled off us and we became chilled. As darkness fell, we finally made The Gunsight. "We're OK," we radioed our boss. "We can see the Valley and have a boulder for shelter, a small fire, and we'll sit on snowshoes and ropes." Then began the worst storm of the season: for us it was an all-night mix of rain and snow.

HELP ARRIVES—WITH CHEESE! The next morning I broke five drill bits—all we had—due to icy water trickling down the cliff face, so we weren't able to place an anchor. So, no rappel. A fellow ranger advised us by radio to go up canyon to another exit spot requiring no rappels; it took us a second grueling day of hiking across the snowshoe-grabbing manzanita to get there. The storm began again and our escape spot became hidden by low clouds. A second bivouac.

With a tiny fire, the boulder we sheltered by gave us just enough refuge. "We're still OK," we radioed. This time, however, our boss did not believe us. Unbeknownst to Mark and me, he pulled together seven of the leading local mountaineers to bring us home. Also in the rescue party was another ranger friend; his job was to bring the emergency food. Not known for his wilderness skills, he lugged in 20 cheeseburgers—which arrived all smashed together!

Splitting into two teams and approaching from different directions, our rescuers climbed all night, battling the deep snow and driving wind. But until we heard their faint voices on the radio, we did not even know they were nearby. They were definitely beat, but we were truly glad to see them and the cheeseburgers. We were down 12 hours later.

THE TAKEAWAY

Now it's the author's turn to fess up to some lessons learned.

+ **We were caught off guard by a serious, potentially life-threatening storm.** Weather forecasting is far superior to how it was 45 years ago, but always check it. If it is good, do not believe it; if it is bad, believe it and go prepared.

+ We were lucky. **Had we not found those sheltering boulders, we might have died.** With today's lightweight space blankets for retaining body heat and nylon tarps for shelter, there is no excuse not to carry them.

+ **Stay dry; wet will kill.** Prevent hypothermia. Only a month before, we had gone through a basic winter survival course in the park. Today, there are many such courses available.

SO YOU WANT TO SEARCH AND RESCUE

For those of you interested in positions in the national parks, visit nps.gov/aboutus/how-to-apply.htm.

If you're still in college or between careers, consider applying for a volunteer or intern position in a busy park, ideally one with SAR. Several of the more active parks have a PSAR program, which may be a valuable starting point.

If you already have a career but have spare time, check out your local county SAR team (see the sheriff's website). This team may also be a game-changing activity for teenagers.

For further information on the NPS volunteer programs go to: nps.gov/getinvolved/volunteer.htm.

To find parks in your area, go to: nps.gov/findapark/index.htm.

My first search took place in mid-November of 1958. I found myself wading through waist-deep snow, early in the largest SAR in southern Arizona history. At a conservative estimate there were eventually 750 searchers, mostly soldiers and airmen from nearby bases.

MY START IN SAR

When three Boy Scouts—a classmate of mine and two younger kids—began a day hike up 9,450-foot-high Mount Baldy, south of Tucson, it was sunny and warm. But the weather turned deadly that afternoon. Although there was no snow in the forecast, a surprise storm started, and by the next morning five feet had fallen on the mountain. Even though I was an Eagle Scout, I had no real idea what was going on. I was 16, my buddies were also Eagle Scouts, and while we were into organized climbing and caving, we had few technical skills. In fact, as part of a search organization, none of us knew what we were doing, although everyone was giving it their best. On December 4, 19 days after it began, the search came to an end when three bodies were found. It is believed all three boys—ages 11, 12, and 16—fell asleep that first night and never woke up.

▲ Working alongside two rangers, four of the six responders in this June 2016 photo are volunteers. A woman suffered a broken lower leg from a ground-level fall, a typical accident on park trails. NPS photo by Alan Hageman.

▲ Depending on the nature of the upcoming mission, all rescues and trainings will involve safety briefings, review of role and task assignments, assessment of the requisites of specialized techniques, and highlighting of any unusual demands of the incident. NPS photo by David Pope.

In today's world, with well-trained, well-organized, and well-equipped search and rescue teams seemingly everywhere, if a teenager like me were out there, dressed in water-absorbing cotton jeans and sweatshirt, with zero training and no communications, my parents could be considered negligent, and rightfully so—not to mention the sheriff's department that had recruited my Scout troop to join the operation. Fortunately, you do not need to start out the way I did.

GETTING INTO SAR So, how do you get into SAR today? The first thing to know is that there is no single, cookie-cutter secret to success. People who are deep into SAR came to it in different ways, mostly as part of larger missions and disciplines. SAR can be a significant part of law enforcement, firefighting, emergency medical first response, the U.S. Coast Guard, the U.S. Border Patrol, and many other professions. If you want to get into SAR in the National Park Service, the best way is to become a seasonal ranger or firefighter and tell everyone who will listen that you are interested in SAR. And while you do, learn as many related skills and disciplines as possible.

NEED TO KNOW Is SAR occasionally glamorous? Yes! Rewarding and fulfilling? Yes! But is it also often mundane, tedious, hard, demanding, scary, frustrating, and dirty? Yes! Does every aspect of SAR require a great amount of physical fitness? Not always, but mostly. Will it take you away from your families and your jobs and your friends? Will it eat up your spare time? Is it—far more than you will expect—ugly? Yes, yes . . . and yes!

TOTAL SARs PER YEAR IN YOSEMITE

These are the total number of Yosemite SAR events recorded during each calendar year. They come from the annual SAR logs housed in the Yosemite Search and Rescue Office and the SAR records in El Portal. Prior to 1976 these figures were tallied for the federal government's fiscal year (FY), July 1 through June 30. From 1976 to present, the FY is October 1 through September 30. The figures below are for the actual calendar year. Annual summaries could not be established prior to 1967.

Year	Count	Year	Count
1967	46	1992	245
1968	55	1993	190
1969	70	1994	229
1970	94	1995	188
1971	85	1996	192
1972	96	1997	154
1973	89	1998	141
1974	121	1999	164
1975	107	2000	147
1976	131	2001	168
1977	110	2002	181
1978	143	2003	181
1979	124	2004	230
1980	151	2005	231
1981	138	2006	219
1982	144	2007	241
1983	110	2008	250
1984	174	2009	242
1985	189	2010	245
1986	194	2011	202
1987	208	2012	216
1988	162	2013	175
1989	133	2014	181
1990	181	2015	216
1991	225	2016	236

THINGS TO CONSIDER You need to be a self-starter, as well as assertive, persistent, inquisitive, and a team player. You need to like people and enjoy helping them. Start by honestly assessing your capabilities and/or potential. Here's a checklist of questions to ask yourself:

+ What do you want out of joining SAR?

+ Are you as physically fit as you need to be?

+ Have you been interested for some time and are you committed for the long term? Achieving SAR certifications can take years.

+ If so, have you done anything about it? If not, why not?

+ Have you checked out the countless websites on the subject?

+ Are there local SAR teams you can contact?

+ What do you have to offer them? Are you a caver, diver, mountaineer, climber, boater, skier, hiker, dog handler, camper, communications or GIS whiz, kayaker, or skilled horseback rider? Are you a pilot, public speaker, computer geek, videographer, or EMT?

Focus on one or more skill(s) and become great at them, and then begin to pick up other skills as you progress. If you are none of the above, you'd better get started!

In 2005, YOSAR responded to two climbers on Higher Cathedral Rock, one of whom was dehydrated and needed help getting to safety. YOSAR helped them both after dark. Rescuers, including Scott Ring (in green) and Ben Blanton (foreground), were then forced to spend the night (bivouac) in place. Early the next morning, the CHP helicopter was able to lift off the one climber, and the other descended to the Valley on his own. NPS photo by Keith Lober.

TIM SETNICKA REMEMBERS

Yosemite SAR Officer, December 1975 to October 1978

" The SAR community both within Yosemite and around the country, particularly in the mountainous West, had been developing over a few decades. In the early 1970s, there was limited printed material available about SAR techniques for interested individuals and SAR teams to use as training references.

Back then, SAR operations in Yosemite reflected the adaptation of climbing ropes and related basic gear, along with rock climbing techniques, for SAR work. Technical SAR operations can be intense and, in some ways, unique, so it was a natural evolution to begin putting these "lessons learned" down on paper.

After each training session, I would always get requests for a handout showing the techniques and riggings used during the class. The NPS had no handouts, so I decided to create some. Fortunately, I knew Valerie Cohen, an accomplished artist and Yosemite climber, and prevailed on her to help. Not surprisingly, there was no way the National Park Service could hire and pay for an artist's illustrations, so I paid for her work myself.

Over time the pile of illustrations grew and grew, as did my written descriptions of each. For example, I described the basic steps and information that anyone involved in taking a report of a lost or injured person needed to obtain. That was the beginning of information about the search portion of a SAR operation. Eventually, these handouts became the genesis of my book, *Wilderness Search and Rescue*, which was published by the Appalachian Mountain Club in 1980.

Wilderness Search and Rescue was popular within the SAR community. After saturating the

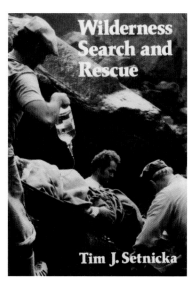

▲ The art and science of SAR tactics and techniques are always evolving. Texts on "how to SAR" began with Field Manual FM 70-10, *Mountain Operations* (see page 36). Produced in 1944 for the U.S. Army, it combined elements of mountaineering, climbing, and related rock rescue. Four years later, Wastl Mariner wrote *Mountain Rescue Techniques,* which quickly

market, the book eventually went out of print in the late 1980s; however, it still serves as a basic primer in SAR techniques. These foundational principles have held true even though the methods of accomplishing various tasks in SAR operations have greatly evolved. Modern SAR operations now involve the use of drones, computers, the Internet, cell phones, Google Earth, more sophisticated helicopters, etc. "

---

became noteworthy for this country's burgeoning SAR community, although it was not translated into English until 1963. In 1973, Dennis Kelley, a pioneer in our understanding of how people go missing in the outdoors, wrote *Mountain Search for the Lost Victim*; the book became a primer on how to look for them. Then, in 1980, Tim Setnicka, readied by hundreds of SAR missions during his nine years in Yosemite, put the basics of *both* search and rescue in one place. His book helped pave the way for the many quality texts now available.

If you look at the cover of Setnicka's book shown here, you will see the *glass bottle* (today, a plastic bag) of IV fluid being held by Ranger Jim Brady in August 1975. Luckily for the 29-year-old man who fell 20 feet while rock hopping at the base of Bridalveil Fall, a visiting medical doctor was willing to start the IV. Thankfully, SAR and emergency medical response in Yosemite has come a long way over the years. Photo of book by Butch Farabee.

RESOURCES

◄ Despite the stunning backdrop of Half Dome and Clouds Rest, YOSAR is all business while preparing to rescue an 18-year-old climber who broke a leg after falling 30 feet in June 2010. NPS photo by David Pope.

SAFETY TIPS FOR STAYING ALIVE

We suggest carrying a photocopy or photograph of these pages when you visit Yosemite and other outdoor areas. They will help guide you to have a safer, more enjoyable visit. However, every situation is different, and these short lists can't cover all contingencies; you must always use your own judgment.

THE HIKING (OR TEN) ESSENTIALS

Here is the minimum equipment to carry with you, even for short day hikes.

1. **Clothing:** for potential weather extremes, e.g., cold, moisture, and wind, as well as footwear for rocky and slippery trails, including traction devices for snow and ice

2. **Sun Protection:** long-sleeved shirt and pants, sunglasses, sunscreen, lip balm, and a hat with a brim/neck cover

3. **Water:** carry at least two water containers (in case one is broken or lost) and more water than you think you'll need, or have a water-treatment system and knowledge of reliable water sources along the trail

4. **Food:** enough for an unplanned overnight, including salty snacks for electrolyte replacement

5. **First Aid Kit:** for common occurrences such as blisters, wounds, sprains, and minor pain, as well as your personal medications

6. **Illumination:** a bright LED headlamp (preferred) and/or a flashlight (ideally two lights), and spare batteries

7. **Navigation:** compass and detailed topographic map (GPS optional)

8. **Repair Kit and Tools:** multifunction tool with a knife blade, duct tape, and anything specific to gear carried

9. **Emergency Shelter:** a brightly colored, ultralight, pitchable tarp, bivy sack, or space blanket, plus parachute cord

10. **Fire and Signaling:** fire starter, cell phone with extra power pack, signal mirror, whistle, and brightly colored items such as clothing, bandanas, and/or your shelter

There is an 11th Essential: your brain, which is always your most powerful tool. The best equipment is only dead weight in your pack unless you know how to use it; you owe it to yourself and to potential rescuers to be knowledgeable and competent with your gear. And remember that the best survival gear won't help if you are incapacitated by injury or separated from your pack or if your cell phone battery runs out and you can't read this when you need to. You still need to hike safely.

TELL SOMEONE WHERE YOU'RE GOING!

Provide a map to a reliable friend, showing your route, your goal, and when to call for assistance if you don't return. This simple step could save the lives of hikers, and save time and expense for searching in wilderness areas across the country.

LOST THE TRAIL? WHAT TO DO NOW

There are only two kinds of hikers: those who have lost the trail and those who are going to lose the trail. What you do next is more important than how you lost the trail in the first place. Here are a few tips:

+ Expect to lose the trail. Whether you're hiking on trail or off, turn around frequently and check the route you've been following (your back trail), especially in confusing areas. Remember landmarks as you hike, so that you can always go back the way you came.

+ If you're not sure that you're still on the trail, stop! Look around—the trail is often only 50 feet away. But if you have no clue which way to go, choose a nearby feature as a point of reference, e.g., a unique and prominent tree. Now explore in any safe direction while keeping this reference point always in your sight. Start with your back trail, and if that doesn't work, return to your reference point and try another way, until you learn the area around you and can pick another reference point. Always be able to go back to your original reference point, because that may be the closest place to where you weren't lost.

+ Shortcuts in rugged country are almost always a bad idea, if you can't see every step of the way. A 20-foot cliff can stop you, so there is no guarantee you'll reach your goal. If you have the option of going down a slope that would be hard to climb back up, don't do it—it probably isn't the route you took before you lost the trail. If you become stranded, you will be at the mercy of the elements and completely dependent on searchers.

+ Don't push on blindly. It is wishful thinking that this will somehow solve your problem. If it's getting dark, find a secure, sheltered, and comfortable spot to rest and wait for daylight.

+ If nothing works, consider asking for help before you make your problem worse.

GETTING FOUND:
HOW TO HELP YOUR RESCUERS

If you are hopelessly lost or unable to return from your hike for any reason, your best option is to ask for help and to make it easy for others to find you. Most stranded hikers are surprised at how difficult it is to be seen, even by helicopter. So keep these tips in mind:

+ If you have a cell signal, first try a voice call to 911 (there is no text-to-911 in Yosemite). If that fails, try voice or text to a friend. A 911 call usually provides the dispatcher with your location. If not, you may be able to use the phone's location app and read the coordinates from the screen or simply consult your map.

+ Do not wander aimlessly. Move only to improve your safety and/or detectability, e.g., better cell reception or visibility.

+ If possible, be out in the open and not surrounded by vegetation. Sometimes, however, you may need to take shelter from weather.

+ Whether or not you are visible, wear bright or contrasting colors and/or place brightly colored items where they can be seen from as many directions as possible, but especially from the air.

+ Use rocks and sticks on the ground or tracks in the snow to spell a large "SOS" or simply an "X." Any unnatural pattern will stand out against nature's clutter.

+ Wave your arms when a helicopter flies by. Movement will help you be spotted.

+ Signal mirror: If aircraft are visible, or if you can see any place where people might gather, even miles away, use anything reflective to repeatedly reflect the sun's rays in their direction. A signal mirror designed for the task is far more accurate and effective than an ordinary mirror like the one on your compass.

+ Fire: Build a visible smoke column by piling green branches on a hot fire—but only if you are sure you can contain the fire and that fire conditions are safe.

+ Lights: Use your light in continuous flash mode, or in groups of three flashes, or by waving it in a circle. A bright light may even be seen from a helicopter in the daytime. In a pinch try your cell phone light or your camera flash, but remember that your cell phone's battery may be critical for calls.

+ Whistle: Use your whistle frequently. It will save your voice.

SWIFT WATERS:
BEAUTIFUL BUT DEADLY

Every year, people die in Yosemite and other recreation areas due to water-related accidents. Most victims were *not* attempting to swim. Some were "merely" wading, some simply standing on shore when they slipped in. Swift-water rescues are difficult and dangerous, even for trained teams, and untrained civilians have died trying to be Good Samaritans.

SWIFT WATER IS ESPECIALLY DANGEROUS DUE TO:

+ water-polished rock next to and in the water that is slippery even when dry.

+ currents that are much stronger than they appear, even in shallow water, and often powerful enough to push a car.

+ aerated (white) water that you cannot swim or float in.

+ cold temperatures that quickly sap your strength.

+ submerged rocks and branches that trap you beyond any hope of escape.

+ cascades and waterfalls with boulders waiting at the bottom.

THE GOOD NEWS IS THAT YOSEMITE'S WATERS ARE VERY SAFE WHEN:

+ viewed from the security of the trail or other developed areas.

+ you stay far enough away from the water that you could never fall in if you slip.

+ you check the park's website nps.gov/yose for allowable seasons and locations before boating.

+ you always wear a Coast Guard–approved personal flotation device (PFD) when boating or floating. Having your PFD quickly accessible (versus on your body) is not safe—mishaps occur so suddenly that you won't have time to put it on.

Yosemite's waters are a beautiful part of the park's scenery, but do not let water tempt you into a disaster. The best way to enjoy the park, while protecting yourself and those under your care, is to always stay on the trail or other developed areas.

SAR GLOSSARY

This is a brief overview of some of the terms and key pieces of equipment commonly used in SAR. It is not exhaustive, nor will it provide thorough descriptions of the items' uses and/or design, but it will provide basic knowledge of these essentials to help you better understand this book.

AID CLIMBING Hanging on or climbing up a cliff face (to ascend) by means of climbing devices attached to the rock.

ANCHOR A strong attachment point for a rope or rescue system, such as a tree, boulder, or bolt.

ANCHOR SYSTEM Carabiners, webbing, ropes, knots, etc., attached to an anchor in an orderly manner. See photo on page 25.

ASCENDER A hand-sized metal device that, when on a rope, will slide one way but will grip tightly when pulled the other way. Used by climbers to go up a rope, but when utilized on rescues, can keep lines under tension while managing raising systems.

BELAY A safety system, typically a rope, intended to catch a person during a fall.

BIVOUAC To shelter temporarily, e.g., due to darkness or weather. The timing, location, and/or level of comfort may be planned or unplanned.

BODY BAG A heavy-duty coated-fabric bag designed for conveying a deceased person.

BOLT As used in SAR, a metal device installed into a hole pre-drilled into the rock. Similar in size to a machine bolt, it is designed to be fitted with a hanger and used as an anchor for a carabiner.

BOLT HANGER A metal link with holes allowing it to connect a carabiner to a bolt.

BONG A type of piton. Bongs come in various lengths and are for cracks up to 2 or 3 inches in width. The name comes from the sound made as they are pounded into a crack with a hammer.

BRAKE-BAR RACK (aka rescue rack; descending rack) A type of descending device used for rescue loads, e.g., rescuers and patients, and also for long rappels. See page 130.

CAMP 4 A campground near Yosemite Valley Lodge, popular with hikers and climbers. Historically known as Sunnyside Campground, it dates back to at least 1941; in 1974, vehicles were banned from it.

CARABINER (aka "biner") See sidebar on page 127.

CARRY OUT To transport a nonambulatory litter patient by hand, on or off trail. See photo on page 94.

CHEST HARNESS A strap system often used in conjunction with a seat harness for suspension from a rope for safety purposes.

CHOCKS Small metal blocks, usually of aluminum, that are wedged into cracks in rock up to a few inches wide to act as anchor points.

CLIMBING ROPE A nylon rope, 8 to 11 millimeters in diameter, 50 to 70 meters in length, able to stretch when arresting the fall of a person.

CRUTCH OUT To allow a patient to walk along a trail with crutches while accompanied by the medical provider. See photo on page 82.

DESCENDING DEVICE A metal device that, when rigged to a rope, provides variable friction, allowing the user to rappel or lower a load under control.

EDGE ROLLER A roller over which the rescue rope runs. Placed at cliff edges, it protects the rope from rock abrasion and reduces friction when raising a load.

EMT (Emergency Medical Technician) A medical certification between First Responder and Paramedic. Usually the lowest level required for an ambulance crew member.

EVAC (Evacuation) To transport the subject of a SAR from point A to point B.

EXCLUSIVE JURISDICTION When the federal government displaces the state government's authority. Yosemite has partial exclusive jurisdiction, which means that the federal government has been granted some of the state's authority and the state has reserved some.

EXPOSURE Vulnerability to danger. In both climbing and rescue, this would include the extent of a potential fall, loose rock, adverse weather, poor equipment, and inexperience.

EXTRACTION Removal of a person from a situation, often by helicopter.

FLAKE (GRANITE FLAKE) A piece of rock—from inches to many feet in size—partially separated from the cliff face. If pulled loose, it could fall and injure someone and/or damage equipment.

FREE CLIMBING When ropes and anchors are not used for direct support but may be used for safety.

FREE RAPPEL A rappel when your feet do not touch anything, such as on an overhanging cliff or from a helicopter.

GRID SEARCH To search an area systematically, often in parallel strips. Variables will determine the area size and the resources and techniques to be used.

H-551 The radio call sign for the Yosemite helicopter.

H-40 The radio call sign for the California Highway Patrol helicopter, based in Fresno.

HARNESS A device made of webbing, buckles, and cloth that allows the wearer to connect to a belay system.

HASTY SEARCH A quick, nonthorough search of likely places, e.g., trails, campsites, scenic attractions, common trouble spots. Done at the start of a search and as needed thereafter.

HELI-RAPPEL A rappel from a helicopter. Inserts a rescuer into a scene quickly.

HELITACK A fusion of "helicopter" and "attack." This is the support crew for all helicopter operations, including SAR and fire. See photo on page 185.

HELMET Worn for protection from falling rocks; a lighter version is used in water rescues.

HIGH ANGLE A technique used where the slope is steep enough to require workers to be belayed for safety.

HOIST To raise rescuer or victim, usually referring to use of helicopter cable winch.

HORSE OUT The evacuation of a patient by horse or mule. The animal is led by a rescuer.

ICS (Incident Command System) Internationally recognized program for managing events. In Yosemite, it is used for any sized SAR. See pages 192–94.

INSERTION Delivering a rescuer or firefighter to the scene by any means. Typically refers to helicopter insertion.

LEAD CLIMBING When two or more climbers ascend, one climbs first (lead) and places protection.

LEDGED OUT The predicament of getting off course while hiking or scrambling and becoming stuck on a ledge or spot where you cannot safely retreat.

LEMOORE Shorthand for the helicopter search and rescue function out of Naval Air Station Lemoore, located south of Fresno, California.

LITTER Any of several designs of rigid stretcher for protecting and transporting patients. A Stokes litter is one basic type used by many rescue teams.

MEDEVAC Evacuation to advanced medical care or hospital, generally by helicopter.

MRA (Mountain Rescue Association) A U.S. and Canadian organization of wilderness SAR teams.

PARAMEDIC The highest level of training in emergency, pre-hospital care. Also, a person certified to this degree who can work with advanced medical protocols, often without immediate medical supervision.

PARKMEDIC Pre-hospital EMS provider level between EMT and Paramedic, found primarily in the NPS. Similar to AEMT. See page 49.

PERSONAL FLOTATION DEVICE A life jacket worn when in or around water, often called a PFD.

PITCH A section of a rock-climbing route between two belay points, often the length of a climbing rope (50 to 70 meters). One route on El Capitan, for example, is 31 pitches long.

PITON Metal spike hammered into a rock crack for an anchor or other support point. Sizes vary from knife-blade width to several inches.

PITON HAMMER A hammer primarily for placing and removing pitons and bolts.

PROTECTION Any item that provides secure anchoring for climbing or rescue systems, e.g., bolts, pitons, nuts, cams, vehicles, trees, and boulders.

PROTECTION RANGER A traditional term for a park ranger who is expected to perform not only law enforcement, but also other protective functions, e.g., SAR, EMS, and fire control.

PSAR (Preventive Search and Rescue) The effort, primarily educational, to keep people from requiring search, rescue, or recovery.

QUESTAR A brand of telescope used by YOSAR for viewing rescue scenes from a distance. See page 128.

RAISING (aka technical raising) Lifting up a person, often in a litter, generally by rope. Frequently the raising will be by ropes and pulleys employing mechanical advantage.

RAPPEL To descend a rope employing one of several types of metal devices, using friction.

RESCUE RIVER BOARD A Styrofoam, 52-inch-long surfing board with handles, used by swift-water rescuers. See pages 148–49.

RESCUE ROPE Very low-stretch rope, usually nylon or polyester, designed to safely support rescuers and patients. Has insufficient stretch for safe lead climbing. See page 125.

SAR Search and Rescue.

SAR-SITER A climber who is a member of the Yosemite Search and Rescue Team and lives for free usually in either Camp 4 or Tuolumne Meadows Campground while involved in SAR. See pages 56–57.

SCREAMER SUIT A nickname for a Vietnam-era nylon harness for lifting a person, originally by helicopter cable hoist.

SHIP In this book, it is a synonym for helicopter.

SHORT-HAUL The act of inserting or extracting rescuers and victims who are suspended beneath a helicopter on a rope. See photo on page 12.

SOCIAL TRAIL An unofficial pathway created over time by climbers, scramblers, or hikers.

STOKES LITTER (aka basket) A litter design made of metal tubing, sometimes with a plastic bottom, which provides a rigid framework for packaging and moving patients. Some models can be disassembled for transport by backpack or packhorse. See illustration on page 82.

TECHNICAL In SAR this usually refers to the use of rope or cable systems, e.g., technical raising or lowering, technical rescue.

THROW BAG The item used as part of a way of throwing the end of a rope or cord to another person. Different designs and uses exist. See illustration on page 148 for water-rescue throw bag. See pages 106–7 for helicopter throw bag.

VICTIM (aka patient; subject) A person in need of assistance.

WEBBING High-strength woven straps of nylon or other synthetics. Used for harnesses and connecting rigging components.

WHITE WATER Moving water that has become aerated, e.g., by waterfall or other turbulence. The resulting bubbles appear white.

YOSAR Yosemite Search and Rescue.

Z-RIG A Z-shaped system of mechanical advantage made of ropes and pulleys. See illustration on pages 146–47.

FRIENDS OF YOSAR

MISSION STATEMENT: Friends of YOSAR is a nonprofit philanthropic organization dedicated to soliciting funds, goods, and services for the benefit of Yosemite Search and Rescue (YOSAR). Our vision is to help YOSAR be a world-class search and rescue organization. Our mission is to actively solicit monetary and in-kind donations from private sources to bridge the gap between public funding and YOSAR's actual budgetary needs.

Friends of Yosemite Search and Rescue (FOYOSAR) assists with training funds, helps secure grants, and provides public outreach and safety-education materials in Yosemite National Park. The FOYOSAR website (friendsofyosar.org) is great! It features high-quality photos of team members performing exciting SAR missions; informative accounts of search and rescues over the years; clear suggestions on safety while in the park; trouble-shooting of problems visitors may have while hiking and climbing; and alerts about potential hazards around water and wildlife. The site also provides updates on weather and conditions on roads and trails and even links to various webcams in the park. It is a handy complement to the Yosemite National Park website (nps.gov/yose).

Donations made to Friends of YOSAR are administered through an independent board of current and former YOSAR members and others who have worked in and around the park. Donations have provided stipends for medical and technical trainings, funds for improvements to facilities, and an endowment to support additional training and website maintenance to provide timely information on important incidents and related conditions in the park. If you wish to make a tax-exempt donation, you may do so on the website. To donate by check, please mail to:

Friends of YOSAR
PO Box 611
Yosemite National Park, CA 95389

◀ On August 21, 2007, YOSAR team member James Thompson nears the overhanging top of Half Dome with David, 31, in the litter. The day before, David accidentally got off route on the strenuous climb and fell 80 feet, seriously hurting his back (see the photo on page 120 for more information). NPS photo by David Pope.

NOTES

The notes and references for the statistics, quotes, and other material in this book are linked to each page by page number and the italicized text.

INTRODUCTION

13 *From the little two-way radio:* "Injured Climber Safe in Yosemite," *Merced Sun-Star,* July 31, 1976.

14 *Yosemite by the Numbers:* Yosemite National Park Reports, National Park Service Visitor Use Statistics, collected at irma.nps.gov/Stats/Reports/Park/YOSE.

15 *The first real record:* Michael Ghiglieri and Charles R. "Butch" Farabee Jr., *Off the Wall: Death in Yosemite,* 6th ed. (Flagstaff, AZ: Puma Press, 2007), 184.

19 *To quote one of the near-legendary thoughts:* Albright, Horace M., *Oh, Ranger! A Book about the National Parks* (Palo Alto, CA: Stanford University Press, 1928), vii.

20–25 *2010: A Typical Year:* The 23 SARs highlighted were selected from the 245 of that year as an overview of the range of incidents that occur. Complete records are available in the Yosemite SAR records in the Valley and in El Portal.

PART 1: THE ADVENTURE BEGINS

28–39 The role of the United States Army in Yosemite's early days draws on two sources: John W. Henneberger, "The History of the National Park Ranger," February 29, 1959, 48–52. Referenced here is a three-volume unpublished manuscript in the Yosemite National Park Research Library. Also: Harvey Meyerson, *Nature's Army* (Lawrence, KS: University of Kansas Press, 2001).

29 *While both sheep and cattle herders:* John Muir, *The Mountains of California* (New York, NY: The Century Company, 1894), 349.

30 *In fact, "state officials had made it abundantly clear":* Linda Wedel Greene, *Yosemite: The Park and Its Resources: A History of the Discovery, Management, and Physical Development of Yosemite National Park, California: Historic Resource Study,* vol. 1 (U.S. Department of the Interior, National Park Service, September 1987), 413.

31 *Between Captain Wood and Major Benson:* Henry G. Benson, *Acting Superintendent of the Yosemite National Park—1906* report to the Department of the Interior, 652.

34 *On May 20 of 1913, Austin Pohli:* W. T. Littlebrandt, *Acting Superintendent of the Yosemite National Park—1913* report to the Secretary of the Interior, in the collection of the Yosemite National Park Research Library.

34 *As the* San Francisco Chronicle *told it:* "A. R. Pohli Falls to His Death in Yosemite," *San Francisco Chronicle,* May 21, 1913.

35–36 Charles R. "Butch" Farabee Jr., *Death, Daring, and Disaster: Search and Rescue in the National Parks,* (Lanham, MD: Taylor Trade Publishing, 2005), 139–40.

37 *You Never Know:* For a history of how Charles Manson and the Manson Family were captured, read Bob Murphy's *Desert Shadows* (Morongo Valley, CA: Sagebrush Press, 1993). Murphy was superintendent of Death Valley National Monument at the time.

38 *Contractors Add Air Power:* Official Website of Yosemite Helitack, sites.google.com/site /yosehelitack50th.

39 *The First Helicopter Medevac:* Originally reported in the *San Francisco Chronicle;* articles appeared daily between August 2 and August 5, 1949.

43 *Pete Thompson Remembers:* Letter to the author, March 24, 2006.

44 *"I came to the Big Wall rescue business":* Letter from Pete Thompson to the author, September 7, 2015.

45 *SAR Officers from 1970 to Today:* Personnel records for federal employees are difficult to access. Despite personal knowledge of these former SAR officers, I did not know their precise dates. Over some 12 years I was able to contact everyone listed here. I asked each to confirm the dates they served in Yosemite SAR, who served before them, and who took over after them. The challenge of remembering details was compounded by individuals' spotty access to their own records.

46 *As Seen on TV:* Richard Yokley and Rozane Sutherland, *Emergency! Behind the Scene* (Sudbury, MA: Jones & Bartlett Publishing, 2008), 1–22.

47 *Defining a New Type of Expert:* American Academy of Orthopaedic Surgeons (AAOS), *Emergency Care and Transportation of the Sick and Injured* (Chicago, IL: The American Academy of Orthopaedic Surgeons, 1971).

52 *Founded in 1968:* For a detailed account of the history of rock climbing in Yosemite National Park, particularly Yosemite Valley, read *Camp 4: Recollections of a Yosemite Rockclimber* by Steve Roper, published by Mountaineers Books in 1998.

52–53 *The Yosemite Mountaineering School:* "Yosemite Guide Service," *Summit Magazine,* June 1967.

53 *Wayne Merry Remembers* and all other quotes from Merry in this section: Email correspondence with the author, April and September 2015.

58 *Michael A. Nash Remembers:* Email correspondence with the author, June and September 2015.

60 *The Ultimate Sacrifice:* Statistics are from an 1,814-person database of deaths in Yosemite maintained by the author for the park's Investigative Services Branch, accessed April 2017.

60–61 *Vernal Fall Claims a Hero:* Ghiglieri and Farabee, *Off the Wall,* chapter 1.

61 *Please do not interpret these thoughts:* Ghiglieri and Farabee, *Off the Wall,* chapter 10.

62 *The Best of Intentions:* Ghiglieri and Farabee, *Off the Wall,* chapter 10.

64–65 *When a SAR Turns Deadly:* Farabee, *Death, Daring, and Disaster,* 271–272 and 534.

PART 2: IN THE FIELD

75–77 *Robin's Winter Hike:* Yosemite Search and Rescue Incident Report #8804-114.61, completed by the author on January 21, 1973, archived in the El Portal SAR records.

77 *In 2012 he orchestrated:* Robin Baxter, "A Winter Experience," a detailed account of this incident sent to the author, January 13, 2005; and Robin Baxter in email correspondence with the author, October 2015.

78–79 *Even a Simple Hike Can Go Wrong:* From the YOSAR presentation in the Yosemite Theater and John Dill in email correspondence with the author, December 24, 2016, and February 14, 2017.

83 *More Than 50 Years:* Fred Koegler in email correspondence with the author, November 2015.

89 *The local newspapers quickly began: The Fresno Bee,* July 1964 (exact date of article not recorded).

89 *Unconsciously, subtly, many of them started:* Related by Ranger Tom Thomas, who participated in the original search, in a letter to the author, March 25, 1986.

89 *It was the most desperate moment:* Doug Warnock, interviewed by the author at the Yosemite Alumni Reunion, October 27, 2008. Warnock was the search boss (incident commander).

90 *Little Boy Lost:* Bill Halainen, ed., *National Park Service Morning Report,* September 7, 2004, and Keith Lober in email correspondence with the author, July 12, 2016.

91–93 *Race against Time and Temperature:* Ghiglieri and Farabee, *Off the Wall,* 139–142; and Dan Ellison and John Dill in email correspondence with the author, July 5, 2016, and April 2017 respectively.

94–95 *Hal Grovert Remembers:* Email correspondence with the author, August and September 2015 and October 2016.

96–101 *YODOGS: Scent-Powered Search*: Evan Jones and Mike Freeman in email correspondence with the author, March and April 2016.

99 *The Case of Randy Morgenson:* Eric Blehm, *The Last Season* (New York: HarperCollins, 2006).

99 *The Search for David Paul Morrison:* Yosemite National Park News Page, Public Information Office, May 27–29, 1998; and Rescue Forum #30, Journal of Mountain Rescue Association, November 1998.

105 *Lisa Hendy Remembers:* Email correspondence with the author, April 2016.

106–7 *Michael Murray Remembers:* Email correspondence with the author, October 2015 and April 2016.

108–9 *Thumbs Up!:* Ranger Eric Gabriel, "Yosemite National Park Operational Leadership Review of a 2011 Helicopter Short-Haul Rescue of an Injured Climber from The Nose Route on El Capitan," January 10, 2012. Gabriel provided additional details in email correspondence with the author, April 2015.

110 *First Military Chopper in the Park:* James Wrightson, "Rescued Coeds Were Busy, Not Worried in Snow," *The Fresno Bee,* April 1, 1958; and *San Francisco Chronicle,* "Girl's Theory Proved: Her Sex Is Hardy," April 1, 1958; and *San Francisco Chronicle,* "One-Legged Pilot, Copter Men Heroes," April 1, 1958.

111–12 *It was 1981 and we were called to assist:* Dan Ellison, in email correspondence with the author, September 2015 and March and July 2016.

111 *A Towering Achievement:* Deactivation Ceremony Program, NAS Lemoore Search and Rescue Unit, July 15, 2004.

113 *A Fatal Fall:* Yosemite Search and Rescue Incident Report #8804-1033-100-110, completed by the author, June 16, 1975, archived in El Portal SAR records; and *Yosemite Case Incident Record* #75-1107, completed by Ranger Dan Sholly June 17, 1975, archived in El Portal SAR records.

114 *Everything Goes Sideways: Yosemite Case Incident Report* #78-0851, completed by SAR Officer Tim Setnicka, archived in El Portal SAR records.

114 *A Singular Award*: The Lemoore Search and Rescue Helicopter Crew, United States Navy, was awarded the Secretary of the Interior Citation for Valor on October 10, 1979, by Secretary Cecil D. Andrus.

115 *Witness to Tragedy*: Donna Sisson in email correspondence with the author, December 2016.

116 *An Inherent Risk*: Brandon Latham in email correspondence with the author, February 2017.

117 *How Climbs Are Rated*: Steve Roper, *Climber's Guide to Yosemite Valley* (San Francisco: The Sierra Club, 1971), 21–32.

118–19 *A Rescue with Multiple Challenges*: Pete Thompson, "Rescue on El Capitan," *Summit Magazine*, October 1972. Additional details provided by Thompson in a letter to the author, November 23, 1986.

120 *From the Top of El Capitan*: Donna Helmbold in email correspondence with the author, July and August 2015.

121–22 *An Epic Rescue on Half Dome*: Robert Pederson, *American Alpine Club—Mountain Rescue Association Accident Report—1968*; and Galen A. Rowell, ed., "Rescue on the South Face of Half Dome," collected in *The Vertical World of Yosemite* (Berkeley, CA: Wilderness Press, 1974), 147–59.

123 *Hollywood Comes Knocking*: Personal recollection of the author, with additional details provided by Rick Smith, Tim Setnicka, and others.

123–25 *A Technical Challenge on Lost Arrow*: Yosemite Search and Rescue Incident Report #120137.37, completed by SAR Officer Pete Thompson, April 16, 1970, archived in El Portal SAR records; and "Rescue," *Summit Magazine*, June 1960.

124 *Loyd and I roped*: Wayne Merry in a letter to the author, April 2, 1989.

126–28 *Trouble on the Leaning Tower*: Dan Horner in email correspondence with the author, April and June 2016.

128–32 *Triumph and Tragedy on El Capitan*: Daniel Duane, "Six Nights on the Dark Tower," *Adventure Magazine*, February 2005; and Keith Lober in email correspondence with the author, June 2016; and Peter Takeda, "The Rescue . . . " (full article title unavailable), *Rock and Ice Magazine*, March 2005.

134–37 *Keith Lober Remembers*: Email correspondence with the author, November 2014 and February 2016.

138 *A Brave Attempt*: Yosemite Case Incident Record #11-1747 and SAR #069, completed by Chris E. Smith, archived in El Portal SAR records.

138 *Swept Away*: Ghiglieri and Farabee, *Off the Wall*, 386–87.

139 *A Tragic Sacrifice*: Yosemite Case Incident Record #97-3342, completed by Brian S. Smith on October 19, 1997, archived in El Portal SAR records; and Carnegie Hero Fund Commission Case Summary titled "News Release: Arjuna D. N. Babapulle—72166-8243," Carnegie Hero Fund Foundation of Pittsburgh, PA, on February 25, 1999.

140 *After the Fact*: Ghiglieri and Farabee, *Off the Wall*, 392–93.

140–41 *Don't Be a Casualty*: Ghiglieri and Farabee, *Off the Wall*, chapter 10.

142–43 *Whitewater Tragedy*: Yosemite Case Incident Record #83-8400, completed by Pete J. Dalton, September 2, 1983, archived in El Portal SAR records.

142 The Yosemite National Park Rescue Team was awarded the Secretary of the Interior Award for Excellence of Service in 1983 by Secretary Donald Paul Hodel.

144 *Fatal Waterfalls*: Ghiglieri and Farabee, *Off the Wall*, chapter 1.

144 *Amazingly, however, while taking a drink*: Article in the *Mariposa Gazette*, July 26, 1951.

146–148 *A Beautiful Death Trap*: Joe Sumner in email correspondence with the author, August and September 2015.

150–53 *Scuba in the Park*: The information comes from thousands of hours of original research. Together with former chief of the NPS's Submerged Cultural Resources Unit, Dan Lenihan, I submitted a history of diving within the NPS to the Service's Submerged Resources Center. Charles R. Farabee and Daniel J. Lenihan, *National Park Service Divers: Protecting Nature, Preserving the Past, Recovering the Dead*, forthcoming from Best Publishing.

154–55 *Dope Lake*: Yosemite Search and Rescue Incident Report, #77-0133, completed by Bruce McKeeman, January 29, 1977, archived in El Portal SAR records; and Ghiglieri and Farabee, *Off the Wall*, 128–37.

156 *A Horse to Water*: Bill Halainen, ed., *National Park Service Morning Report*, 95-373, July 6, 1995.

156 *Mule Plunge*: Bill Halainen, ed., *National Park Service Morning Report*, July 12, 2004.

157 *A Doggone Rescue*: Bill Halainen, ed., *National Park Service Morning Report*, June 16, 2011.

158 *The First BASE Jump*: Johnny Utah, "Mike Pelkey: A BASE Pioneer," johnnyutah.com.

159 *Later that year, Jan Davis*: Jeff Sullivan, NPS Criminal Investigations Unit, *Jan M. Davis Investigation, Occurred 22 October 1999, Yosemite Case Number YOSE 99-3481* (Freedom of Information Act

Request), and Jeff Sullivan in email correspondence with the author, April 2017.

161 *Hang Glider Meets Tree; Tree Wins: Yosemite Case Incident Record #08-2106* and *SAR #08-109*, completed by Michael Foster on August 15, 2008, archived in the Yosemite SAR records.

162 *The first person interred where he fell was Franklin Johnson:* "Intern Killed in Yosemite Fall Buried on Cliff," *Mariposa Gazette,* June 7, 1956.

163 *A Hopeless Endeavor:* "Helicopter Spots Victim at Base of 300 Foot Drop," McClatchy Newspapers Service, September 2, 1956.

164 *Death on Lost Arrow Spire:* Steve Roper, *Camp 4: Recollections of a Yosemite Rockclimber* (Seattle, WA: The Mountaineers, 1994), 110–111.

165–67 *A Mysterious Disappearance:* Ghiglieri and Farabee, *Off the Wall,* 468–70.

167–69 *Over the Falls:* Ghiglieri and Farabee, *Off the Wall,* 32–33; and *Yosemite National Park Supplemental Case Incident Record #95-2284* and *SAR #95-113*, completed by Ranger G. P. Jablonski on August 15, 1995, archived in El Portal SAR records.

168–169 *The day after the accident:* Steven Yu in email correspondence with the author, February 2016.

PART 3: BEHIND THE SCENES

172 *Into the Deluge:* Mary Hinson and Keith Lober in email correspondence with the author, August 2004.

172 *An Expensive Hike:* Bill Halainen, ed., *National Park Service Morning Report*, March 24, 2015, and John Dill in email correspondence with the author, February 15, 2017.

173 *The Priciest SAR:* Farabee, *Death, Daring, and Disaster*, 276–78.

173 *The largest search for a missing person:* Dwight McCarter and Ronald G. Schmidt, *Lost!: A Ranger's Journal of Search and Rescue* (Yellow Springs, OH: Graphicom Press, 1998), 22–43.

174–75 *A Wild Ride:* Mike LaLone in email correspondence with the author, in October 2016.

174 *The Annual Tally: NPS National Search & Rescue Annual Report—2014*, coordinated by Ken Phillips, National Search and Rescue Coordinator, made available to the author by Ranger Phillips via email in June 2015; and *NPS Park Search & Rescue Annual Report—2015*, Yosemite National Park.

176–77 *Jim Reilly Remembers:* Email correspondence with the author, November 2015 and December 2016.

176 *On November 16, 1980:* Mike Durr in email correspondence with the author, October 2015 and December 2016.

178 *lost for two and half-days: Yosemite National Park Superintendent's Monthly Report,* June 1934.

178 *The National Park Service's 1934 Annual Report:* Report of the Director of the National Park Service to the Secretary of the Interior for the Fiscal Year ended June 30, 1934.

178 *The Dawn of Wireless:* "Wireless Sent from Aeroplane During Flight," *Arizona Daily Star,* January 22, 1911; and "Wireless to Aid Forest Fire Fights," *Arizona Daily Star,* January 7, 1912.

178 *However, minds had: Yosemite National Park Superintendent's Monthly Report,* May 1934.

178 *The Modern Era:* Nancy Phillipe in email correspondence with the author, January 2017.

179 *Cell Phones: Yosemite National Park Visitor and Resource Protection Annual Reports*, 2013 and 2014.

182 *An Incident in El Portal:* Deron Mills in email correspondence with the author, February 2017.

184–85 *A Record-Breaking Incident: Yosemite Case Incident Record #08-4370* and *SAR #08-230*, completed by SAR Officer Keith Lober on October 18, 2008, archived in Yosemite SAR records.

186 *Rangers as Coroners:* A wealth of information was provided by Jeff Sullivan, Assistant Special Agent in Charge, Investigative Services Branch, National Park Service. Sullivan coordinates the park coroners.

187 *No Duty to Rescue:* Hugh B. Johnson Jr., as personal representative of the Estate of Ben Johnson, Deceased v. United States of America, Department of Interior, 949 F.2d 332 (10th Cir. 1991).

188–89 *A Case of Jurisdiction: Yosemite Search and Rescue Incident Report #8804-1033-100-76*, completed by the author on February 14, 1975, archived in the El Portal SAR records; and Ghiglieri and Farabee, *Off the Wall*, 127–28.

190 *According to one source:* "The Fires that Created an Incident Management System," by Dale D. Rowley, Director, Waldo County Emergency Management Agency, Belfast, ME.

192 *A New Threat:* Donna Sisson in email correspondence with the author, October and December 2016.

193 *Incident Management Teams:* Steve Frye in conversation with the author, March 5, 2017. Frye was the senior FEMA Type I Incident Management Team Incident Commander.

196 *My Start in SAR:* For an in-depth review of this incident, read Cathy Hufault's book *Death Clouds on Mt. Baldy: Tucson's Lost Tragedy* (Arizona Mountain Publications, 2011).

199 *Tim Setnicka Remembers:* Email correspondence with the author, December 2016 and January 2017.

IMAGE CREDITS

The author has made every effort to identify and acknowledge the photographers who took the photos in this book, nearly all of whom were National Park Service employees at the time. These credits are placed with the photo captions. If a photo is listed simply as "NPS photo," the photographer is unknown. If the author or the publisher are alerted by the photographer, the book will be updated in a future printing. When necessary, names have been changed in the text and faces obscured in the photographs.

Page 6: map of Yosemite National Park showing district boundaries by Eric Knight.

Page 117: Ten classic routes on El Capitan graphic by Mona Reilly.

Pages 33, 35, 74, 82, 107, 127, 128, 130, 146–47, 148, 180: Illustrations by Dov Pope.

THE FOLLOWING IMAGES ARE COURTESY OF THE YOSEMITE NATIONAL PARK ARCHIVES, MUSEUM, AND LIBRARY:

Page 8: RL 008706. Image of "Overhanging Rock with Warning Sign." Photographer unknown, 1924.

Page 10: RL 007829. Image of "Chief Ranger F.S. Townsley Using Radio." Photograph by Ralph H. Anderson, May 21, 1934.

Page 24: RL 19975. Image of "Safety Sign from 1947: Be Careful and Live." Photograph by Ralph H. Anderson, 1947.

Page 29: YM 007259. Image of "Park Regulations." Photographer unknown, 1902.

Page 30: YM 004650 (YOSE/WML-230). Image of "Troop F, 6th U.S. Cavalry, on Fallen Monarch, Mariposa Big Tree Grove." Photograph by Tibbets for the Southern Pacific Railroad Co., 1899.

Page 31: RL 005701 (YOSE/WASO 82-39). Image of "Negro Troopers of 24th Cavalry." Photograph by Celia Crocker Thompson, 1899.

Page 32: RL 004405. Image of "U.S. Army Pack Train No. 6 near Camp Yosemite, Yosemite Valley." Photographer unknown, 1909.

Page 35: RL 004066. Image of "Two Howitzers at Tunnel Parking Area. 30th Field Artillery from Camp Roberts." Photograph by Ralph H. Anderson, October 22, 1941.

Page 37: RL 007370. Image of "Mr. and Mrs. Charles McNally, Rangers at Tuolumne Meadows." Photographer unknown, 1926.

Page 46: RL 023451. Image of "The First Rangers." Photograph by George Fiske, 1915.

Page 52: RL 18769. Image of "Ranger Frank Betts Glacier Point Rescue." Photograph by *The Fresno Bee*, August 21, 1958.

Page 54: RL 014258. Image of "Galen Clark." Photographer unknown, date unknown.

Page 70: YOSE 049311. Image of "Do Not Feed the Bears—Lantern Slide." Photographer unknown, date unknown.

Page 85: RL 12974. Image of "Girl Lost Overnight from Camp 14." Photographer unknown, June 1932.

Page 157: RL 12754. Image of "Getting Ready for a Pack Trip. Forest Townsley on Left." Photographer unknown, 1926.

THE FOLLOWING IMAGES ARE COURTESY OF THE NATIONAL PARK SERVICE HISTORY COLLECTION:

Page 8: HPC-000211. Image of "Rock Climbing Accident Victim." Photograph by Ralph H. Anderson.

Page 36: HFCA 1607. Carl P. Russell Photo Collection.

Page 38: HPC-001075. Image of "Using a Helicopter to Search Cliffs for Lost Hiker." Photograph by Robert N. McIntyre.

THE FOLLOWING IMAGE IS COURTESY OF THE LIBRARY OF CONGRESS, PRINTS AND PHOTOGRAPHS DIVISION:

Page 28: LC-DIG-ppmsca-36413. "Theodore Roosevelt and John Muir on Glacier Point, Yosemite Valley, California, in 1903." Photograph by Underwood & Underwood, © 1906.

INDEX

ACKNOWLEDGMENTS

When asked by Yosemite Conservancy if I would be interested in doing a book on Yosemite Search and Rescue, I jumped at the chance. A book like this was absolutely needed and eminently worthy, and I was thrilled to even be considered. Then reality set in. Could I do justice to it all? To the people, their efforts and legacies? To the thousands of missions and the stories behind them? To the overall history of Yosemite SAR? Ultimately, you will have to judge how well we all did. But regardless, I need to say thank you to a bunch of people.

First, thank you to the talented men and women over the years who have been saving lives, finding missing kids, and, in general, making Yosemite Search and Rescue internationally renowned. Thanks are due to Yosemite Conservancy, whose donor-supported grants make possible a summer-long PSAR volunteer program, which has contributed to the dramatic decline in incidents the last several years. Additional Conservancy grants have sponsored replacement tent cabins for Yosemite's dedicated search and rescue volunteers in historic Camp 4. Thank you, too, to the Yosemite Conservancy book team in El Portal, Adonia Ripple and Katie Manion, who supported this project from the get-go. Without editor Nicole Geiger's critical eye, organizing abilities, patience, and hand-holding through this process, I might have given up. Then I would like to thank Mariah Bear, developmental editor, and Nancy Austin, designer, both of whose book-construction skills and great instincts for details and photos make this book what it is. Also on this book team were Eric Ball, the book's cover creator, as well as Katie Moore, Eric Knight, Brittany Bogan, Molly Woodward, and Mona Reilly.

▲ The 2009 Helicopter Rescue Team Recertification: (back row, left to right) Jack Hoeflich, David Pope, Eric Gabriel, Pilot Richard Shatto, Jason Ramsdell, Dov Bock, Matt Stark; (front row, left to right) Jeff Webb, Chris Bellino, Keith Lober, Aaron Smith. NPS photo.

How about those photos? If it weren't for Keith Lober, David Pope, Tim Setnicka, Barry Smith, Tom Evans, and Josh McNair, among others who gave photos freely and graciously, this book could never have been done. I constantly pestered them for follow-up information, and I think many of their shots are world-class. Dov Pope, former SAR officer as well as the accomplished illustrator here, had an insight into the subject second to none. Then there are the book's "Remembers" sections contributed by former Yosemite search and rescue officers. I am sorry we could not fit all of you. As for Jack Morehead and his foreword— what a legacy he has left for all the young rangers following in his footsteps. Always available to me for background information and support were Linda Eade, Bill Halainen, Steve Shackelton, Jeff Sullivan, Jim Tucker, and Steve Yu. Chief Ranger Kevin Killian, PSAR Operations Supervisor Alan Hageman, and VIP Michael Hernandez all read the drafts and gave us many constructive thoughts.

Last, I need to single out Ranger John Dill. A SAR technician since 1974, John was willing and gracious in reviewing the drafts of this book and answering our questions. He has a critical eye and an amazing memory for SAR missions. Way too many times I was embarrassed by my mistakes— the ones that John caught and politely corrected. Thank you, John.

There were a lot more people who assisted in this project, and I wish to thank you all. If I have overlooked even one person, I am truly sorry.

Paul Anderson
Tony Anderson
Paula Andress
Robin Baxter
Barbara Beroza
Jim Brady
Merrie Braun
Werner Braun
Cathy Buckingham
Dennis Burnett
Julie Byerly
Linda Campbell
Gary Colliver
Ellen Croll
Glen Denny
Sabrina Diaz
Aaron Dick
George Durkee
Mike Durr
Jan Eagle
Dan Ellison
Mark Faherty
Jennifer Fetterley
Mark Forbes
Mike Freeman
Steve Frye
Eric Gabriel

Scott Gediman
Michael Ghiglieri
Tom Griffiths
Hal Grovert
Bryan Harry
Donna Helmbold
Lisa Hendy
Steve Hickman
Jack Hoeflich
Dan Horner
Evan Jones
Dani Julien
Kristin Kirschner
Kathy Komatz
Mike LaLone
Brandon Latham
Dan Lenihan
Maura Longden
Joy Marschall
Kelly Martin
Christy McGee
Joanne Cross McGill
Tom Medema
Wayne Merry
Michael Michener
Dave Mihalic
Deron Mills

Mike Murray
Michael Nash
Mike Osborne
Nancy Phillipe
Ken Phillips
Jeff Pirog
Loyd Price
Jim Reilly
Katrina Reyes
Leslie Reynolds
Anne-Marie Rizzi
Claudine Ronay
Steve Roper
Ginny Rousseau
Virginia Sanchez
John Seymer
Heidi Schlichting
Donna Sisson
Sally Sprouse
Joe Sumner
Pete Thompson
Michelle Torok
Kim Tucker
Bill Wade
Ray Warren

ABOUT THE AUTHOR

Photo by Adam H. Farabee

In his 34 years with the National Park Service, **Charles R. "Butch" Farabee** rose from ranger to superintendent, working in 10 NPS areas, including the Grand Canyon, Death Valley, and Glacier. He was the agency's first emergency services coordinator, responsible for SAR, EMS, diving, and aviation. He went on his first SAR in 1958, and subsequently responded to some 900 search and rescue missions; 10 years and 800 of those missions were in Yosemite National Park. Butch is the recipient of the Harry Yount Lifetime Achievement Award for exemplifying the best of the National Park Service ranger tradition. He was granted an Honorary Lifetime Member of the Mountain Rescue Association for his contributions to search and rescue. The Coalition of NPS Retirees presented Butch with the George B. Hartzog Jr. Award for "increasing public knowledge about the National Park Ranger profession."

He authored *Death, Daring, and Disaster: Search and Rescue in the National Parks* and *National Park Ranger: An American Icon.* He coauthored *Off the Wall: Death in Yosemite* and *National Park Service Divers: Protecting the Resource, Preserving the Past, Recovering the Dead.* Butch was also a Tucson, Arizona, police officer for three years, is a graduate of the FBI Academy, and holds B.S. and M.A. degrees. He says he is most proud of having raised, as a single father, two fine sons, and he is now the proud grandfather of four grandchildren. Butch lives in Tucson, Arizona.

ABOUT THE ILLUSTRATOR

Photo by David Pope

The illustrations of rescue techniques and equipment by **Dov Pope** (née Bock) enliven this book, and it is the background of this capable artist that makes her uniquely qualified to illustrate it. With a B.S. in botany and a graduate degree in scientific illustration, Dov may seem like an unlikely candidate to be dangling 150 feet below a rescue helicopter, but during her hundreds of SAR missions between 2004 and 2015, she did just that. Dov was the first woman to hold a permanent Yosemite SAR technician position and was a veteran member of the park's elite Helicopter Rescue Team. Between 2011 and 2012 she was the interim Yosemite SAR program manager. She served as the medical services manager from 2012 through 2015, leading the Yosemite Medical Clinic and park-wide emergency-medical-service program.

Dov says, "I was honored to have the opportunity to serve among some of the world's finest mountain rescue technicians. The YOSAR team is an incredibly capable group of individuals with a wide range of backgrounds and skill sets. On any given operation there would often be hundreds of years of combined rescue experience represented among the decision makers. I loved the challenging and exciting nature of rescue work and found the collaborative team dynamic immensely rewarding."